CAREERS
IN TRAVEL, TOURISM,
AND HOSPITALITY

VGM Professional Careers Series

CAREERS
IN TRAVEL, TOURISM, AND HOSPITALITY

MARJORIE EBERTS
LINDA BROTHERS
ANN GISLER

VGM Career Horizons
NTC/Contemporary Publishing Group

Library of Congress Cataloging-in-Publication Data

Eberts, Marjorie.
    Careers in travel, tourism, hospitality / by Marjorie Eberts,
Linda Brothers, Ann Gisler.
        p.   cm. — (VGM professional careers series)
    ISBN 0-8442-4462-7 (cloth)
    ISBN 0-8442-4463-5 (paper)
    1. Tourist trade—Vocational guidance.   I. Brothers, Linda.
II. Gisler, Ann.   III. Title.   IV. Series.
G155.5.E24   1997
338.4'791023—dc21   96-47296
                                                   CIP

Cover photo courtesy of United Airlines.

Published by VGM Career Horizons
A division of NTC/Contemporary Publishing Group, Inc.
4255 West Touhy Avenue, Lincolnwood (Chicago), Illinois 60646-1975 U.S.A.
Copyright © 1997 by NTC/Contemporary Publishing Group, Inc.
Printed in the United States of America
International Standard Book Number: 0-8442-4462-7 (cloth)
                                    0-8442-4463-5 (paper)
19   18   17   16   15   14   13   12   11   10   9   8   7   6   5   4   3   2

CONTENTS

worker. Looking at the future. On-the-job responsibilities for fast-food restaurant managers. Working conditions. Training for becoming a fast-food restaurant manager. Advancing up the career ladder in the fast-food industry. Salary and fringe benefits. Looking at the future in fast-food management. For more information.

DEDICATION

To the Eberts, Brothers, and Gisler families, with whom we have shared so many delightful travel, tourism, and hospitality experiences.

ABOUT THE AUTHORS

Marjorie Eberts has co-authored more than 60 books, primarily in the field of education. This is her tenth career book. She is a graduate of Stanford University and Butler University. Eberts drew upon her experiences as a frequent traveler to Europe, Asia, Latin America, and the Caribbean in writing this book. Travel is her favorite avocation.

Dr. Linda Brothers is an associate professor and chairman of the Department of Restaurant, Hotel, Institutional and Tourism Management at Indiana-Purdue University, Indianapolis. She has developed courses in hospitality management and works with restaurant managers in central Indiana to provide seminars to update both managers and employees. Brothers is a graduate of Purdue University as an education major, with a related area of study in hospitality management.

Ann Gisler is a student at Indiana University-Purdue University, Indianapolis. She has co-authored a book on tourism. Gisler has gained travel experience through exploring the eastern half of the United States and visiting Caribbean islands. She has also lived in Scotland.

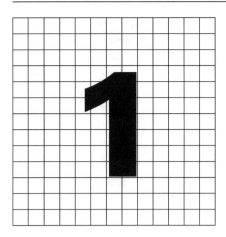

AN INTRODUCTION TO WORKING IN TRAVEL, TOURISM, AND HOSPITALITY CAREERS

Today, the largest industry in the world is the travel, tourism, and hospitality industry. It also is the world's fastest-growing industry and the greatest generator of jobs. A continuing bright job outlook for the future is predicted in these career areas in the United States and around the world because people now have more leisure time and greater disposable income to enjoy travel, tourism, and hospitality experiences. More than ever before, people are flying and taking cruises to all corners of the earth, joining tour groups to see places as disparate as New York City and Antarctica, and eating out in restaurants and staying in hotels, motels, and inns.

One of the great appeals of careers in these areas is the opportunity for motivated people of all ages and backgrounds to move up the career ladder rapidly or even to own one's own business. For example, Julie and Bill Brice managed a frozen yogurt stand in their late teens. When the owner put their unit and the one he managed up for sale, they bought both units with the $10,000 they had saved for college, and the I Can't Believe It's Yogurt chain was founded.

Lack of experience is no barrier to employment or advancement in many travel, tourism, and hospitality careers. A large number of today's fast-food company executives started out as hourly workers. John Hyduke, who became vice president of franchise development at Dairy Queen, started out working in the store owned and operated by his parents.

Of course, some careers in travel, tourism, and hospitality require specialized training, such as pilot, flight attendant, travel agent, and chef. Also, specialized training and education beyond high school can help individuals get ahead faster. Many two-year and four-year colleges, universities, and vocational/technical schools have hospitality and tourism programs that prepare young people to move into management positions.

The three career areas of travel, tourism, and hospitality provide many other special opportunities. Individuals choosing careers in these areas can stay in their own community or explore fascinating locations around the world. There is the possibility of setting up a health club in a hotel in Africa or one next to a hometown airport; the chance to cook in Paris, France or Paris, Kentucky; and the opportunity to lead tours to South America or to local historic spots. Here is a list of just some of the places at home and abroad where people can find careers in travel, tourism, and hospitality:

adventure travel companies	publishing houses
airlines	railroad and bus companies
amusement parks	riverboats
camps	sit-down and fast-food restaurants
cruise ships	tour companies
hotels and motels	tourist attractions
national, state, and local parks	travel agencies

Another advantage of these careers is that they give people opportunities to work with or play host to just about everyone. Movie stars and sports heroes fly on planes, eat in restaurants, stay at hotels, and visit tourist attractions. So do ordinary citizens, politicians, foreign dignitaries (kings and ambassadors), and affluent business executives.

CAREERS IN TRAVEL, TOURISM, AND HOSPITALITY

Selecting a career in travel, tourism, and hospitality is rewarding because these careers involve helping others have a good time. While experience and education determine where people start in these careers, once they begin there is no limit to where their talents and ambition can take them. Brief descriptions of the career areas explored by this book follow.

Careers Working as a Travel Agent

Part of the lure of working as a travel agent is the opportunity to travel free or for reduced rates to places in the United States and around the world. While a love of travel attracts many people to this profession, success is based on a genuine desire to serve people by helping them arrange transportation, lodging, tours, and other travel services. In the course of their job, travel agents must "wear many hats," for they need to be salespeople, bookkeepers, ticketing agents, file clerks, receptionists, and computer and geography experts. To handle this complex job they need specialized training either on the job or from a college or vocational school.

Careers Working for the Airlines as a Pilot or Flight Attendant

The airlines are the backbone of public transportation in the United States and many places around the world. The most glamorous airline jobs are those of pilots and flight attendants. These individuals are highly trained professionals.

The work of pilots is not limited to transporting passengers; pilots also work for airlines devoted to carrying freight, packages, and mail. And a small percentage work as corporate pilots transporting businesspeople. Flight attendants have the responsibility of ensuring that all passengers have safe, comfortable, and enjoyable flights. Both pilots and flight attendants appreciate that they have jobs that allow them considerable free time and the opportunity to travel.

Careers Working as Reservationists, Customer Service Representatives, Mechanics, and in Other Airline Jobs

One of the perks of working for airlines is receiving free or reduced-fare flights for the employee and family members. Both reservationists and customer service representatives spend their days dealing with the public. They need superb communication skills to secure and keep customers for their airline. Mechanics need to have a high degree of mechanical aptitude because they have to diagnose and solve complex mechanical problems. Both jobs are likely to involve shift work, as airlines operate around the clock.

Careers Working Aboard a Cruise Ship

Most employees aboard cruise ships—from ship's officers to crew members—are not Americans but citizens of other countries. However, those jobs that involve dealing directly with the passengers are largely held by Americans, since most passengers are from the United States. This includes jobs on the cruise and purser's staff as well as service jobs such as gift shop personnel, beauticians, casino dealers, and photographers. Cruise ship employees may stay aboard a ship for as long as six to eight months. During that time, they will have the opportunity to disembark at many ports. So this is one occupation that truly lets people see the world. It is also a hard job, for many employees must work ten- to fifteen-hour days. Because cruising has become so popular and there is considerable turnover in jobs, the opportunity for employment on cruise ships should remain good.

Careers Working in Even More Travel Jobs

Certainly, it is not essential to work for an airline or directly in the travel industry to have a job that involves travel. Many possibilities now exist for traveling to other countries. American companies have salespeople and offices throughout the world to sell products like computers, food, clothing, automobiles, telephones, bicycles, tools, steel, farm equipment, film, and lumber. Anyone who joins the armed services has the chance to live and work in another country. Almost every country has an American embassy or consulate that needs to be staffed.

Careers Working for a Tour Company as a Guide and in Other Jobs

"On the road again" could be the theme song of guides who lead tours in America and throughout the world. For some this is a full-time job; however, for more people it is a part-time or seasonal job. While it is exciting to see new places and meet new people on each trip, being a tour guide involves working long hours and dealing continually with problems that might lower guest satisfaction. Not all tour guides travel. Some work at historic sites like Williamsburg and Gettysburg.

Tour companies employ far more people than just guides. They have tour planners, reservationists, a sales and marketing staff, and a support staff in the business arena.

Careers Working in Amusement Parks

People go to amusement parks like Disney World, Universal Studios, Opryland, Magic Mountain, and Busch Gardens to have fun. In turn, it can be fun working at these places and helping people enjoy themselves. There are jobs for entertainers, ride operators, store salespeople, safety engineers, maintenance workers, ticket takers, food outlet employees, parking attendants, bus drivers, and business support staff employees, to name just a few workers. While Disney parks are huge and have tens of thousands of visitors daily and thousands of employees, across the country there are much smaller amusement parks with far fewer employees, like the 100-acre Holiday World and Splashing Safari in Santa Claus, Indiana. Smaller parks may offer only seasonal employment, except for the few employees on the business staff.

Careers Working in National, State, and Local Parks and Organized Camps

National, state, and local government units have set aside lands to preserve the environment, to showcase the nation's history, and to offer recreation for visitors. Within the United States, there are magnificent national parks such as Yosemite and Yellowstone that display all the grandeur of nature. There are also parks that provide a view of America's past, like Monticello, Mount Vernon, and Hyde Park. All employees at these parks try to create a memorable experience for park visitors. There is considerable competition for positions as rangers in these parks. However, there are many other park jobs, since these facilities often have stores, restaurants, lodgings, and service stations.

Careers Working at Tourist Attractions

The Empire State Building is a tourist attraction, so is an alligator farm in Florida. Just about anything that interests people can become a tourist attraction. This includes such things as museums housing James Dean memorabilia or hubcaps; Southern mansions; sports halls of fame; and ghost towns in the West. A staff is needed to describe what each tourist attraction offers, to maintain the facility, and to sell food and souvenirs. Attractions may be open year-round, only during the summer, or just on weekends or by appointment.

Careers Working in Adventure Recreation

Some people want to climb mountains, raft down turbulent rivers, sky dive, scuba dive, and hike or canoe through wilderness areas. On land, sea, and air these people seek challenging adventures. People working in adventure recreation organize and lead trips for these intrepid adventurers. They also run survival schools; whitewater, scuba, and sky-diving schools; and camps for adventure recreation. Besides being skilled in one or more adventure recreation activities, these people also must be safety experts and be skilled in first aid procedures. Most adventure recreation companies are small and offer only seasonal employment except for their owners/operators and office personnel.

Careers Working in Meeting Planning

Being a meeting planner is a relatively new career. It involves organizing all the events for the meeting of a business, professional, or social organization, from the arrival of those attending the meeting to their departure. It can involve finding speakers and entertainers, arranging meals and lodging, setting up displays, selecting meeting sites, creating a theme, planning the budget, and coordinating all efforts with needed support groups, such as airlines, bus companies, hotels, and restaurants. Meeting planners work for large companies and meeting planning firms, and many are self-employed.

Careers Working in Hotels and Motels

More and more people are traveling for pleasure and business. This makes the hotel and motel industry a leader in creating new jobs and offering long-term career growth. Workers in this industry have the task of making their workplace a "home away from home" for travelers. Within this career, there are two basic categories of jobs. Employees who work directly with guests have "front-of-the-house" jobs, and those who work in housekeeping and maintenance have "back-of-the-house" jobs. Both offer employees opportunities to move up fast. While entry-level employees once moved up the ranks to management positions, more managers are now being selected from those who have post-secondary training in hotel management.

Careers Working in Restaurants

The restaurant business has become the leading retail employer in the United States, and the future of the industry appears extremely bright because people are eating more meals out each year. Today, more than thirty percent of the adults in America are patrons of restaurants on a typical day, and twenty percent more are customers for carryout or delivery. The National Restaurant Association predicts that, by the year 2000, the majority of meals will be prepared outside the home. Because there is a wide variety of employers, work locations, and work schedules, the restaurant industry gives its employees an enormous number of career choices. It also gives them the opportunity to work in a fast-paced career that allows hard-working, ambitious employees to be promoted swiftly to positions of increasing responsibility. The restaurant business is one place where it is realistic for the entry-level employee to dream of owning his or her restaurant some day.

FINDING OUT MORE ABOUT CAREERS IN TRAVEL, TOURISM, AND HOSPITALITY

The best way to become acquainted with the vast number of opportunities in many of these career areas is by taking a part-time job. This demonstrates at once what so many jobs in hotels, motels, restaurants, amusement parks, tourist attractions, and national, state, and local parks are like. And it also lets individuals assess if this is a career that they would enjoy and that is appropriate for them.

An excellent source of information for many careers in travel, tourism, and hospitality is the *Occupational Outlook Handbook,* compiled by the United States Department of Labor. This book gives information about working conditions, employment opportunities, training required, advancement opportunities, earnings, and future job outlook. And throughout *Careers in Travel, Tourism, and Hospitality,* readers should look for the "For More Information" sections, which list helpful sources for more career information.

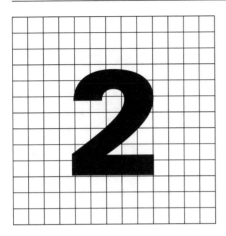

WORKING AS A TRAVEL AGENT

Being a travel agent is certainly not a new profession. In fact, it is a very old one. There have always been people who help others travel, whether the trips are for business or pleasure. When cave dwellers went out to hunt, someone had to organize these trips. When the Romans became the first people to travel for pleasure and ventured to places like Athens, Alexandria, and Naples, Roman slaves arranged their masters' trips. After the fall of the Roman Empire, guides organized and led religious pilgrimages to holy shrines like Bethlehem and Jerusalem. During the time of the Crusades, which lasted from A.D. 1096 to 1270, commercial agents organized these complicated expeditions. Then in the Middle Ages, innkeepers took on the role of travel agents, arranging safe travel for groups of people staying at their inns. In the 16th century, people began traveling in greater numbers not just for business but also to see great cultural centers. Careers opened up for travel advisors who provided information about transportation, places to visit, and prices for these trips.

Perhaps the first true travel agent was a Parisian doctor and philanthropist who opened an office in the early 1600s to provide detailed information on transportation. Subsequently, other entrepreneurs opened businesses to book passages on stagecoaches, ships, and trains, and the profession of travel agent emerged. Besides serving individuals, these precursors to the modern travel agent oversaw the movement of military troops when they undertook expeditions. As transportation improved in the 1800s, the number of individuals arranging travel for others rapidly accelerated in both Europe and America. However, it was not until the 1920s that the term "travel agent" was used to describe people who arranged trips for others.

Two

TRAVEL AGENCIES

Thomas Cook, an English man, is often called the father of the travel agency industry. He organized his first tour in 1841, and his company is still serving travelers throughout the world. In 1879 Cook's agency became the first foreign agency to establish offices in the United States. Cook established the way most travel agencies would operate. He did not charge customers for his travel services. Instead, he received commissions from rail companies on each ticket he sold. Most travel agencies still derive their income primarily from commissions paid by hotels, resorts, airlines, cruise lines, rental car companies, and other places where they make reservations for clients.

Today, there are more than 22,000 travel agencies in more than 44,000 locations in the United States. Some of these agencies are parts of large chains like American Express and the Carlson Travel Network, but more are independent operators. Nearly one-half of the travel agencies are located in suburban areas; about forty percent are in large cities; and the rest, in small towns and rural areas. Within these agencies, more than 250,000 trained personnel have jobs. Most travel agencies are small, with fewer than ten employees. Today's travel agents are not so different from the very first travel agents; the major duty of people in this profession is now and has always been to help travelers reach their destinations safely and efficiently.

According to the American Society of Travel Agents (ASTA), the largest and most influential travel trade association, the majority of travel agencies specialize in certain services or destinations. One important aspect of specialization concerns the type of clientele that a travel agency serves. In this respect, there are corporate (commercial) agencies and vacation (leisure) agencies. The commercial agency caters predominantly, or perhaps exclusively, to the travel needs of business travelers. This type of agency actively seeks new corporate accounts and may enter into contracts with companies as their travel arranger. The leisure agency, on the other hand, assists individuals or groups in making vacation or other leisure travel plans. Many individual travel agents have specialized skills and work exclusively as either corporate or leisure agents. And, of course, there are travel agencies that provide services for both business- and vacation-oriented travelers.

LOOKING AT A CAREER AS A TRAVEL AGENT

Americans now make over one billion trips a year. The average traveler is confronted with many alternatives for transportation, accommodations, and other travel services. Today's travel agents give travelers advice on destinations and make arrangements for transportation, hotel accommodations, tours, car rentals, and recreation. They may also advise on weather conditions, restaurants, and tourist attractions and recreation and sell travel insurance. For international travel, agents also provide information on customs regulations, required papers (passports, visas, and certificates of vaccination), and currency exchange rates. Travel agents who plan conventions and other meetings are usually called meeting planners and are discussed in Chapter 12.

Most travel agents work at agencies and sell travel arrangements directly to clients. Besides business or leisure travel, they may specialize in an area such as cruises or adventure travel. Travel agents can also work for corporations arranging travel for employees, universities with travel programs for students and alumni, membership organizations or associations offering travel programs for members, and banks with travel departments. Many agents are self-employed.

WORKING CONDITIONS

Travel agencies are found in every part of the country; few towns are too small to have a travel agency. These agencies are located everywhere from stand-alone offices, to mini-malls, to department stores, to huge skyscrapers. Typically, all the agents work in one large room; however, in larger agencies managers may have private offices. Each agent's desk usually has a telephone and computer on it and has several chairs nearby for clients. Also in the room are file cabinets with travel brochures and racks displaying tour information. Quite often the room is noisy, with phones ringing, keyboards clicking, printers operating, and clients and agents holding conversations.

Travel agents tend to work forty-hour weeks. They may start at 9:00 a.m. and work to 5:00 p.m. Or they may start later in the day and work until the agency closes, which could be at 8:00 or 9:00 p.m. This job frequently involves working on Saturdays. In fact, work hours are dictated by the clients' needs. If a clientele consists solely of businesspeople, work hours will mirror the typical business week. If most clients are making personal travel plans, then the agency is likely to be open later in the evening and on Saturdays. No matter where a travel agent works, it will often be necessary to work longer hours during vacation seasons and/or periods of heavy business travel to finalize travel plans and to get tickets to customers. Agents who are self-employed usually work longer hours.

ON-THE-JOB RESPONSIBILITIES

Beginning travel agents may not have all of the responsibilities of more experienced agents. More of their time may be spent greeting customers and directing them to other agents, handling routine office mail, filing brochures, and handling simple travel requests. They may also assist experienced agents in expediting complicated orders.

The major responsibilities of travel agents are to handle requests for information and to make travel arrangements. Their clients will either come into their office or call on the phone. Here are some examples of the types of requests agents will handle:

Business

- "Please book me on a flight next Friday from Oakland that arrives in San Diego by 9:00 a.m. and returns to Oakland around 8:00 p.m. the same day."
- "I need a business-class flight to Chicago for three members of our firm. We'll require three rooms at the Drake Hotel and a mid-size rental car.

We want to leave at the end of the workday on March 18 and return on the earliest flight on the 21st."

Personal
- "Our family wants to go to Hawaii during the Christmas holiday. What is the most economical tour package that offers a rental car and a condominium with two bedrooms?"
- "What is the best season of the year to go to Thailand? Is there ever a time when it is cool in Bangkok?"
- "Our ten-year-old son wants to visit his grandmother in Florida. What special arrangements will we have to make with the airline?"

SOURCES OF INFORMATION

Whether a request is simple or complex, travel agents must be very skilled in finding the information quickly. Simple requests for airline, hotel, and automobile reservations can be handled easily by using one of the reservation systems on the computer, but complex requests require agents to use a variety of sources. Agents may rely on tourist offices, reference books, guidebooks, trade publications, brochures, and their own experiences through familiarization trips, as well as travel videos, newspaper and magazine articles, and experiences of clients and other agents.

Tourist Offices

Cities and states in the United States have tourist offices, as do foreign countries that seriously promote travel. Besides answering routine questions on such topics as climate, things to see, and accommodations, these offices also have or will research other information travel agents need. This might include finding out how to conduct business, take a bus between two cities, or stay with a local family.

Reference Books

Atlases give agents a tool to identify where both major and minor destinations are located. Almanacs provide useful statistics as well as information about recent events in an area. Hotel guides describe accommodations and frequently have pictures of the facilities.

Guidebooks

While most guidebooks are designed more for tourists than travel agents, agents need to be familiar with these books so they can make recommendations about the books to clients. Also, guidebooks contain useful information for agents wanting to know more about a tourist location.

Trade Publications

ASTA's publications, as well as trade newspapers like *Tour and Travel News, Travel Weekly, Travel Agent,* and *Travel Trade,* provide current information about destinations and what is happening throughout all aspects of the travel industry. Their coverage includes changes in industry rules and regulations. In addition, there are journals for many segments of the industry, such as hotels and restaurants.

Brochures

Travel agencies constantly receive brochures promoting different travel options from airlines, tour companies, cruise lines, and hotels.

Familiarization Trips

Known as "fam" trips to travel agents, these trips are sponsored by airlines, tour operators, and even governments to acquaint agents with what a region has to offer. Typically, these trips are short and very busy, with visits to a great number of hotels, restaurants, and tourist attractions in one or more areas. Through these trips, agents get a firsthand look at an area and the opportunity to experience the local culture. These trips are an inexpensive way to learn about an area. They are not a vacation.

Other Sources

Travel agents continually learn more about different destinations through their clients and other agents who have visited these places. In addition, whenever they are reading books, magazines, and newspapers, they may find material relating to travel. Television has travel channels and programs that give an intimate look at a variety of destinations. Travel videos do the same.

PROMOTING SALES

People may not realize that part of the job of being a travel agent is promoting sales. For any agency to be successful, there must be repeat clients and new clients. Handling a client's travel needs successfully can lead to that client not only coming back to the agency but referring his or her friends there too. It can also lead to securing corporate accounts. Travel agents find additional clients by approaching groups such as fraternal, religious, or social organizations and offering to put together a vacation package that can be sold only to the membership. One way for agents to court business travelers is by contacting corporations and describing their services. By getting to know meeting planners, travel agents can find opportunities to make travel arrangements for these professionals.

PREPARATION FOR BECOMING A TRAVEL AGENT

Formal or specialized training is becoming increasingly important for travel agents, since few agencies are willing to train people on the job. Consider for a moment some of the many things a travel agent is expected to know, and it becomes clear how important this training is. A travel agent needs to know:

air travel regulations

computer skills

configurations of airplanes and cruise ships

general business skills

government paperwork for visas and passports

organizational skills

sales skills

ticketing procedures for planes, trains, cruise ships, tours, rental cars, and hotels

world climate

world geography

Training Opportunities

Many vocational schools offer six- to eighteen-week full-time programs, as well as evening and Saturday programs. Travel courses can also be found in public adult education programs and in community and four-year colleges. A few colleges offer a bachelor's degree and a master's degree in travel and tourism. Although few college courses relate directly to the travel industry, a college education is sometimes desired by employers. Courses in computer science, geography, foreign languages, and history are most useful. Courses in accounting and business management also are important, especially for those who expect to manage or start their own travel agencies. The American Society of Travel Agents and the Institute of Certified Travel Agents offer a travel correspondence course. Travel agencies also provide some on-the-job training for their employees, a significant part of which consists of computer instruction. Employees must have computer skills to operate airline reservations systems.

Choosing a Travel School

Travel agents clearly need certain skills and knowledge. Attending a school to help acquire these skills should make prospective agents more marketable. ASTA suggests that the following questions be asked of the representatives of the educational institutions that individuals are considering attending.

1. *Has the school been "approved," "registered," or "licensed" by the State Postsecondary Education Bureau or a recognized accreditation association?* If there is no such indication of "approval," "registration," or "license" in the school's catalog or brochure, check with the state department of education in the state where the school is located. For additional information, you may also want to contact the Better Business Bureau in the city/town where the school is located.

2. *Who teaches on the faculty?* How many members of the faculty have recent travel industry experience or certified travel counselor (CTC) designation? Are they professionally active within the travel and tourism industry?

3. *What does the curriculum offer?* Does it offer travel courses in geography, fares/ticketing/tariffs, industry forms and procedures, automation, sales, marketing, and travel industry operations? Does the school provide for internships? Does the school offer extracurricular activities? *Is the course of study of sufficient duration to cover adequately the curriculum advertised?*

4. *What kind of hands-on airline computer training is available?* Does it teach both domestic and international reservations? Does the training cover accessing airline availability, pricing, selling, and creating a passenger name record (PNR), as well as booking hotel, car rental, and rail reservations?

5. *How long has the school been in operation?* Is the school a member of ASTA? Does the school have a good relationship with the local travel agency community? Does the school have an advisory board of active travel industry professionals?

6. *Does the school offer placement assistance for graduates?* If so, what is their success ratio? Feel free to ask if there are any graduates of the school who are working in the area whom you can contact. Ask working graduates for their evaluation of the program.

Certification, Licensing, and Advancement

Travel agents with five or more years of experience can take an advanced course leading to the designation of Certified Travel Counselor (CTC). The course is part-time and takes eighteen months to complete. The CTC certification indicates that an agent has gone beyond the ordinary agent in education. It is the hallmark of a truly professional agent. Owners and managers of agencies tend to have this certification. The Institute of Certified Travel Agents also offers courses leading to certification, called designation of competence, in North American, western European, and Caribbean, or South Pacific, tours. This certification indicates that an agent has an in-depth knowledge of one or more of these travel areas.

There are no federal licensing requirements for travel agents. However, certain states require licensing, and several have registration requirements.

Some employees start as reservation clerks or receptionists in travel agencies. With experience and some formal training, they can take on greater responsibilities and eventually assume travel agent duties. In agencies with many offices, travel agents may advance to office manager or to other managerial positions. Many agents advance up the career ladder by moving from one agency to another. The key to advancement in all cases is a demonstrated ability to attract new clients and to do work at such a level that most clients become repeat clients.

Travel agents who start their own agencies usually have experience in an established agency first. They must generally gain formal supplier or corporation approval before they can receive commissions. Suppliers or corporations are organizations of airlines, ship lines, or rail lines. The Airlines Reporting Corporation, for example, is the approving body for airlines. To gain approval, an agency must be in operation, be financially sound, and employ at least one experienced manager/travel agent.

Continuing Education

No one should ever become a travel agent unless he or she is willing to learn continually throughout his or her career. Change is a constant in this profession. Agencies change the computer programs they use. New databases are constantly being added to computer systems. Tour companies and cruise lines offer new tours each year. And airline rates may change almost daily, even to the same destination. New hotels are built throughout the world, and tourist "hot spots" for travel change. The Institute of Certified Travel Agents offers courses that agents can use throughout their careers.

SPECIAL ATTRIBUTES OF A TRAVEL AGENT

Sales Skills

Travel agents are salespeople. And to be successful in this facet of their jobs, they must demonstrate these characteristics:

- an ability to close a sale
- an ability to get along with clients
- an ability to handle complaints
- an engaging telephone personality
- enthusiasm for travel
- integrity (to earn the client's confidence)
- patience
- persistence
- solid listening skills
- a talent for discovering what clients really want
- thorough knowledge of travel options

No one is born with a sales personality. These are skills that can be developed.

Technical Skills

Every year more sophisticated computer systems are used in the travel industry. Travel agents must be sufficiently skilled to access air, rail, cruise, tour, and accommodations information and to book reservations.

Organizational Skills

Travel agents must know how to prioritize their work so that clients receive tickets and information when needed. Some ticketing must be done immediately, while other ticketing can be postponed for days or even weeks.

Business Skills   Every travel agent must understand how his or her agency functions. In addition, agents must possess such basic business skills as letter writing, filing, and handling money.

SALARY AND FRINGE BENEFITS

It is important for future travel agents to understand that travel agencies earn their income primarily from commissions paid by airlines, travel suppliers, and tour operators. While commissions vary, those for domestic travel arrangements, cruises, hotels, sightseeing tours, and car rentals are about ten percent of the total sale. Recently, some airlines have placed a cap on the total amount of the commission for a transaction. Some agencies may also charge clients a service fee for the time and expense involved in planning a trip.

Agencies have what are known as inside sales agents, outside sales agents, or both inside and outside sales agents. Outside agents may rent a desk at an agency, but typically they work on commission. This commission is usually split with the agency. Inside agents are hourly employees. They usually do not receive commissions.

According to ASTA, the annual salary of an entry-level agent averages $11,000. In 1995, the average salary for sales agents, regardless of length of employment, was $22,700; for Certified Travel Counselors (CTC), the average was $24,100. Travel agents' salaries depend on experience, seniority, and the size and location of the firm. In addition, good salespeople can earn bonuses or free/discounted trips. ASTA reports that the average travel agency manager receives an annual salary of $22,270. Those with less than one year of experience understandably earn less (an average of $17,370) than those with more tenure. Managers with more than fifteen years of experience are paid an average salary of $28,200; CTC managers with more than fifteen years of experience are paid an average salary of $29,000. Benefits may include medical insurance plans, sick leave, paid holidays and vacation days, and familiarization trips. And according to ASTA, one travel agency in five offers its employees a retirement plan.

Earnings of travel agents who own their agencies depend mainly on commission. During the first year of business or while awaiting corporation approval, self-employed travel agents usually have low earnings. Their income is generally limited to commissions from hotels, cruises, and tour operators and to nominal fees for making complicated arrangements. It needs to be pointed out that even established agents have lower profits during economic downturns.

THE PERKS AND PRESSURES OF BEING A TRAVEL AGENT

The major perk of being a travel agent is free or inexpensive travel. The familiarization trips that were described earlier in the chapter generally require agents to pay a small amount. These trips rarely include travel companions. Airlines do give free and discounted tickets. This represents an enormous saving on international travel because the agent's ticket cost is often discounted seventy-five percent, and a companion's fare is frequently discounted fifty percent. Tours and hotels also offer discounts; however, they are frequently only ten percent off the established price.

Although the travel perks can be impressive, there are downsides to this career. Prospective travel agents must realize that they will be spending a great portion of their day at a computer. This can cause agents to suffer from wrist injuries and eye and back strain. There is also stress in this job because of the rapid work pace in many agencies and the fact that agents cannot control such things as cancelled flights, overbooked hotels, and tour destination changes that affect their clients' satisfaction. And in this job there is also the continual challenge of dealing with demanding and difficult clients.

THE PERSONAL STORY OF A TRAVEL AGENT

Being a travel agent is an occupation in which there are far more women than men. One of these women is Sylvia Porter, who has been a travel agent for more than eight years. After graduating from college with a bachelor's degree in English, Sylvia had the unusual job of training teachers from throughout the world to operate the Opticon, a device that allows the blind to read by feeling print. This job, which involved some travel in the United States as well as a trip abroad to Greece, instilled in Sylvia a desire to travel and to have a career that involved travel.

Sylvia went back to school, enrolled in a community college, and received a degree in tourism. Over the years, she has observed that most agents have received training as she did because it is absolutely necessary for this job. She explains that this training teaches prospective travel agents two valuable skills: how to use the computer in a travel agency and how to research destination information.

Eight years ago, it was easy for Sylvia to get her first job as a travel agent. She was older, and in this profession age is considered a plus. Her first position was in a small travel agency with three inside agents. Sylvia primarily handled leisure clients, selling tours and creating foreign travel packages for those who wanted to travel independently. As an inside agent, she handled clients who walked in the door and at the same time tried to build a client base of repeat customers. She received an hourly salary and no commission. After one year, this agency folded and Sylvia was seeking a job again.

In her next job, she became an outside agent. Her income was now based solely on the commissions she earned. No longer did she have the luxury of being assigned walk-in clients; now she had to attract her own clients. Some of these clients were individuals for whom Sylvia had made travel plans at her former agency; others were friends and people who had heard of her through other clients. Also, she would write to people that she knew in some way to solicit new business. Unlike some other agents, Sylvia did not make "cold" calls to people she did not know in order to secure their business. At this agency, she spent most of her time working with clients, helping them make leisure travel plans, although she did have some corporate accounts. As an outside agent, Sylvia was able to make more money than she did in her previous job as an inside agent. After five years, however, this firm folded too. (This is one of the downsides of a job as a travel agent—many firms go out of business each year.)

Again, Sylvia was able to find a job easily as a travel agent. For the past two years, she has worked as an outside agent. Although she works independently, four of the other agents in the firm cover for her and each other so all are able to take vacations and still serve their clients. In this job, she splits her commission with the agency.

A Typical Day

Sylvia's hours are flexible. Some days she works from 9:00 a.m. to 5:00 p.m., and others from 10:00 a.m. to 4:00 p.m. If she doesn't go in to work, she monitors her calls from home. Every day she spends a lot of time on the phone with clients, considerable time on the computer, and some time with clients who come into the office. Sylvia compares her job to that of a fireman, as she is constantly responding to the calls she receives.

Here is a look at the diversity of tasks this travel agent handled on a recent workday:

- arranged a trip to Mexico for some clients
- consulted with clients who were planning a trip to Italy
- handled several calls for tickets (routine work)
- made a phone call to arrange a Hawaiian package for a client
- talked with a consolidator about a ticket to Switzerland
- searched for a nonstop flight from San Francisco to Philadelphia for a couple and their show dogs

The Good and the Bad

While perks allow a travel agent many opportunities to travel inexpensively, Sylvia sees several negatives to her career choice. This is a job with a lot of stress, and the pay is poor. Also, she doesn't know what will happen in the future, with the advent of ticketless travel and the dollar cap on airline commissions.

LOOKING AT THE FUTURE

The future is generally bright for those seeking a career as a travel agent. This occupation is expected to grow much faster than the average for all occupations through the year 2005. Spending on travel is expected to increase significantly: more people are expected to travel and to do so more frequently. In fact, many people now take more than one vacation a year. In addition, the employment of managerial, professional specialty, and sales representative occupations—those that do the most business travel—is projected to grow rapidly. Many job openings will arise as new agencies start up and existing agencies expand to meet the needs of these additional travelers, but most will occur as experienced agents transfer to other occupations or leave the workforce.

As a result of airline deregulation in 1978 and other industry factors, the travel agency business has become increasingly competitive. New industry trends have forced travel agencies to become more creative in their marketing and advertising efforts. Travel agents have found it necessary to cultivate new fields to keep their profits high enough to sustain their agencies. Group travel, incentive travel, travel clubs, and corporate contracts are more important to travel agents than they were a decade ago.

Caution: The travel industry generally is sensitive to economic downturns and political crises, when travel plans are likely to be deferred. Therefore, the number of job opportunities fluctuates. While a love of travel attracts many people to this field, it is important to remember that to succeed, a travel agent must have a genuine desire to be of service.

FOR MORE INFORMATION

Individuals who are thinking about a career as a travel agent need to become acquainted with the American Society of Travel Agents (ASTA) for information about becoming a travel agent and what is happening in the industry. In appendix A, there is a list of schools from ASTA that offer training for becoming a travel agent. Also, for more information on training opportunities, contact:

> American Society of Travel Agents
> Education Department
> 1101 King Street
> Alexandria, VA 22314

For certification information, contact:

> The Institute of Certified Travel Agents
> 148 Lindon Street
> P.O. Box 82-56
> Wellesley, MA 02181-0012
> Phone: 1-800-542-4282

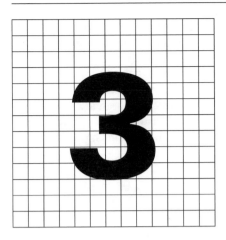

WORKING FOR THE AIRLINES AS A PILOT OR FLIGHT ATTENDANT

Throughout the course of civilization, people have looked at birds flying in the sky and wished that they, too, could fly. The invention of the airplane has turned this dream into a reality for more than 400 million airline passengers each year, and this number is expected to climb steadily. Being able to fly is a relatively new experience for humans. The first person to fly was actually a French balloonist who flew over Paris for thirty minutes in 1783. Then, more than 100 years later, the Wright Brothers made the first manned, powered flight at Kitty Hawk, North Carolina. In 1926, commercial air passenger service began in the United States. And shortly thereafter, familiar airlines like TWA, United, and American started.

AIRLINE DEREGULATION

In the early years of commercial air passenger service, airlines in the United States operated much like utilities. The government regulated ticket prices and assigned routes to the airlines. All of this changed dramatically in 1978, when President Jimmy Carter signed the Airline Deregulation Act. This meant that new carriers could easily start up and airlines could charge fares according to what the market would bear. They could also compete for routes. Many innovative new airlines, like People's Express, were launched within the first few years of deregulation, and passengers became accustomed to searching for and finding bargain fares and innovative new services. The competitive atmosphere of deregulation caused a number of airlines to merge together to form very large carriers (like Delta and Northwest) while at the same time, some carriers (Eastern, Braniff) disappeared after suffering financial difficulties. Another aspect of deregulation was the emergence of the hub-and-spoke system, in which major airlines use a city as a central point (hub) and funnel traffic from secondary cities (spokes) to the hub for connecting flights to other cities. Also, many commuter airlines carried passengers to the hubs for major airlines. These commuter carriers also took a substantial number of passengers away from the major carriers.

Today, those who want to work in the airline industry can find a variety of jobs. For those who are lured to the skies, there are jobs as pilots, copilots, flight engineers, and flight attendants. Then there is the greater number of people employed by airlines as reservationists, customer service representatives, and mechanics, as well as all of the people in operations, finance, sales, and marketing.

LOOKING AT A CAREER AS A PILOT

Pilots are highly trained professionals who fly airplanes and helicopters. While the vast majority of pilots work for airlines transporting passengers and cargo, others are involved in more unusual tasks, such as testing aircraft, monitoring traffic, rescuing and evacuating injured persons, firefighting, and crop dusting.

Being a pilot is one career choice that was not available until the twentieth century. Even then the early leaders of commercial aviation were in Europe, not the United States, because the distances commonly to be flown were much shorter there. Nevertheless, in the 1920s many of today's prominent U.S. carriers began to conquer the skies. Delta Airlines started as a crop-dusting company and then began carrying passengers in 1929. Charles Lindbergh, one of America's pilot pioneers, flew for a company that joined with others to form American Airlines in 1930 (the same year that TWA was formed from the merger of several airlines).

Cockpit Positions

There are three positions for professional pilots in the cockpit. The captain commands the aircraft, supervises all the other crew members, and is responsible for the safety of the passengers, crew, and cargo. The copilot (first officer) assists the captain in communicating with air traffic controllers, monitoring the instruments, and flying the aircraft. The flight engineer (second officer) assists the other pilots by monitoring and operating many of the instruments and systems, making minor in-flight repairs, and watching for other aircraft. Being a flight engineer is an entry-level position at many airlines and does not include flying the airplane. While some large aircraft still have a flight engineer in the cockpit, virtually all new aircraft now fly with only two pilots, who rely more heavily on computerized controls.

WORKING CONDITIONS

By federal law, airline pilots cannot fly more than 100 hours a month or 1,000 hours a year. Most airline pilots fly an average of 80 hours a month and work an additional 80 hours a month performing nonflying duties before and after flights. Since airlines operate flights at all hours of the day and night, pilots can expect irregular hours. They can also expect layovers away from home.

During these layovers, they receive hotel accommodations, transportation be-tween the hotel and airport, and an allowance for expenses.

Pilots employed outside the airlines often have irregular schedules; they may fly as few as 30 hours one month and as many as 100 hours the next. For example, corporate pilots do not usually fly scheduled routes. Instead, they are on call most of the month and fly when businesspeople schedule trips. Because these pilots are transporting corporate employees, they are usually home each evening and will not often fly on holidays. They will frequently have many nonflying responsibili-ties and much less free time than airline pilots.

ON-THE-JOB RESPONSIBILITIES

Commercial airline pilots must arrive at the airport a set amount of time before each flight. After checking in, the pilots typically receive a computer printout from the flight planning computer, listing things such as weather at takeoff, weather at destination, in-route weather, time of trip, routing, winds at cruise altitude, and fuel load. The computer also predicts the plane weight, winds, and temperature at takeoff and gives the optimal runway and takeoff speed. If computerized flight information is not provided, the pilots will confer with flight dispatchers and avia-tion weather forecasters about weather conditions en route and at their destina-tion. Based on this information, they choose a route, altitude, and speed that should provide the fastest, safest, and smoothest flight.

Once aboard the aircraft, the pilots use a checklist to thoroughly check their aircraft to make sure that the engines, controls, instruments, and other systems are functioning properly. They also make sure that the baggage or cargo has been loaded correctly, and they brief flight attendants about the trip.

Takeoff and landing are the most difficult parts of the flight, requiring close coordination between the captain and copilot and the flight engineer (if aboard). For example, as the plane accelerates for takeoff, the captain concentrates on the runway while the copilot, not flying, scans the instrument panel. The mo-ment the plane reaches takeoff speed, the copilot tells the captain, who then pulls back on the controls to raise the nose of the plane into the air.

During the flight, the captain pilots the aircraft along the predetermined route with the assistance of autopilot and the flight management computer. In the past, pilots guided the plane's course constantly. Today, planes are flown mechanically throughout most of the flight. The pilots, however, will periodi-cally scan the instrument panel to check their fuel supply, the condition of their engines, and the air-conditioning, hydraulic, and other systems. The po-sition of the plane is monitored by the air traffic control radar stations that are being passed along the way. During the flight, the pilots may request a change in altitude or route if the circumstances warrant it. For example, if the ride is rougher than expected, the pilots may ask air traffic control if pilots flying at other altitudes have reported better conditions. If so, they may request a change. They may also follow the same procedure to find a stronger tailwind or a weaker headwind to save fuel and increase speed. If visibility is poor, the pilots will need to rely completely on their instruments. Very sophisticated equipment is now available that enables pilots to land completely "blind." In fact, a computer on board the aircraft, which is taking in information from all over the plane, can actually land the plane in very bad weather. (Not all planes have this sophisticated equipment.) Once on the ground, pilots must complete records on the flight for their airlines and the Federal Aviation Administration (FAA).

The number of nonflying duties that pilots have depends on where they are employed. Airline pilots have the services of large support staffs; however, pilots employed by other organizations such as charters or corporate operators have many other duties. They may load the aircraft, handle all passenger luggage to ensure a balanced load, and supervise refueling. Other nonflying responsibilities include keeping records, scheduling flights, arranging for major maintenance, and even performing minor maintenance and repair work on their aircraft.

PREPARATION FOR BECOMING A PILOT: REQUIREMENTS AND TRAINING OPPORTUNITIES

Whether they are employed by major airlines, commuter airlines, corporations, or cargo airlines, all pilots must meet very specific requirements. The FAA sets the standards for pilots and other people working in the aviation field. Following is a look at some of the requirements future pilots must meet.

Experience Requirements

For pilots, experience is judged in two ways: hours of flying and kind of flying. Certain levels must be reached in both categories for an individual to qualify for any of the basic pilot certificates issued by the FAA. For example, commercial pilots need to have at least 250 hours of flight time and an instrument rating, and air transport pilots need 1,500 flight hours and an instrument rating. Most applicants exceed the minimum experience requirements.

Personal Requirements

The FAA has set minimum ages for pilots. There is also a maximum age of sixty for commercial airline pilots. To earn a pilot's certificate, applicants must meet very stringent physical requirements, which include having 20/20 vision with or without glasses, good hearing, good health, and no physical handicaps that could impair their performance. Furthermore, pilots must continue to pass periodic medical examinations to maintain a valid certificate. It is advised that prospective pilots have a physical examination by an FAA-designated aviation medical examiner to make sure they meet the physical requirements for a pilot's certificate before beginning a formal training program. According to the Air Line Pilots Association, a candidate's heart, lungs, physical dexterity, and eyesight are the main concerns. Pilots must also demonstrate to airline companies that they can make quick decisions and accurate judgments under pressure by passing required psychological and aptitude tests.

Educational Requirements

Some small airlines will hire high school graduates. While larger airlines require two years of college, more than ninety percent of the pilots with major airlines have four-year college degrees. Furthermore, airlines prefer to hire college graduates. College graduates may choose to major in aviation; however, airlines do not specify a particular major.

License Requirements

To qualify for one of the five main types of pilot certificates (student, recreational, private, commercial, airline transport), applicants must meet age, physical, education, and skill level requirements set by the FAA. Applicants must pass a written test that includes questions on the principles of safe flight, navigation techniques, and FAA regulations. They also must demonstrate their flying ability to FAA or designated examiners.

The Air Line Pilots Association points out that all categories of licenses require recency of experience, and that all pilots must take a flight review with an instructor at least every two years. In addition to taking regular six-month or annual FAA and company flight checks, and simulator and medical exams, an airline pilot is subject to unannounced spot checks by FAA inspectors. Here is a brief look at requirements for the commercial pilot and air transport pilot certificates as described by the Air Line Pilots Association.

Commercial Pilot

Minimum age: 18

Privileges: May act as pilot in command of any aircraft for which a rating is held and may receive compensation.

Physical standards: Must hold a valid and current second class medical certificate. Must get a new certificate each year.

Aeronautical experience: Must have at least 250 hours of flight time, including at least 100 hours as pilot in command, 50 hours of cross-country, 10 hours of training in control of a complex (retractable landing gear and adjustable props) aircraft, 10 hours of instrument instruction, and an instrument rating.

Aeronautical skill: Must pass a detailed written examination and demonstrate to an examiner most of the skills required for a private certificate but performed with a higher degree of precision.

Air Transport Pilot

Minimum age: 23

Privileges: May serve as pilot in command of an aircraft. (Captains must hold this certification.)

Physical standards: Requires a current and valid first class medical certificate, which must be renewed every six months.

Education: High school diploma or its equivalent. (Most employers prefer a college degree.)

Aeronautical experience: 1500 flight hours, 500 of which are cross-country, 100 at night, 75 in instrument category, of which 50 will be in actual instrument weather conditions. An instrument rating is required.

Aeronautical skill: Must successfully pass a written examination and demonstrate to an examiner his/her ability to pilot an aircraft under the complex situations applicable to airline-type flying.

Company Requirements   Besides the above requirements, pilots who want to work for airlines must also meet the individual requirements of the airlines. Airlines publish requirements; however, successful job candidates typically have more education, ratings, and flight hours than the minimum requirements.

Training Opportunities   Many pilots get their training in the armed forces. Military pilots get extensive flying experience on jet aircraft and helicopters. At the end of their tours of duty, many pilots leave the military for civilian jobs. Because of budget reductions, it is expected that fewer pilots will be able to receive military training in the future and more pilots will receive their training at FAA-certified schools. At the present time, the FAA has certified about 600 civilian flying schools, including some colleges and universities that offer degree credit for pilot training.

A LOOK AT OTHER PILOTING JOBS

Jobs as pilots are not limited to transporting passengers. Many pilots work for airlines devoted to carrying freight, packages, or mail. For example, the overnight delivery services have fleets of planes flying each night. In addition, some of the major airlines have freight operations. Cargo pilots will tend to fly regular schedules. Like passenger airline pilots, cargo pilots must have the appropriate FAA pilot's certificates.

About 10,000 pilots work as corporate pilots, transporting businesspeople to meetings and work sites. These pilots need to be trained to fly a wide range of aircraft, since corporations fly everything from single-engine planes to large jets. The basic requirement for this job is to have a commercial certificate with an instrument and multi-engine rating. Many corporations, however, prefer applicants who have experience in the type of craft they will be flying most frequently.

Helicopter pilots, like airline pilots, frequently receive their training in the armed forces. They must also hold a commercial pilot's license with an instrument rating issued by the FAA. Some helicopter pilots fly passengers on short runs from airports to other airports and to city centers as well as over tourist sites. But helicopter pilots are engaged in many other activities besides transporting passengers. They give traffic reports for radio stations, evacuate injured and sick people to hospitals, aid in fighting fires, spray and dust crops, and carry heavy equipment to job sites.

ADVANCING UP THE CAREER LADDER

New airline pilots usually start as flight engineers unless the company does not have any planes requiring three pilots in the cockpit. At organizations other than airlines, new employees usually start as copilots or flying less sophisticated equipment. Helicopter pilots typically start by flying a single-engine aircraft.

Advancement for all pilots generally is limited to other flying jobs. In the airlines, advancement usually depends on seniority provisions of union contracts. After two to seven years, those who start as flight engineers advance according to seniority to copilot and, after five to fifteen years, to captain. Seniority also determines which pilots get the more desirable routes. In a non-airline job, a copilot may advance to pilot and, in large companies, to chief pilot or director of aviation in charge of aircraft, maintenance, and flight procedures. Merit can be more important than seniority for corporate pilots in climbing up the career ladder. Seniority is usually important in advancement for helicopter pilots. They frequently advance to flying larger aircraft as they gain experience and flight time.

SALARY AND FRINGE BENEFITS

One of the best-paid positions in the travel, tourism, and hospitality industry is that of airline pilot. Most pilots are members of the Air Line Pilots Association. According to this organization, the average captain with twenty years of service earns about $110,000 annually. Some captains may earn in excess of $200,000. Copilots with ten years of service typically earn a yearly salary of about $58,000. Flight engineers with six years of service will earn approximately $38,000; their entry-level salaries range from $12,000 to $25,000. Earnings for airline pilots also depend on factors such as the type, size, and maximum speed of the plane, and the number of hours and miles flown. Extra pay may be earned for night and international flights. Typically, pilots working outside the airlines earn lower salaries.

Airline pilots generally are eligible for life and health insurance plans paid for by the airlines. They also receive retirement benefits. If they should fail the FAA physical examination at some point in their careers, they get disability payments. In addition, some airlines provide allowances to pilots for purchasing and cleaning their uniforms. As an additional benefit, pilots and their immediate families usually are entitled to free or reduced-fare transportation on their own and other airlines.

THE PERSONAL STORY OF A PILOT

An interest in flying in college has turned into a career as a pilot for Kit Darby. Like so many other pilots, he learned to fly in the armed forces. During his eight years in the military, he was able to get an air line transport certificate, so he was qualified to seek a job with an airline upon returning to civilian life. His first job was with a flight training company, teaching various aspects of flying. While working at this job, Kit also obtained a rating to fly 727s. Within a few months, he landed a job with Braniff and began the company's training program. (Every airline has its own training program, which all new company pilots must complete.) First, he went to ground school for about four weeks, and then he worked with a flight simulator for almost two weeks. His training was complete after he spent twenty-five hours flying in the cockpit with experienced Braniff pilots. Kit was briefly assigned to a B-727 as a flight engineer before he began flying DC-8s. After nine months, he became a copilot. Unfortunately, deregulation brought increasing financial difficulties to Braniff, and Kit was furloughed. He worked briefly for a family business before joining Capitol Airlines as a DC-8 copilot. In this job, his home base was New York City and he flew to Europe and the Caribbean. After $1\frac{1}{2}$ years, he became a DC-8 captain. When Capitol Airlines encountered problems staying in business, Kit again had to look for another job. He was then hired by United Airlines as a flight engineer; however, a strike threatened, so he was placed in a reserve group. While waiting for this situation to be resolved, he worked for six months at Republic as a copilot on a DC-9. The fall of 1986 was decision time for Kit. He was recalled by United, had the opportunity to remain with Republic, and was offered a position with Piedmont. He chose United because it offered the best retirement program. He has remained there ever since. At United he began as a flight engineer, because of the seniority system that exists in the airline industry. After four years in this position on a B-727, he served as a copilot for three years, then became a B-737 captain.

A Pilot's
Work Schedule

Kit now lives in Atlanta, Georgia; however, his home base is Chicago, so he must commute to work. Since the flight between Atlanta and Chicago takes only $1\frac{1}{2}$ hours, he spends less time commuting in a week than many who drive to work each day. Once a month he bids for routes. Currently, he works three or four days a week and has the rest of the time off. His work week begins with an early morning commute to Chicago and includes layovers of two or three nights. Fortunately, at present one of his layover nights is spent at home in Atlanta. Because Kit flies a 737, which is not a long-distance plane, he will typically fly to three or four cities during a day's work and usually will change planes at least once during that time.

On flight days, Kit shows up at the flight planning area at the airport one hour before his plane is scheduled to depart. He checks in on a computer and then with his copilot looks over a computerized version of the flight plan, the plane's maintenance record, and the weather report. If he agrees with the flight plan, he signs the computerized report. He can make conservative changes on his own—such as adding more fuel—but must talk to the flight dispatcher if he wishes to be less conservative.

From the flight planning area, Kit goes to the gate, a considerable distance away at some airports. He meets the flight attendants and the gate agent and checks if the plane is clean or needs any maintenance. If it is a continuing flight, he will talk to the previous pilot about any problems that are not yet on the computer. And he always asks this pilot about the weather and whether the ride was smooth. Typically, the copilot checks the plane's exterior. Once inside the plane, Kit and his copilot check their areas. Then Kit begins a formal check of the instruments, using a checklist. Once he gets the final weather report and weight of the plane, usually from a computer, he will make any final adjustments that are necessary. Then he will taxi out to the runway.

Either Kit or his copilot will take off. Pilots and copilots usually alternate taking off and landing throughout the day. Once the plane reaches cruising altitude, the plane is normally flown by a computer as the captain and copilot monitor the instruments. Throughout the flight, Kit is always looking for ways to make the flight smooth and fast. According to Kit, landing is the most demanding time for pilots. Typically, this is "handflown" (done by the pilots) rather than controlled by computer. While computers can land some planes, the computer can only bring Kit's plane to 200 feet from landing at the airport. If visibility is poor, Kit uses the computer as much as possible because it is easier to monitor the instruments this way. Once the plane lands, Kit is already planning for the next leg of the trip as he taxis to the gate. Typically, he will have between thirty and sixty minutes between flights.

Kit sees being a pilot as a blend of headwork and handwork. When flying is automated, he must constantly be monitoring what is happening. When he is handflying the plane, it is close to being a sport. Kit believes that, because of his love of flying, he is almost being paid to enjoy himself.

LOOKING AT THE FUTURE

There will be considerable competition for pilots through the year 2005 because the number of applicants for new positions is expected to exceed the number of openings. Pilots have a strong attachment to their occupation, with its high earnings, glamour, prestige, and travel benefits. They rarely change occupations; however, because of the large number of pilots who will reach retirement in the next decade, replacement needs will generate several thousand job openings each year. Furthermore, additional jobs will be created by a rising demand for pilots. The outlook is for employment to increase faster than the average for all occupations through the year 2005. It is expected that new two-pilot aircraft with their computerized flight management systems will all but eliminate the demand for flight engineers; however, the expected growth in airline passenger and cargo traffic will create a need for more airlines, pilots, and flight instructors. Employment of corporate pilots is expected to grow more slowly than in the past, as businesses opt to have employees fly with regional and smaller airlines serving their area rather than buy and operate their own aircraft. The need for helicopter pilots, on the other hand, is expected to grow more rapidly as the demand for this type of service increases.

There has been a glut of pilots in the recent past, as more pilots left the armed forces and the pilots who lost their jobs during the restructuring of the airline industry looked for jobs. Prospects for future pilots are improving dramatically. Pilots who have logged the greatest number of flying hours in the most sophisticated equipment generally will have the best prospects for jobs. Prospects will also be good for the jobseekers with the most FAA licenses.

The employment of pilots is always sensitive to cyclical swings in the economy. During times of recession, pilots are often temporarily furloughed because there is a decline in demand for air travel. At these times commercial and corporate demand for pilots is also reduced.

FOR MORE INFORMATION

Before getting started on a career as a pilot, it is often helpful to visit the nearest airport to talk with a flight instructor. Also, the Air Line Pilots Association has a program designed for aspiring airline pilots, the Pilot Information Program (PIP). For information about PIP membership, write or call for a brochure:

> Pilot Information Program
> Education Department
> Air Line Pilots Association
> 535 Herndon Parkway
> Herndon, VA 22070
> Phone: (703) 481-4452

Aviation Information Resources, Inc. has an airline pilot starter kit with career information. Call or write to this organization to learn more about this kit:

> Aviation Information Resources, Inc.
> 4002 Riverdale Court
> Atlanta, GA 30337
> Phone: (800) AIR-APPS

For a copy of the List of Certificated Pilot Schools, write to:

> Superintendent of Documents,
> U.S. Government Printing Office
> Washington, DC 20402

LOOKING AT A CAREER AS A FLIGHT ATTENDANT

While the image of a flight attendant is that of a glamorous individual in uniform who travels to places most people dream of visiting, the reality is a hardworking individual who has the job of seeing that all passengers have a safe, comfortable, and enjoyable flight. At times, this job means being a nanny, a short-order cook, a waiter, a bartender, a psychologist, an instructor, a janitor, a librarian, a linguist, an emergency coordinator, a travel consultant, and even a paramedic. Flight attendants wear many "hats" in the course of their work. But it is also true that the combination of free time and free or reduced air fares offered by this profession provides them with a great opportunity to travel and see new places.

WORKING CONDITIONS

Flight attendants may find themselves on small commuter planes with 10 or fewer passengers, or on jumbo jets with close to 500 people on board. Since airlines operate around the clock all year long, attendants must be prepared to work at night and on holidays and weekends. They usually fly an average of seventy-five to eighty-five hours a month and spend about the same amount of time on the ground preparing planes for flights, writing reports following completed flights, and waiting for planes that arrive late. During very long flights, they may have breaks to rest for up to two hours. Because of the way flights are scheduled and the limitations on their flying time, attendants can have eleven or more days off each month.

Flight attendants have a home base that is typically a major city, such as New York, Minneapolis, Dallas/Fort Worth, Chicago, San Francisco, Los Angeles, St. Louis, Miami, or Atlanta. This job may take attendants away from their home base at least one third of the time. During layovers, the airlines provide transportation to and from airports, hotel accommodations, and an allowance for meal expenses. To be home every night, it is usually necessary to fly short routes for feeder airlines.

Being a flight attendant can be strenuous and trying work. Short flights require speedy service if meals are served. And full flights on small planes can make it difficult to maneuver food and drink carts in the aisles. A turbulent flight can also make serving food and drinks difficult. Flight attendants on long flights may suffer jet lag. And they are susceptible to injury because of the job demands in a moving aircraft. There is also the risk of exposure to contagious illnesses from being in close contact with so many people in a confined area.

ON-THE-JOB RESPONSIBILITIES

A flight attendant's job begins when he or she arrives at the airport at least an hour before the plane is scheduled to depart. Then it is time to check a personal mailbox, read bulletin boards, and attend a flight briefing with the other attendants. At this meeting, responsibilities will be assigned by the lead attendant or purser. Attendants will find out where they will sit for takeoff and landing, in which cabin they will work, and how the meal service will be done. Then a supervisor who has talked to maintenance will come in and talk about any problems there may be, such as an inoperative seat or a balky coffee maker. If movies will be shown, the attendants will learn their titles. And they will be told about any passengers with special needs, such as an individual with breathing difficulties who needs supplemental oxygen. They will also learn if there are any authorized individuals carrying firearms, such as F.B.I. agents or Secret Service personnel. From the lead attendant or purser, they will find out the names of the cockpit crew, the flying time, and the departure gate. After the completion of the briefing, the attendants will gather their belongings and proceed to the plane.

Once aboard the plane, the flight attendants typically have the following responsibilities before takeoff:

- see that the passenger cabin is in order
- check that supplies of food, beverages, blankets, and reading materials are adequate
- make sure that first aid kits and other emergency equipment are aboard and in working order

- greet passengers and help them find their seats
- assist passengers in storing coats and carry-on luggage
- pass out newspapers and magazines
- instruct passengers in the use of emergency equipment and the location of emergency exits
- check to see that all passengers have seat belts fastened, seat backs forward, and tray tables in the stored position

Once the plane is airborne, the flight attendants will try to make the passengers' trip enjoyable by providing some or all of these services:

- answer questions about the flight
- distribute pillows and blankets
- help care for small children, the elderly, and disabled persons
- serve cocktails and other refreshments
- heat and distribute precooked meals
- answer questions about the destination
- provide information about arrival and connections
- distribute headphones for movies
- sell duty-free items on international flights
- help passengers fill out entry and custom forms on international flights

Before landing, the flight attendants will pick up headsets if movies have been shown, gather trash, and check that the passengers have fastened their seatbelts, stowed items away, and returned their seats and trays to their original positions. After landing, they will help the passengers deplane, prepare necessary reports, and may straighten up the plane's cabin.

Helping passengers in the event of an emergency is the most important responsibility of the flight attendant. This may range from reassuring passengers during occasional encounters with strong turbulence to directing passengers in evacuating a plane following an emergency landing.

QUALIFICATIONS FOR BECOMING A FLIGHT ATTENDANT

The airlines want to hire poised, tactful, friendly, and resourceful men and women who can deal comfortably with strangers. They are also looking for people who can stay calm in emergencies and reassure others. For international routes, a knowledge of a foreign language may be essential. Applicants must usually be at least nineteen years old; however, some airlines have higher minimum age requirements. Furthermore, applicants must fall into a specific weight range depending upon their height and must have excellent health, good vision, and the ability to speak clearly.

Flight attendants need to have a high school diploma; however, those who have several years of college or experience in dealing with the public are preferred. Today, more and more attendants who are being hired have college degrees.

PREPARATION FOR BECOMING A FLIGHT ATTENDANT

Most large airlines require that newly hired flight attendants complete four to six weeks of intensive training in their own schools. The airlines that do not operate schools generally send new employees to the school of another airline. Transportation to the training center and an allowance for board, room, and school supplies may be provided. At these schools, trainees learn emergency procedures such as evacuating an airplane, operating an oxygen system, and giving first aid. They are also taught flight regulations and duties and company operations and policy. The future flight attendants learn how to prepare meals, handle the beverage service, speak on the intercom, and relate effectively with the passengers. Instruction is given on personal grooming. Toward the end of their training, students go on practice flights. Flight attendants who will be flying international routes get additional instruction in passport and customs regulations and dealing with terrorism. Throughout their careers, flight attendants will receive twelve to fourteen hours of training in emergency procedures and passenger relations each year.

ADVANCING UP THE CAREER LADDER

After flight attendants complete their training, they are assigned to one of their airline's bases as reserve flight attendants. They do not have regular assignments but instead are called on either to staff extra flights or to fill in for attendants who are sick or on vacation. Reserve attendants on duty must be ready to fly on short notice. New attendants usually remain on reserve for at least one year; however, it may take up to five years or longer to advance from reserve status in some cities. The length of time depends on the airline and on the routes that the reserve attendant flies. Once attendants are no longer on reserve, they bid for assignments on a seniority basis. Usually only the most experienced attendants get their choice of base and flight.

Advancing up the career ladder takes longer today than in the past because so many attendants are remaining in this career longer than they used to. The first step is to become a lead attendant in charge of the other attendants on the flight. Some airlines have pursers, who are in charge of all the money collected during a flight; this is also a step up. Beyond that, if they wish to advance, flight attendants must move into nonflight positions, such as instructors, supervisors, and recruiters.

SALARY AND FRINGE BENEFITS

Flight attendants are generally paid by the hour. According to the Association of Flight Attendants, the median income for beginning flight attendants in 1996 was $13,000 a year. With six years of experience, attendants were earning about $18,500 a year, while some senior flight attendants earned as much as $40,000 a year and a few earned even more. Extra compensation is paid for overtime and for night and international flights. Benefits packages are also offered, including health insurance and pension plans. Most flight attendants belong to unions, which have played an important role in securing improved salaries and benefits for them as well as recognition of the professionalism of this career.

Flight attendants and their families are usually entitled to free or reduced fares on their own and most other airlines. While attendants may have to buy their uniforms, uniform replacement items are usually paid for by the company. And the airlines generally provide a small allowance for cleaning and upkeep of the uniforms.

THE PERSONAL STORY OF A FLIGHT ATTENDANT

Linda Curtis Olinger flew domestic routes for United Airlines until she started flying internationally four years ago. Because she has been with this airline for more than twenty years, Linda has sufficient seniority to fly the routes and times that she wants. She has been a purser but now prefers to work as a flight attendant in first class. Based in San Francisco, Linda is currently alternating between flying to Hong Kong and London. She will fly either three times in a month to Hong Kong, a fifteen-hour flight, or four times in a month to London, an eleven-hour flight. Her layover time abroad ranges from twenty-four to forty hours. From San Francisco, Linda also has the opportunity to fly to Sydney, Paris, Honolulu, Korea, and Japan—all options she has taken.

On a flight day, Linda arrives at the airport $1^3/_4$ hours before her flight is scheduled to depart. Her first stop is always to check her mailbox. Once a month, she will get revisions to her manual, and frequently there are safety updates. Next, she looks at the bulletin boards, which will have hotel information, United Airlines news, and safety news. After checking herself in, she attends the briefing with the entire crew of flight attendants. Linda usually flies a 747 that has a crew of eighteen attendants (unless fewer are needed because of a smaller number of passengers). At the briefing, she will get her flight assignment. Since the assignments are based on seniority, she usually is able to work in first class.

After the briefing, Linda has quite a long walk to the international terminal, where she goes through security and boards the plane. Her first task is to stow her gear. Then she goes to her seat and takes out the United manual, which she must always carry with her on flights. Using the manual as a guide, she checks out the emergency equipment around her assigned area. Her next task is to get the first class cabin ready for the passengers. This means checking the cleanliness of the cabin and ensuring that there are enough headsets, amenities kits, pillows, blankets, and current newspapers. Then she is ready to welcome and seat passengers in her area.

During Linda's international flights, as many as three movies may be shown. And Linda will serve beverages several times, as well as two meals and a snack or breakfast, depending on the time the plane is scheduled to land. All of the flight attendants get a two-hour break during the flight, which they take in a bunk room in the tail of the 747. Six attendants at a time are able to rest there. After landing and saying goodbye to the passengers, Linda goes through customs and takes a company bus to a hotel. Another flight has been completed.

Being a flight attendant is the only job Linda has ever had, and it's a job she says that she can't seem to get out of her system. She likes the flexibility of this job, which offers her so much time off and lets her trade flight times with other attendants so she can fly when she wants. Moreover, Linda finds it exciting to visit international destinations and to be continually meeting new crew members and passengers. For her, the only downsides to this job are being in the airplane so long on international flights and coping with jet lag. Linda, like so many other flight attendants, plans to continue in this career, which she started by flying short hops out of Newark, New Jersey.

LOOKING AT THE FUTURE

Turnover was once very high among flight attendants. This is no longer the case because this occupation has become more professional. Still, employment of flight attendants is expected to grow much faster than the average for all occupations through the year 2005. Thousands of openings will arise each year to replace flight attendants who transfer to other occupations or leave the labor force. In addition, airlines are enlarging their capacity by increasing the number and size of planes in operation; according to FAA safety rules, there must be one attendant for every 50 seats. It is expected that competition for jobs as flight attendants will remain very stiff because the number of applicants exceeds the number of job openings and because of the glamour of this job.

FOR MORE INFORMATION

To learn about job opportunities at a particular airline and the qualifications required, write to the personnel manager of the company. Appendix B has a list of airlines and their addresses. For a fee the Future Airline Professionals of America (FAPA) has job information including books, directories, and newsletters. Contact FAPA at (800) JET-JOBS.

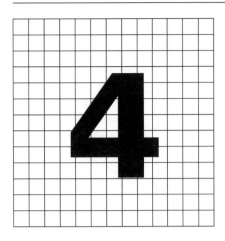

WORKING AS A RESERVATIONIST, A CUSTOMER SERVICE REPRESENTATIVE, A MECHANIC, AND IN OTHER AIRLINE JOBS

Each year millions of Americans travel by plane, train, ship, bus, and automobile. Because so many people are traveling, wise travelers make plans in advance for these trips, as well as making reservations. Reservationists and customer service representatives help them accomplish this. Customer service representatives also assist passengers in the many activities involved in boarding and leaving planes, trains, ships, and buses. Travelers depend on the airline mechanics to maintain and repair aircraft to ensure the safety of their flights. In addition, many other airline workers have jobs that keep the airlines operating smoothly.

LOOKING AT A CAREER AS A RESERVATIONIST

Reservationists play an essential role in the transportation industry. They ensure that there will be seats on planes, trains, and buses; cabins on cruise ships; rooms at hotels and motels; and rental cars for the travelers who need them. The majority of reservationists are employed by airlines. However, cruise lines, railroads, bus companies, tour companies, hotels and motels, travel agencies, and car rental companies also employ reservationists. And some reservationists work for membership organizations like automobile clubs and other companies that provide transportation services.

WORKING CONDITIONS

Reservation agents usually work in large central offices. While these offices used to be in the downtown areas of major cities, increasingly they are found in suburban areas and even rural areas where rents are cheaper and travel companies can economize. On the job, reservationists wear headsets all day so they can take calls from customers. They generally have computer terminals so they can quickly obtain information needed to make, change, or cancel reservations at the customer's request. Their workplace is loud, as it is filled with the voices of other reservationists and the clicking of computer keys. Typically there isn't much privacy in these large open offices, although some reservationists may have their own cubicles.

Most reservationists will work 8 or 8½ hours a day five days a week. Because airlines and other travel companies keep their phone lines open 24 hours a day, reservationists often work shifts. Beginning workers typically will have the least desirable shifts because reservationists bid for their work times based on seniority. Some overtime work should be expected, especially around holidays and when travel promotions are offered. Many airline reservationists are part-time employees who may work full time when there are sales promotions or during periods of high demand.

ON-THE-JOB RESPONSIBILITIES

Each phone call connects reservationists to new travel customers with requests for their help. Typically, reservationists will have these duties:

- answer calls from customers
- arrange for tickets to be mailed, picked up, or handled as ticketless travel
- book travel reservations
- compile and record reservation information
- confirm or change travel reservations
- help customers plan trips by answering questions and offering suggestions on travel arrangements
- keep up with the latest changes in fares, schedules, and other arrangements that travel companies are constantly making
- provide information about fares, schedules, and the booking of flights, trips, cruises, accommodations, or rental cars
- record method of payment

PREPARATION FOR BECOMING A RESERVATIONIST

No matter where a reservationist elects to work, there will be on-the-job training to learn the company's product, automated reservations system, and sales procedures. Travel school or community college courses in using a reservations system may be required to obtain jobs with many companies. Reservationists must be good typists. In addition, companies like to hire individuals who have sales experience. Knowing how to use a computer is definitely helpful, and a college degree is also an advantage in this job market.

SPECIAL ATTRIBUTES OF RESERVATIONISTS

Not everyone has the aptitude to be a reservationist. For this job, it is absolutely essential to be able to work fast and accurately and to deal effectively with people. During the course of the day, reservationists will encounter difficult, indecisive, and belligerent customers whom they must convince to purchase their company's travel product. Being a reservationist is a job for a salesperson who can remain upbeat and enthusiastic through as many as several hundred customer calls in a day. This requires having a pleasant telephone manner and a thorough knowledge of the travel product.

ADVANCING UP THE CAREER LADDER

No matter where reservationists work, they essentially do the same job. Some reservationists will move to other companies that offer more interesting assignments or better pay. Reservationists in large companies have the opportunity to transfer laterally into positions in international or frequent flyer travel or advance to positions as senior agents, supervisors, or managers. Agents can also elect to move into another department in their company, such as sales and marketing, to advance their careers.

SALARY AND FRINGE BENEFITS

Airlines once paid high salaries for reservationists; however, because of the emphasis on cost-cutting this is no longer true at some airlines. Depending on where they work, entry-level reservationists may earn from $12,000 to $20,000 a year. Experienced reservationists can make more than $40,000 a year, while the few who work overtime constantly (eighty-hour weeks) can earn up to $100,000. Full-time reservationists will receive benefits such as health insurance, paid vacations, and discounted and free travel; part-time employees will typically get only travel benefits.

THE PERSONAL STORY OF A RESERVATIONIST

John Sticht, Jr. has been a reservationist for America West Airlines for less than a year. Originally, he obtained this job because it offered him a flexible time schedule so he could complete his master's degree. Now he thinks of continuing with America West because the airline is growing so rapidly that the opportunities for advancement are excellent. He also likes the fact that America West promotes from within. John can envision himself moving into reservation planning, administration of the reservation center, or other administrative responsibilities. John found out about his current job by calling the company's job hotline. After sending in his resume, he went to a group interview (about 100 job candidates) and took a typing test before being hired. The next step was the airline's five-week training course. All new reservationists are paid to attend the eight-hour-a-day, five-day-a-week course. This is quite a rigorous course, and future reservationists have to pass tests to reach the next level or retake the course. During the first three weeks, John learned how to use the airline's computerized reservation system, talk to customers, make sales, and help customers understand how the reservations system works. Because John had solid computer skills, he found the instruction on using the computer a breeze; however, trainees without this experience found it quite challenging. The final two weeks of the training period involved taking customer calls under the direction of facilitators.

John considers this job a sales job in which he is the direct link between the airline and the public. He also sees it as an excellent stepping stone to other jobs at America West. Most reservationists at this airline are full-time employees who have full benefits, including travel benefits.

A DAY IN THE LIFE OF A RESERVATIONIST

Carol Love is an experienced reservationist who has worked in domestic, international, prepaid tickets, and group sales for a major airline. Her career began just before computers were incorporated into the job, so much work was done manually. Even when the first computers were introduced in the early 1970s, not every part of Carol's job was automated. It wasn't until the mid-1980s that she began working on a "totally modern" system. Soon she will be working on the most up-to-date computer reservations equipment in the airline industry. Over the years Carol's job has become more complex because travelers' options have increased with the introduction of so many different fares and the greater number of flights to each destination.

A Typical Day

Carol's current shift as a reservation sales agent is from 3:00 p.m. to 11:30 p.m. on Sunday through Thursday. On workdays, she must arrive at the reservations center located near a major airport in time to run her card through a reader, get work gear from her locker, and be at a work station by precisely 3:00. Her gear consists of a new state-of-the-art headset, which prevents customers from hearing any background noise, and a company manual with reference telephone numbers and information on how to access different computer entries. Company policy forbids having food or reading material not related to her job in the work area; nevertheless, most reservationists eat on the job. Carol's workplace is a large room with stations for about 125 agents. When the company has sales promotions, all the places will be filled. Every reservationist tends to have a favorite spot.

Carol works in domestic sales. Her customers can be from anywhere in the United States, since the company routes calls between its six centers to even the workload. She does not deal exclusively with customers wanting to purchase tickets, although that is certainly the most common call she receives. Carol provides information to people who cannot or do not want to use the automated flight information system. During periods of bad weather, she answers a lot of questions about plane arrivals and departures and the cancellation of flights. And she refers callers who want to complain about or compliment airline employees or policies to customer relations.

During her shift, Carol is given a thirty-minute break for a meal and two ten-minute breaks which can be taken as one twenty-minute break. Sometime during the shift, she is expected to use her computer to read the latest company memos on topics such as personnel news, flight delays, fare updates, and events in other cities and airports. There is also a news wire with information about the company, ranging from the price of its stock to the purchase of new planes. Carol can even get updates on soap operas and Broadway and Las Vegas shows, world-wide weather, and other information on her computer.

Once Carol puts on her headphones and sits down in front of her computer terminal, the company expects her to be plugged into the phone ninety-five percent of the time when she is not on a break. Her average is a high ninety-seven percent. The company keeps track of this, as well as how many seconds each call lasts. While the company goal is for agents to spend 180 seconds (3 minutes) on a call, Carol usually averages 300 seconds (5 minutes) per call. She spends this extra time because she wants to be sure her customers understand all aspects of purchasing a ticket, including whether the ticket can be changed or is refundable. She tries to be very thorough with each customer. The calls that take the most time are those where certificates are being used for discounted fares and companion travel. Although Carol's call time is above average, this is not frowned upon by the company because she sells a lot of tickets. The company also notes how long the agents spend between calls finishing the processing of tickets. The standard time is twenty seconds; however, Carol's time is a mere nine seconds. Once her shift begins, the phone calls never stop coming. Only occasionally are there lags between calls. This is a job that truly requires employees to stay on task. Warnings are given when employees are not meeting the various company time standards. Help is also given when individuals are having trouble meeting these standards.

Carol continues to enjoy her job as a reservationist. The money is great, and she loves the flexibility of shift work, which has allowed her to get a college degree as well as take classes in personal interests like photography. Having a six-week paid vacation is another benefit of this job, along with the ability to change shifts and days and to travel worldwide at a nominal cost.

LOOKING AT A CAREER AS A CUSTOMER SERVICE REPRESENTATIVE

Customer service representatives are the smartly uniformed individuals who are seen dealing directly with the public at airports, train stations, and bus terminals, and aboard ships. At airlines, they are the employees behind the ticket counter, at the gate, in baggage service, at the ramp, and in the baggage room. They are also the people behind the counter at car rental sites and central city ticket offices. Depending on their job responsibilities, they are also known as customer service agents, ticket agents, passenger agents, gate agents, passenger-booking clerks, ticket sellers, ramp agents, or baggage agents. No matter what their title is, they help smooth the way for travelers.

ON-THE-JOB RESPONSIBILITIES

Customer service representatives at major air terminals are not likely to have as wide a range of duties each day as those at small terminals, who may be expected to sell tickets, check in passengers and baggage, take tickets at the gate, direct in the plane, and load and unload the baggage for each flight. Here is a look at the wide range of duties that customer service representatives can be called upon to handle:

- answer questions about fares and schedules
- check baggage
- check in passengers
- collect tickets at the gate
- direct the arrival and departure of planes
- direct passengers to boarding areas
- examine passports and/or visas
- help passengers board
- issue boarding passes
- load and unload luggage
- make boarding announcements
- provide flight information
- resolve problems ranging from lost luggage to medical emergencies
- sell tickets
- supervise the loading of passengers and cargo

The job of airline customer service representatives is performed at ticket counters, gates, ramps, baggage rooms, and baggage service areas. Depending on the airline, customer service representatives may alternate where they work or be permanently assigned to one station. Typically, customer service representatives learn their job through formal training programs and on-the-job training after they are hired. Computer skills are a necessity for many of the tasks customer service representatives handle, and a certain amount of physical strength may be required because lifting luggage is often part of this job.

SALARY, FRINGE BENEFITS, AND ADVANCEMENT

At present, customer service representatives generally start as probationary employees and become part-time employees before achieving full-time status. Entry level employees can expect to receive about $7.00 an hour, while the top salary for customer service representatives is about $21,000 a year. Supervisors will receive from $22,000 to $33,000 a year. Full-time employees typically receive health, vacation, and travel benefits. Part-time employees usually receive travel benefits but may not be eligible for any other benefits.

Job assignment is based on seniority, and employees bid for the shifts that they want. They can generally switch with other customer service representatives to get the work hours and work assignments they want. Like reservationists, they can become supervisors and then managers if they wish to advance.

THE PERSONAL STORY OF AN EARLY CUSTOMER SERVICE REPRESENTATIVE

When Grace Knight first started as a customer service representative working up front at the ticket counter in the San Francisco Airport for a major airline in 1968, there were no computers. She had to write out tickets by hand and use tariff books to figure out the price. To make her job easier, she memorized many of the fares that were charged to frequently traveled cities. The job was quite different then compared to today. Grace would bid for her work schedule but could find herself working in lost and found baggage or at the gate instead of at her regular assignment. Today, customer service representatives at her airline tend to have the same job responsibilities each day.

After computers became an integral part of the airline industry, Grace's job at the ticket counter became far simpler and less challenging. When someone wanted to purchase a ticket, she would use the computer to find out if the person had a reservation, check the form of payment, do the necessary bookkeeping, and print the ticket. Then she would check the traveler's luggage and go on to the next customer.

Grace's last assignment as a customer service representative was working as a passenger or gate agent. Here everything happens in the last fifteen minutes before departure. The pressure is to get the flight out on time, a leading concern of passengers. The job becomes quite stressful when there are 100 people in line waiting to get boarding passes and it's just a few minutes to departure time. This job also includes printing and taking passenger lists to the captain, taking tickets at the entrance to the jetway, as well as moving the jetway into the proper position for arriving and departing planes. Grace was one of the first women to drive a jetway when it was essential to have a heavy equipment operator's license for this job. Today, a group of people in central control with computers and TV monitors make decisions about holding flights. When Grace first began this job, the passenger agent had the responsibility for the flight as long as it was on the ground.

Grace's workday always began with a ten- to fifteen-minute briefing with the duty supervisor, at which she would learn about the passenger load, any irregularities, and the weather. It was extremely important to be on time for this briefing, and late employees would have their wages docked. She worked an $8^1/2$ hour day with two 15-minute breaks and a half-hour break for meals. When these breaks occurred depended on passenger traffic, so there could be long stretches of work without breaks or no coffee breaks at all.

After many years as a customer service representative, Grace left this career. She felt that it had become too routine, and that computers were making the decisions that she had once found such a challenging part of her job. In addition, she was working long and hard hours, which necessitated her getting up as early as 4:00 a.m. every day. She notes that today few full-time representatives are being hired at her airline, and more employees are part-time workers.

THE PERSONAL STORY OF A CURRENT CUSTOMER SERVICE REPRESENTATIVE

Cynthia Jones (not her real name) is thoroughly delighted with her job of more than five years as a customer service representative for America West. It lets her travel (she especially enjoys trips to Hawaii and Europe), use her knowledge of Spanish, and deal with the public. Before finding what she calls her perfect career niche, this college graduate worked at a bank, a wind energy company, and a pharmaceuticals firm. She sees herself working in her current job for many years.

Cynthia started her customer service career as a ramper (also known as ramp agent). This began after 40 hours of training, which included classroom work, videos, and going over the job with a trainer, followed by on-the-job training. A minimum of four rampers is required to handle the arrival and departure of each America West plane. The operations agent is in charge of the paperwork as well as the arrangement of the cargo. The load must be balanced, with the appropriate amounts of cargo in the front and back of the plane. If the load is too heavy, some of the cargo will have to be unloaded. One worker is assigned to the baggage room to sort the baggage by flight and destination. There will be at least two rampers planeside but could be as many as four. Their duties include marshalling the plane in with wands, connecting ground power, loading and unloading baggage, and doing other services like restocking snack carts. To be a ramper requires a certain amount of physical strength; Cynthia had to demonstrate that she could pick up seventy pounds and turn around while holding it. After a ninety-day probationary period, Cynthia did part-time work for one month before becoming a full-time employee.

America West likes its customer service representatives to be cross-utilized—that is, capable of handling several of the jobs that these representatives customarily do. So after her probationary period was completed, Cynthia decided to take the training to become a ticket/gate agent. One of the prerequisites was the ability to type at least twenty-five words a minute. Her three weeks of classroom training included:

- a condensed version of the training reservationists receive, so she would know how to handle reservations
- instructions on how to issue and reissue tickets and handle frequent flyer tickets
- learning automatic checking-in, which includes handling seat assignments, luggage, and customers' questions
- familiarization with gate procedures like how to open a gate computer and reconcile coupons with passengers on the plane

- some instruction on baggage service procedures, including working in lost and found, filing claims, tracing luggage, and working with other airlines

- instruction on hazardous materials—what can and cannot be carried on the plane

- training in security procedures and FAA regulations

Throughout her career as a customer service representative, Cynthia has continually received training. This is because changes are constantly being made in procedures ranging from security to baggage handling. And she has also taken part in motivation programs offered at the company headquarters. Part of the company's continuing education program is the new quiz she finds in her mailbox each week to make sure she is abreast of current procedures. Furthermore, Cynthia can expect FAA checks from time to time to make sure her company is complying with all airline regulations.

Current Work Schedule   Cynthia bids periodically for work time periods. Her shift currently begins at 5:30 a.m. and ends at 3:00 p.m. Supervisors who know her work and preferences assign her to a work schedule resembling the one she is now following:

> Saturday—baggage service (lost and found)
>
> Sunday—ticket counter
>
> Monday—baggage room
>
> Tuesday—ticket counter
>
> Wednesday—gate

Cynthia is able to trade these assignments with others to get time off.

Baggage Service.   This is a very customer-oriented service. Cynthia finds it challenging to find missing baggage and assuage unhappy travelers. She also must assess the damage done to luggage by the airlines.

Ticket Counter.   Working here is Cynthia's favorite job because it is so challenging. Every time she says "Next in line" she has no idea of whether she will be issuing or reissuing tickets, making a reservation, checking in a passenger, or handling a more complicated request.

Baggage Room.   Working in the baggage room (located behind the ticket counter) is a low-stress job. However, it is quite physical. Cynthia will take baggage off the belt and place it in the appropriate cart by flight and destination. Then she will drive each cart down to a plane, where she may help load the luggage. For each flight, she will have to go back to the baggage room to check if additional baggage has come for the flight. If she is gone from the baggage room for any length of time, bags may get jammed up on the belt.

Gate. Approximately one hour before a plane is scheduled to depart, Cynthia's job at a gate begins. Here she will check in passengers; make announcements; assist the elderly, children, and disabled to board; tear the ticket stubs of boarding passengers; and reconcile the tickets to the number of passengers on the plane. This job also involves pulling the jetway up to the plane door and helping to open the plane door when necessary.

LOOKING AT THE FUTURE FOR RESERVATIONISTS AND CUSTOMER SERVICE REPRESENTATIVES

Most applicants for positions as reservationists and customer service representatives are likely to encounter considerable competition for jobs because the supply of qualified applicants exceeds the demand. Many people satisfy the entry requirements, and many applicants are attracted to these jobs by the travel benefits and the glamour associated with the industry. Nevertheless, overall the number of jobs for reservationists and customer service representatives is expected to grow faster than the average for most jobs, because both business and personal travel is likely to remain strong. In the event of a downswing in the economy, travel companies will be less likely to hire and even may lay off these employees.

FOR MORE INFORMATION

For information about job opportunities as reservationists and customer service representatives, write to the human resources departments of individual airlines. Addresses of airlines are given in appendix B. Also, a brochure with career information about reservationists is available from:

> Air Transport Association of America, Suite 1100
> 1301 Pennsylvania Avenue NW
> Washington, DC 20004-1707

LOOKING AT A CAREER AS AN AIRLINE MECHANIC

More than three-fifths of all aircraft mechanics work for airlines. Most will work at major airports near large cities. Their workdays will usually be spent in hangars or in other indoor areas unless they have to make immediate repairs or preflight checks on aircraft, which can put them outside in very unpleasant weather. Airline mechanics frequently work under time pressure to maintain flight schedules. At the same time, they have the overwhelming responsibility to maintain safety standards.

Mechanics generally work forty hours a week on eight-hour shifts around the clock. Their work frequently involves standing, lying, or kneeling in awkward positions to do inspections, maintenance, and repair work; occasionally they work in precarious positions on scaffolds or ladders.

ON-THE-JOB RESPONSIBILITIES

Mechanics have the responsibility of keeping aircraft in peak operating condition by performing scheduled maintenance, making repairs, and completing inspections required by the FAA. Maintenance work involves inspecting such things as engines, landing gear, instruments, pressurized sections, brakes, valves, pumps, and air conditioning systems and then doing the necessary maintenance. An engine may need to be removed from a plane and taken apart, and then the mechanics may use precision instruments to check it for wear and use x-ray and magnetic inspection equipment to check for invisible cracks. Maintenance workers also check the fuselage, wings, and tail for corrosion, distortion, and cracks. Once all the repairs are completed, the mechanics have to test that everything is working properly. While mechanics who are doing maintenance work are following a set protocol, those who do repair work rely on pilots' descriptions of problems to find and fix faulty equipment. These mechanics must work as fast as safety permits so that the aircraft can quickly be put back into service.

Mechanics may work on one or many types of aircraft or just specialize in one area of a particular aircraft, such as the engine, electrical system, or air conditioning system. Because of technological advances, mechanics are now spending more time repairing electronic systems.

Besides mechanics there are many other airline employees who work on the maintenance and repair of aircraft. Included in this group are: machinists, sheet metal workers, carpenters, electricians, painters, electroplaters, drill press operators, and upholsterers.

PREPARATION FOR BECOMING A MECHANIC

There are still some individuals who become aircraft mechanics through on-the-job training. Most learn their jobs in FAA-certified trade schools. Emphasis in these schools is being placed on newer technologies such as aviation electronics and composite materials, including graphite, fiberglass, and boron, which are being used more and more in the construction of new aircraft. Completing a course generally takes from twenty-four to thirty months.

Certain high school and college courses—including mathematics, physics, chemistry, electronics, computer science, and mechanical drawing—are quite helpful to future mechanics because a knowledge of their principles is often necessary to make repairs. Writing skills are also important because mechanics are frequently required to submit reports. Furthermore, as aircraft continue to become more complex, the airlines are requiring mechanics to take ongoing training to update their skills, especially in electronics.

Certification

The majority of airline mechanics are certified by the FAA as either "airframe mechanic," "powerplant mechanic," or "repairer." Airframe mechanics are authorized to work on any part of the aircraft except the instruments, powerplants, and propellers. Powerplant mechanics are authorized to work on engines and do limited work on propellers, and repairers have the authorization to work on instruments and on propellers. Combination airframe and powerplant mechanics (called A & P mechanics) can work on any part of a plane, and those with an inspector's authorization can certify inspection work completed by other mechanics. Uncertified mechanics are supervised by those with certificates.

Advancement

In the airlines, the promotion of mechanics is often determined by examination and experience. Opportunities are best for those who have an aircraft inspector's authorization. Mechanics can climb the career ladder to become lead mechanics (crew chiefs), inspectors, lead inspectors, and shop supervisors. Supervisors may advance to executive positions.

SPECIAL ATTRIBUTES OF AIRLINE MECHANICS

Airline mechanics must have a high degree of mechanical aptitude because they have to diagnose and solve complex mechanical problems. They also need to be self-motivated, hard-working, and enthusiastic. Moreover, they need to be agile in order to handle all the reaching and climbing that are part of this job. And because they work high off the ground, on top of the wings and fuselages of large jets, these mechanics must not be afraid of heights.

SALARY AND FRINGE BENEFITS

Mechanics who work at airlines receive higher pay than other aircraft mechanics. The average hourly pay for beginning airline mechanics with A & P certification ranges from $11.44 to $13.50 an hour. The top salary is currently $22.25 an hour. Those who work at larger carriers earn the most money. Inspectors and foremen will have starting salaries of $46,000 and top salaries of $60,350. Some mechanics at major airlines are covered by union agreements. Airline mechanics have travel benefits along with health insurance and vacation benefits.

LOOKING AT THE FUTURE FOR AIRCRAFT MECHANICS

Employment opportunities for aircraft mechanics are expected to increase more slowly than those for other occupations. While the number of airplanes is expected to grow, employment growth is being restricted by increases in productivity from greater use of automated inventory control and modular systems that speed repairs and parts replacement. Most airline job openings will arise from replacement needs. Aircraft mechanics generally have a strong attachment to this occupation, and many stay in this career until their retirement. Job opportunities for aircraft mechanics are likely to be best in general aviation, where wages are lower and there are fewer applicants for jobs.

FOR MORE INFORMATION

For general information about aircraft mechanics, write to:

Aviation Maintenance Foundation
P.O. Box 2826
Redmond, WA 98073

Professional Aviation Maintenance Association
500 Northwest Plaza, Suite 401
St. Ann, MO 63074

For information about jobs in a particular airline, write to the company's personnel manager. A list of the addresses of these companies is given in appendix B.

LOOKING AT A CAREER IN OTHER AIRLINE JOBS

While jobs like pilot and flight attendant that let airline employees fly during their workday are much sought after and glamorous to most people, there exist within the very large airline industry many other jobs that allow employees to travel. In fact, every airline offers flight benefits to its full-time employees and most part-time employees, which means that airline secretaries, accountants, computer operators, and lawyers can take frequent trips. Furthermore, within every airline, there are the same jobs that are found in most large industries. Individuals can find jobs dealing with technology, research, marketing, sales, human resources, public relations, law, operations, advertising, administration, and finance that offer the additional benefit of travel. In each of these areas, there will be entry-level, middle-management, and senior-management positions.

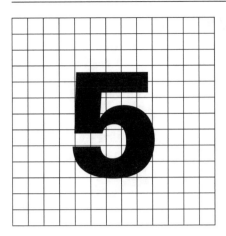

WORKING ABOARD
A CRUISE SHIP

For centuries, travelers journeyed between distant points on great ships. The romance and excitement of this mode of transportation has been documented in many movies. After the debut of the jet airplane in the 1950s, travelers rejected traveling by boat and began making intercontinental trips on the much faster airplanes. Passenger ships almost disappeared except for the few that adapted to the cruise trade.

In the 1970s, the popularity of cruising began to grow, and the number of ship passengers increased dramatically. By the 1980s, new ships were being built once again, and tourist port facilities throughout the world were being improved. Cruising has become so popular that it is anticipated that seven million to eight million people will be taking cruises annually by the year 2000. The Cruise Lines International Association projects significant increases in passenger counts because of the large number of repeat customers and potential new cruisers.

The television show *The Love Boat* gave Americans a glimpse of what cruising was like. They saw the possibility of visiting exotic locales, eating gourmet meals, and enjoying endless shipboard entertainment including shows, movies, dancing, lectures, games, gambling, health spas, and sports. Cruises are now available that last for just a day; however, the hottest market at present is for three- to five-day cruises. In addition, there are cruises lasting for one or two weeks or longer, as well as a few that last for several months. Cruise ships vary greatly in size—from large, oceangoing ships that can carry thousands of passengers, to small ships with less than 100 passengers cruising inland bodies of water and less-frequently visited locales. Today's average cruise ship has about 1,700 berths. Cruising opportunities are also available on much smaller barges and on sailboats.

LOOKING AT JOBS ABOARD CRUISE SHIPS

It is important to understand that very few cruise ships are United States ships. It costs much more to build ships in the U.S. and to staff them with Americans. Most crew members aboard a ship (there is one for every two or three passengers) are not American. Typically, cruise-ship officers are from European countries (England, Italy, Greece, Norway), and the staff working in such employee-intensive departments as food and beverage, hotel, deck, and engine are from Asia. Because the majority of passengers are from North America, most job opportunities for Americans lie in positions that deal directly with passengers, such as cruise staff, the purser's staff, and service jobs such as gift shop personnel, beauticians, casino dealers, and photographers. Only cruise ships that fly the American flag will have exclusively American crews. This includes all ships cruising the inland waters of the United States.

WORKING CONDITIONS

The ship is the home of those who work aboard it. Employees, depending upon their positions, may have to share cabins that are far more spartan than those the passengers enjoy. On older ships, the residents of several cabins may share one bathroom. Newer ships have amenities like employee cabins with their own bathrooms and even television sets; they may also have employee stores, pantries, and laundries. Most cruise-ship employees will eat in crew messes. However, the ship's officers and some members of the cruise staff regularly eat with passengers. They are the only employees that generally have access to passenger areas when not working.

Aboard the ship, most employees wear uniforms that are associated with their jobs. While cruises are a true vacation for passengers, they may require long hours seven days a week for employees. It is not unusual for employees to have to work ten to fifteen hours a day with no time off for six or eight months. How much an employee works depends solely on his or her job. Waiters work long hours, while manicurists, musicians, and photographers may work relatively short hours. The marine crew, which includes the deck and engine departments, will work regularly scheduled hours. There are no long layovers for rests in ports. Typically, ships leave a home port and then stop in different ports before returning to one of several home ports. Passengers disembark in the morning on the last day of a cruise, and new passengers come aboard in the afternoon. Then the ship takes off on the same itinerary or a new one.

ON-THE-JOB RESPONSIBILITIES BY DEPARTMENT

The jobs are much the same from one cruise ship to the next. However, cruise lines will assign responsibilities to different departments and staff members. What follows is a general description of the departments found on cruise ships and the positions in these departments, along with the employees' duties.

Deck Department

The deck department personnel have the responsibility of operating and navigating the ship and handling all sea duties, as well as maintaining the ship. Passengers see deck personnel when they visit the bridge, when the ship is tied to docks, and when lifeboat drills are held. Some of the officers will eat with the passengers. The captain is the head of this department, and all other department heads report to the captain. Positions in this department include ordinary seaman and able seaman as well as marine officers.

Engine Department

The engine department staff operates, maintains, and repairs the engines that propel the ship. It is also responsible for all the electrical, plumbing, and mechanical systems on the ship. The chief engineer is in charge of this department. Within this department, there are jobs for first, second, third, and fourth engineers; electricians; plumbers; machinists; welders; and mechanics.

Food and Beverage Department

Employees of the food and beverage department have much the same titles and duties as they would in a first-class hotel. This is the largest department on a cruise ship and an extremely important one, since passengers will not make repeat trips with a cruise line unless the food is outstanding and the servers helpful and friendly. The person in charge of the entire operation is the chief steward or food and beverage manager, who will be responsible for making menus, purchasing food and beverages, and handling all dining room and bar services. On the food side, some of the positions are:

assistant chefs	dining room manager
assistant maitre d'	dishwashers
busboys	food handlers
butchers	maitre d'
chefs	specialized cooks
cooks	waiters, waitresses

On every cruise ship, the bar is one of the profit makers. Again, the friendliness and competence of this staff is extremely important. The beverage staff will include these positions:

assistant bar manager	dishwashers
bar manager	waiters, waitresses
bartenders	wine stewards
chief wine steward	

Hotel Department

The hotel department workers comprise the second largest department on cruise ships. They hold jobs that are comparable to those found in large hotels or resorts. Heading the department will be a hotel manager; this individual is responsible for every passenger's comfort, the employees in this area, the cleanliness of the ship, and obtaining the necessary supplies and amenities for every cabin. Working in this department are the chief steward (housekeeper), room stewards, cleaners, and bellhops.

Purser's Department

The purser's department employees are ship's officers who wear uniforms at all times. This is the staff headed by the chief purser, who will handle with his or her assistants all of the administrative tasks related to the passengers. They will provide such services as cashing checks, staffing the ship's information desk, running the lost-and-found, storing valuables, handling complaints, changing cabins for passengers, doing the ship's accounting, maintaining accurate passenger records, providing translators, dealing with customs officials, and handling embarkation and disembarkation.

Cruise Department

The cruise department has the task of entertaining the passengers. These employees lead and implement all daily recreational activities, including shipboard activities, shore excursions, and entertainment. This is the department where Americans will find it easiest to obtain employment. A cruise director heads this department and has a staff of assistants, including hosts and hostesses, a shore excursion director, recreation director, children's activities coordinator, the ship's musicians and entertainers, and staff to set up the various activities. Members of this staff will wear uniforms and have access to all the public areas aboard the ship when in uniform. They may be assigned to eat with the passengers. They must be gregarious people who are at home speaking with one person or 500 people.

Service Department

The service department staff includes all those who offer services as photographers, gift shop employees, beauticians, barbers, manicurists, masseuses and masseurs, doctors and other health personnel, and casino dealers and cashiers. These individuals can be hired by the cruise lines but can also be hired by companies that operate these concessions aboard the ship. Their duties are the same as they would be on shore.

PREPARATION FOR BECOMING A CRUISE-SHIP EMPLOYEE

Cruise lines are looking for experienced employees. They want chefs who have worked in first-class restaurants, stewards in housekeeping with work experience in hotels, and musicians who have been in organized groups. Certain employees, including doctors, nurses, and barbers and beauticians, will need to have experience plus the appropriate licenses to obtain jobs.

Deck and engineering officers aboard United States cruise ships must be licensed. To qualify for a license, applicants must have graduated from the U.S. Merchant Marine Academy, or one of the six state academies, and pass a written examination. Individuals with at least three years of appropriate sea experience also can be licensed if they pass the examination, but it is quite difficult to pass without substantial formal schooling or independent study. The academies offer four-year programs (except for one that has a three-year program) in nautical science or marine engineering to prepare students to be third mates or third assistant engineers. With experience and passing of additional examinations, third officers may qualify for higher rank. Deck and engineering officers who seek employment with foreign-flagged ships must demonstrate naval skill and show proof of attendance at an accredited school or a license acceptable to the cruise company.

ADVANCING UP THE CAREER LADDER

To advance up the career ladder, it is essential to be committed to working for a cruise line for longer than a few months or a long vacation. Even those who are experienced in the hotel or restaurant field on land may find it necessary to take a lower starting position than the one they held on shore. However, individuals can begin in entry-level positions in most departments and advance rather rapidly into management jobs. This is because there is considerable turnover. Incidentally, most employees who climb the career ladder in on-shore positions with cruise companies have spent some time working aboard ships.

SALARY AND FRINGE BENEFITS

To most Americans, the pay aboard cruise ships is considered low. However, to those from Third World and southern European countries, who make up the majority of the employees, these wages are better than what they could earn at home. Americans are most likely to work in the cruise department, where entry-level monthly salaries are in the $900-to-$1,300 range. Employees who are waiters, waitresses, and busboys generally receive very low wages (less than $100 a month) but may make very good income from tips. American cruise lines that have unionized employees will pay higher salaries.

In considering shipboard earnings, it is important to remember the many fringe benefits that allow cruise employees to save a considerable portion of their wages. First of all, there is free room and board and laundry service for the duration of employment. Employees who are required to wear uniforms will usually have them furnished by the cruise line, while those who are asked to wear a certain type of garb may have a clothes allowance. While aboard the ship, employees receive free medical service. Vacation time is also provided by many lines after a certain period of service.

THE PERKS AND PRESSURES OF CRUISE-SHIP EMPLOYMENT

This job has one outstanding perk—free travel. Cruise ship employees can truly see the world. And, after being employed for a certain length of time, employees can have guests aboard (family and in some cases friends) for a very nominal daily fee. Some companies also have interline agreements that let employees travel on other cruise ships for a very low daily charge. Another perk of cruise line employment is the opportunity to work with people from many different countries, as well as to meet travelers with diverse interests and occupations.

There are downsides to working aboard cruise ships too. Besides the low pay and long hours, most employees are limited to crew areas in their off hours. In addition, very few employees are able to participate in on-board ship activities. Because time is short in ports and work hours are long, it is not always possible for employees to go ashore in every port.

THE PERSONAL STORY OF A CRUISE LINE EMPLOYEE

Carol Rossi had work experience as a teacher and a medical malpractice investigator when she took a cruise with a friend who worked for Royal Cruise Line. She truly enjoyed the cruise and spent some of her time aboard talking to the staff. The ship's worldwide itinerary piqued Carol's interest, and she decided that, since she was looking for work, she would send in her resume when she returned home. In fact, she sent two resumes—one to operations for the cruise line and one to the person in charge of on-board hiring. For two months, she called frequently inquiring about jobs, only to discover along the way that one of her resumes had been lost. Because her home town was also the headquarters of the cruise line, it was easy for Carol to be persistent in contacting the company for a job. Nevertheless, it was a fortuitous circumstance that led to her employment. After overhearing a conversation in the ship's office about a vacancy for a secretary (administrative assistant) aboard one of the ships, her cruise companion immediately called Carol. Phone calls flew back and forth that day (a Friday), and on Tuesday Carol flew to Lisbon, Portugal to begin working on the Golden Odyssey.

A Starting Job

Carol's position as secretary was the one in which most women started for this cruise line. For six weeks, Carol worked as the ship cruised through the Mediterranean and Black seas. When the cruise ended, Carol returned to her home and looked for another position aboard a Royal Cruise Line ship.

Passenger Service Representative

Carol's next job was as a passenger service representative (PSR). This is a unique position in the cruise industry in that it does not require the staff to live on board the ship for an extended period of time. While Carol held the position of PSR, she was able to maintain her apartment at home while flying around the world to meet the various ships. She could be on board ships for seven to twenty-two days, depending on the length of the cruise and her participation in the post-cruise programs.

Each assignment began at the airport, where Carol would meet the passengers who were flying from San Francisco to the ship. Upon their arrival at the airport in San Francisco, Carol would meet the passengers scheduled on her flight to the ship. She would give these passengers a brief overview outlining the specifics of their air itinerary and the provisions made to transport them from the airport to the ship. She would also discuss any necessary details regarding visas, passports, or customs regulations pertaining to the embarking country. Then she would fly with the passengers, clear customs, and help them board the ship. Carol's first task aboard the ship was to check that all the passengers had their luggage and, if necessary, initiate a search for lost bags.

Aboard the ship, Carol's major responsibility was to prepare all the paperwork for the disembarkation of the passengers. This process began with the creation of a questionnaire to determine each passenger's plans on leaving the ship. Then she had to collect the passengers' airline tickets, secure boarding passes for them, and prepare color-coded tags for every piece of luggage leaving the ship so it would be directed to the proper airline or dockside location. A manifest had to be created for each airline, listing all passengers, any specific seating or meal requests, all connecting flights, and number of checked pieces of luggage. This document was extremely important to the airline officials, and accuracy was imperative due to the high security regulations instituted in many of the international airports. If the number of passengers was noted incorrectly or the amount of luggage was not documented appropriately, a flight could be canceled, costing the cruise line thousands of dollars in overnight hotel stays and the rebooking of flights. It was a very difficult task.

Besides spending the majority of her time working on the disembarkation, Carol also had office hours which she spent answering passengers' questions. Here she dealt primarily with passengers who did not believe that they had received the correct number of shipboard credits (money allocated to be spent on the ship) or the proper gift as a repeat customer.

At the end of the cruise, Carol held disembarkation briefings organized by airplane flights. She would explain how to disembark the ship properly, give out all tickets and luggage tags, and make any corrections that were necessary. Finally, she helped the passengers disembark and returned with a group to her home port, where she continued to assist the cruisers until they were aboard another flight or had left the airport. At this point she was utterly exhausted and suffering from jet lag. However, Carol's job was still not complete. She had to go to the cruise line's headquarters and brief a management team on how the cruise had gone. She would discuss with them such things as the quality of the food of a new chef, passengers' response to shore excursions, interest in ports of call, and the response to an entertainer. Then she would go home for a period of time ranging from three days to two weeks before her next assignment. Carol stayed at this job for eighteen months.

Port Lecturer

As in any large company, once an individual has had a job within a cruise line, it is much easier to learn about and move into different positions. After her jobs on board as the administrative assistant and as a passenger services representative, Carol had proven herself a capable and effective employee and was offered the position of port lecturer. In this job she would be a contract employee and live aboard the ship and have her own cabin. Each day, she was required to give a one-hour lecture on the next port of call—a job that necessitated considerable research, as she had to talk about the region's history, points of interest, exchange rate, and shopping. Because the ship was small, she also served as the assistant shore manager for excursions. Carol's workday never ended at 5:00 p.m. In the evening, she ate dinner with the passengers, went to cocktail parties, and participated in costume parades and a fun-and-games night. When individuals are employed in a service industry, it is important for them to remember that the customer always comes first, even if it is in the employees' "home." Passengers often approach staff with questions or special requests. Cruise ship employees must remember that they are there for the passengers' benefit and are considered a resource. At times, this can be difficult, especially when employees are in port trying to enjoy time off with their friends.

Hostess

Carol's last job aboard a ship was as a hostess in charge of all the social functions on the ship. She organized all the main social events, wrote party invitations, and was in attendance at the evenings' social functions. The purpose of her job was to make sure all the passengers were comfortable and satisfied; however, the job had a tedious side, as she had to hand-write all the invitations and deal frequently with disgruntled passengers. Besides her social duties, Carol distributed and corrected a daily quiz and then awarded prizes to passengers. She also did such diverse things as rolling balls and selling tickets at bingo games, participating in trivia games, and attending gatherings of grandmothers. Then at 5:00 every evening, she would take off her uniform and dress in the appropriate attire for the evening's round of parties and gatherings.

After a vacation of a few months, Carol worked as a passenger service representative and a future sales consultant before leaving the cruise line to pursue other interests. Looking back at her cruise line career, she remembers lots of great times and fabulous trips to every continent, highlighted by cruises up the Amazon, through Indonesia, and to Hong Kong, Ukraine, and Venice. At the same time, she remembers never getting a block of 24 hours off in most of her jobs.

ANOTHER PERSONAL STORY OF A CRUISE LINE EMPLOYEE

After graduation from college, Julee Moser worked in public relations. Expressing her love of travel to a fellow employee led to Julee learning about working for Royal Cruise Line—the same cruise company where Carol was employed. Her first job was serving as a ship's secretary—the same starting position as Carol's. This job required Julie to work very long hours, from as early as 7:30 a.m. to as late as 10:00 p.m. Few Americans were employed on this ship—a small, 450-passenger vessel. Most of the crew was Greek, along with English, Irish, Scandinavian, and Filipino workers.

Julee worked in a small office next to the purser's. Her major responsibility each day was to coordinate all the events and write as well as print the daily program of activities for the ship. This involved conferring with the cruise director, the chief purser, and all the other heads of departments in order to schedule the events. It also entailed fighting with a difficult machine that was reluctant to print the schedule at times. In the evening, she would host and mingle at cocktail parties and attend special events, where she would always have an assigned task, such as handing out prizes at contests. Other duties included collecting passports, cruise documents, and tickets on embarkation days and helping direct passengers and luggage on disembarkation days.

Julee worked as a secretary for a year. This was a contract position, which meant that she worked full time for six to eight months and then could elect to take some time off before signing another contract.

Assistant Shore Excursion Manager

Julee's second contract was for a nine-month stint as an assistant shore excursion manager. Most cruises on this ship lasted from twelve to fifteen days, and there would be a stop at a port every day or two. Stays at ports varied from early morning to afternoon stays to longer overnight visits. Always dressed in a uniform provided by the cruise line, Julee worked part of the time at a desk where she sold tickets for ports of call, answered questions about tours, and told people about local places and transportation. She also went on shore excursions, acting as a supervisor to ensure that everything was going as planned. Then in the evening Julee would attend social events, as in her previous job. She did not have to eat with the passengers but was able to eat with the crew in either the ship's or crew's dining room.

Future Cruise Consultant

After working as a passenger service representative for four years, Julee elected to become a future cruise consultant. While seated at a desk outside of the ship's dining room for two hours in the morning and two hours in the afternoon (times varied depending on port times), she gave information to passengers about the cruise line's ships, cruise prices and promotions, and space availability. She also helped with tours, crowd control at embarkation and disembarkation, and social events which included attending all cocktail parties. In addition, Julee held a travel agent get-together to advise the agents of the cruise line's future plans. When she worked as a future cruise consultant, Julee ate her evening meals with the passengers.

Being a cruise consultant was Julee's last job with the cruise line because it went out of business one month after her contract ended. Altogether Julee worked for eight years with the cruise company—a job she really liked because it gave her a chance to see the world. She was almost always able to work late to get her job done so that she would have a chance to go ashore frequently. Julee recommends that anyone seeking to work aboard ships in jobs like hers have people skills and computer skills, as well as the ability to function on a limited amount of sleep.

LOOKING AT THE FUTURE

Because the number of cruise passengers keeps growing each year, as does the number of cruise ships, employment needs are steadily increasing. This is a very labor-intensive industry—it employs one crew member for every two or three passengers. Furthermore, according to Cruise Lines International Association (CLIA), only about five percent of the American population has taken a cruise. This means there is a very large population of potential cruisers. Reaching even a small percentage of these individuals will increase the number of cruisers, because once people take cruises, seventy-four percent say they will take another cruise within five years. Another reason there will continue to be employment opportunities aboard cruise ships is the high turnover of employees. Americans need to remember, however, that even though the number of employees on cruise ships is steadily increasing, the majority of employees aboard these ships are from other countries.

LOOKING AT OTHER OPPORTUNITIES

Most jobs for Americans associated with the cruise industry are not aboard ships but working for cruise lines. Here it is possible for Americans to work in administrative, sales, marketing, finance, management information systems, and operations areas just like they would at any other company—and still have some opportunity to travel. Most cruise lines will offer their land-based employees cruises for a very nominal daily charge (or even free in some cases). In addition, some employees will need to go aboard ships as part of their jobs. For example, employees in management information systems departments may need to put new or updated programs or systems on the ships' computers, as well as update computer hardware. Another attraction to working for a cruise line is that because this is a rapidly growing industry, opportunities for rapid advancement exist.

FOR MORE INFORMATION

Information on employment opportunities aboard cruise ships can be obtained by writing to the individual cruise lines. These lines are primarily located in New York, Miami, and Los Angeles. A good guide to getting a job with a cruise line is *How to Get a Job on a Cruise Ship* by Don Kennedy, published by CareerSouth Publications.

CAREERS WORKING IN EVEN MORE TRAVEL JOBS

Jobs that involve opportunities for travel are certainly not limited to working as a travel agent or working for an airline or cruise line. Many United States corporations sell their products throughout the country and the world. This necessitates considerable domestic and foreign travel for employees, especially those in sales and marketing. Many companies like hotels, fast-food chains, automobile manufacturers, and banks have offices throughout the world that need staffing. The United States government has employees in foreign embassies. Every branch of the armed services presents opportunities to live abroad. Navy personnel visit foreign ports on cruises. Soldiers are stationed in many countries. Furthermore, there are jobs with railroads, bus companies, and trucking firms that involve almost constant travel. In addition, many professions such as travel writer and travel photographer necessitate frequent travel to exotic locales.

LOOKING AT JOBS WITH RAILROADS: AMTRAK

The railroads were once the number one transportation choice of travelers in the United States. However, after World War II most passengers deserted the railroads for buses and planes. Soon the railroads were trying to get rid of their unprofitable passenger lines. In 1970 the federal government created Amtrak to preserve some passenger lines. The new corporation faced many obstacles, with poor roadbeds, old equipment, inadequate maintenance facilities, a weak ticketing system, and too many routes. Much progress in developing a modern passenger rail system has been made with the introduction of a computerized ticketing system, new cars, high-speed trains, improved roadbeds and facilities, and a reduced number of routes. The system currently operates 216 trains a day over a 23,800-mile system and serves 530 stations in

45 states. Since its inception Amtrak has operated at a deficit and has been under continual pressure from the government to achieve profitability.

Individuals who have dreamed of a life riding the rails should look for jobs that involve traveling with Amtrak rather than with freight lines. Because of work rules, locomotive engineers and conductors on freight trains only work eight hours or 130 miles—whichever comes first. A trip may be as short as two or three hours and does not involve much true travel, as these employees remain within a district.

Engineers

In the cab of every Amtrak train, there are always two employees: the engineer and the assistant engineer. The engineer operates the train by using the throttle to start and accelerate the train and the brakes to slow and stop it. The assistant engineer acts as the second set of eyes and ears in the cab. These assistant engineers watch the track and the signals that indicate track obstructions, other train movements, and speed limits. They also keep in constant contact with the dispatcher and conductor by sending and receiving messages.

Engineer jobs are frequently filled by workers with experience in other railroad operating occupations. Beginning assistant engineers receive six weeks of instruction, which includes hands-on instruction in locomotive operation as well as learning operating rules and regulations. Seniority dictates advancement from newly-trained engineer to assistant engineer to engineer.

Conductors

The responsibility for the safety and well-being of all passengers rests on the shoulders of the conductor. This individual has the following duties: handling tickets, supervising the boarding and detraining of passengers and any baggage, staying in radio contact with the cab, deciding in consultation with the engineer if a train with mechanical or other problems can continue its route, throwing switches, and deciding when a train can leave the station. The conductor is usually aided in these tasks by an assistant conductor. Assistant conductors are given 244 hours of training by Amtrak that covers operations, emergency procedures, ticketing, and handling people.

Service Personnel

Aboard every long-distance train are personnel such as porters and dining car, lounge car, and sleeping car attendants. An on-board service chief is in charge of this entire crew. Occasionally, there will be guides aboard calling attention to points of interest. These are the railroad jobs that truly involve travel, because on-board service personnel work an entire trip—cross-country or within a region.

SALARY AND FRINGE BENEFITS

Almost all railroad transportation workers are members of unions. Amtrak assistant engineers earn between $34,000 and $45,000, while engineers' salaries range from $36,000 to $48,000. Assistant conductors earn between $26,000 and $35,000, while conductors receive between $30,000 and $40,000. Employees receive benefits including health insurance, vacation time, and personal days; and uniforms are provided. Reduced-price travel is available for all Amtrak employees and their spouses, and there are occasional free travel days.

LOOKING AT THE FUTURE

The downsizing of Amtrak in the early 1990s, along with uncertainties about the ability of the corporation to reduce costs, makes it difficult to predict what the demand for employees will be in the future. Many openings will arise as workers retire or leave jobs for other reasons.

LOOKING AT A CAREER AS A BUS DRIVER

The heyday for bus travel was in the 1940s and 1950s. At that time, air service was limited and few families owned cars. As air travel became cheaper and more available and most families purchased cars, fewer and fewer people elected to use bus transportation between cities. Still, today buses transport millions of Americans every day, providing an alternative to the airplane, automobile, and railroad. Modern buses used on inter-city routes and as tour buses and charters provide a very comfortable trip with their wide windows, reclining seats, air conditioning, restrooms, viewing decks, and even movies. Furthermore, buses serve far more communities than the airlines and railroads do, and they manage to do so at very low fares.

Just as airline deregulation spawned the growth of a number of new airlines, bus deregulation in the 1980s brought about the creation of several thousand new companies. The largest inter-city bus company is Greyhound, the only company that offers nationwide service. Gray Line, which operates local and long-distance sightseeing tours, is another major carrier. And in the Northeast, Peter Pan Bus Lines is an important carrier, offering scheduled trips, tours, and charters. Less than 500 of the more than 3,000 bus lines in the United States offer scheduled service; the remaining companies provide tours and charters.

WORKING CONDITIONS

Because inter-city, tour, and charter bus drivers are the drivers who truly spend their working days traveling, the focus of this section will be on them rather than on local route or school bus drivers. Charter and tour drivers, especially, have the opportunity to travel to popular tourist spots. Bus drivers may work nights, weekends, and holidays. They often spend nights away from home, staying at hotels at company expense. Inter-city drivers with seniority will have regular schedules, but others must be prepared to report to work on short notice. In addition, seasonal layoffs are common. Many inter-city bus drivers with little seniority, for example, are furloughed during the winter when regular schedule, tour, and charter business falls off.

ON-THE-JOB RESPONSIBILITIES

All bus drivers face driving through heavy traffic while dealing with passengers, which can be stressful. At the same time, they have the advantage of working long stretches without direct supervision. The length of the workday of bus drivers is strictly regulated by the Department of Transportation. All drivers must keep accurate logs of their duty time and driving time. Before beginning a route, tour, or charter trip, drivers check the cleanliness of their bus and the vehicle's tires, brakes, windshield wipers, lights, oil, fuel, water, and safety equipment, such as fire extinguishers, first aid kits, and emergency reflectors. Along their routes, bus drivers must be alert to prevent accidents, especially in heavy traffic or in bad weather, and to avoid sudden stops or swerves that jar passengers.

Inter-city bus drivers report to their assigned terminal or garage, where they receive tickets and prepare trip report forms. Besides picking up and discharging passengers at terminals, inter-city drivers collect fares; answer questions about schedules, routes, and transfer points; may handle luggage; and sometimes announce stops. Their days are run by the clock as they must adhere to schedules. In a day, inter-city drivers may make only a single one-way trip to a distant city, or they may make a round trip to a nearer city. They may stop at towns just a few miles apart, or only at large cities hundreds of miles apart. Drivers who operate chartered buses pick up groups, take them to their destinations, and generally remain with them until they return, which could be the same day or a week or more later. Tour drivers drive an entire tour and can be gone as long as thirty days.

PREPARATION FOR BECOMING A BUS DRIVER

The first prerequisite for becoming a bus driver is to like to drive and travel. Then it is essential for prospective drivers to secure a commercial driver's license from the state in which they live. This involves taking a written test plus passing a behind-the-wheel road test in the type of vehicle they will be operating. Many inter-city bus companies prefer drivers who are high school graduates at least twenty-four years of age, and some require several years of bus or truck driving experience. Inter-city drivers also are required to submit to drug screening as a condition of employment. Inter-city, tour, and charter companies also expect their drivers to have well-developed people skills that allow them to interact well with others.

SALARY, FRINGE BENEFITS, AND ADVANCEMENT

Earnings of inter-city bus drivers depend primarily on the number of miles they drive. Beginning inter-city drivers who work about six months out of the year will earn more than $20,000, while senior drivers who work all year long can earn more than $48,000. With tips, charter and tour drivers can earn between $50,000 and $75,000 a year.

The fringe benefits that bus drivers receive from their employers vary greatly. Most inter-city drivers receive paid health and life insurance, sick leave, and free bus rides on any of the regular routes of their line or system. Drivers who work full-time also get as much as four weeks of paid vacation annually.

Opportunities for promotion generally are limited. However, experienced drivers may become supervisors or dispatchers, who assign buses to drivers, check whether drivers are on schedule, reroute buses to avoid traffic jams and other problems, and dispatch extra vehicles and service crew to scenes of accidents and breakdowns. A few drivers become instructors and managers.

LOOKING AT THE FUTURE

Individuals seeking jobs as bus drivers through 2005 should encounter good opportunities. Employment of inter-city drivers will grow as bus ridership increases because the population and labor force are growing and incomes are rising. There may continue to be competition for inter-city bus drivers in some areas, since many of these positions offer relatively high wages and attractive benefits. The most competitive positions will be those that offer regular hours and steady driving routes.

LOOKING AT A CAREER AS A TRUCK DRIVER

There are more than two million truck drivers in the United States. Most of them have jobs concentrated in and around large cities. It is only the long-distance truckers who have jobs that involve travel to distant areas of the country. On long runs, drivers may haul loads from city to city for a week or more before returning home. Some companies use two drivers on very long runs, allowing one driver to sleep in a berth while the other drives. Stops are made only for fuel, food, loading, and unloading.

ON-THE-JOB RESPONSIBILITIES

Long-distance truck drivers spend most of their working time behind the wheel but may be required to unload their cargo. Before beginning their trip, they check their trucks for fuel and oil and make sure the brakes, windshield wipers, and lights are working and that all safety equipment is aboard and working correctly. Once underway, drivers must be alert to prevent accidents and to drive their trucks efficiently. At the end of each run, they are required by the U.S. Department of Transportation to complete reports about the trip and the condition of the truck and to give a detailed report of any accident.

PREPARATION FOR BECOMING A TRUCK DRIVER

Drivers must meet the qualifications and standards set by both federal and state regulations. Minimum qualifications include: being at least 21 years old, passing a physical examination, having good hearing, having 20/40 vision with or without glasses, and having normal blood pressure. All drivers of trucks designed to carry at least 26,000 pounds (which includes most long-distance trucks) need to obtain a special commercial driver's license from the state in which they live. Also, drivers must pass periodic random tests for drug and alcohol use. Both states and trucking companies often have higher standards than the ones described here.

To obtain a commercial driver's license as well as learn how to drive trucks, most long-distance drivers attend tractor-trailer driver training programs at private and public technical vocational schools. It is important for drivers to select schools that have been certified by the Professional Truck Driver Institute of America and that have been approved by prospective employers. A list of certified programs can be obtained from: Professional Truck Driver Institute of America, 8788 Elk Grove Boulevard, Suite 20, Elk Grove, CA 95624.

SALARY, FRINGE BENEFITS, AND ADVANCEMENT

The earnings of long-distance drivers of tractor-trailers varies from as little as $20,000 to more than $40,000 per year. Company drivers receive standard benefits. Some long-distance drivers advance by purchasing a truck and going into business for themselves. A few may advance to dispatcher, to manager, or to traffic work—for example, planning delivery schedules.

LOOKING AT THE FUTURE

Job opportunities for truck drivers vary from year to year because the amount of freight moved by trucks fluctuates with the economy. Growth of long-distance trucker jobs should slow somewhat as more trailers are shipped on rails rather than hauled over highways to distant cities. Overall, opportunities for jobs as long-distance truckers should increase as more freight is carried by trucks.

LOOKING AT A JOB AS A TRAVEL PHOTOGRAPHER

Travel photographers take pictures for magazines that feature travel, exotic lands, and wildlife. They work for publications like *National Geographic* and *Travel & Leisure.* They also take pictures that are used in newspapers, calendars, books, greeting cards, tour company brochures, and advertisements. Many photographers work for what are known as stock houses—agencies that have libraries of thousands of slides that are sold to publications and organizations.

This is a very competitive occupation, and pay is low. Most travel photographers are freelancers who are forced to devote a great deal of their time to soliciting jobs and to selling the work that they have done. It is, however, one occupation in which people truly have the opportunity to travel.

LOOKING AT A JOB AS A TRAVEL WRITER

Being a travel writer is decidedly one job that involves a great amount of travel. Some writers will travel as much as seventy to eighty percent of the time. Jobs can be found on the staffs of newspapers, consumer-oriented travel magazines, and travel trade publications. There are also jobs writing and updating travel books;

more than 1,000 new guidebooks are published each year.

Today, travel writing jobs are not limited to publications. Radio, television, and cable television stations need writers for travel programs. Furthermore, job possibilities exist with tour companies, lecture series, tourist offices, and wherever a need for written travel information exists.

Pay can be good for travel writers; however, job competition is fierce. There are a limited number of jobs at newspapers and magazines, and these publications want to hire experienced travel writers—an obstacle for beginning a career with these companies. Guidebook publishers also want experienced travel authors. Generally, travel writers will need to get started in this profession by writing travel articles and having them published in a local newspaper or a small trade publication to establish their credibility as writers. They will usually find it easier to get an initial job with a trade publication writing about what is happening in the travel industry than with a consumer magazine writing about exotic locales around the world. Another obstacle to entering this career is the competition by so many writers for the small number of positions.

Instead of working for publications, many travel writers opt to become freelancers. This adds the additional task of constantly finding a market for one's writing. However, by changing a travel article to fit different audiences, the same basic material can be sold to several publications.

Those who are successful in establishing careers as travel writers find it a most satisfying way of life because they genuinely love to travel. They are the ones who have learned to write about travel in a way that appeals to a variety of audiences. Prospective travel writers should study consumer-oriented travel magazines, travel sections in newspapers, and travel guidebooks to decide if this type of writing appeals to them.

FOR MORE INFORMATION

There are many other travel careers that may appeal to travel lovers, such as careers with the Merchant Marine, tour operators, and car rental companies to name just a few. The following books have more information on travel careers:

Miller, Robert F. *Careers Without College: Travel,* Princeton, NJ: Peterson's, 1993.

Milne, Robert Scott. *Opportunities in Travel Careers,* Lincolnwood, IL: VGM Career Horizons, 1992.

Plawin, Paul. *Careers for Travel Buffs and Other Restless Types,* Lincolnwood, IL: VGM Career Horizons, 1992.

Rubin, Karen. *Flying High in Travel,* New York: John Wiley & Sons, Inc., 1992.

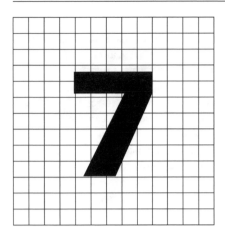

WORKING FOR A TOUR COMPANY AS A GUIDE AND IN OTHER JOBS

Starting in the 15th and 16th centuries and lasting until the 19th century, the Grand Tour was an introduction to the countries of Europe for wealthy young Englishmen. Accompanied by their tutors, they completed their education through these trips. While the Grand Tour has largely disappeared, sightseeing, special-interest, convention, and many other tours are now operated worldwide by tour companies.

Today, tour-operating companies are found in very nearly every town and city across the country. These companies may be very small and owner-operated, or larger in size, with employees in departments such as guiding, planning/operations, sales/marketing, and accounting/managing. Tour companies may package and sell trips on a wholesale basis to smaller travel planning companies, to associations, to meeting planners who may plan a trip as a special function during an annual association meeting, or to businesses seeking trips as bonuses to recognize outstanding employees' performances. Other tour companies sell retail, which means selling directly to the consumer of the trip. Both wholesale and retail tour companies put together travel packages that include such components as transportation, accommodations, and sightseeing.

LOOKING AT TOUR TRAVEL OPTIONS

The means of travel for tours range from bus, ship, train, or plane to any combination such as bus and plane. Tours may be local, perhaps even within the geographic location of the tour company, or they can be long distances from the home base of the tour operation company. Buses are a popular choice for transportation for both local and long-distance tours because bus travel can be very affordable. Passengers stop at many points along the bus tour, so they get to see interesting sites en route to the final destination. An example of a local tour would be one in which a tour guide escorts a group through a historic area of a city. These local tours can be for a partial day or full day of travel. They may take passengers to a nearby attraction or community festival.

Plane travel allows people to take short excursions of a day or two to more-distant locations. Tropical climate sites offer great appeal for winter-weary individuals, as do ski trips to the mountains for Sunbelt residents. These are marketed as getaways and have become very popular, because leisure-time opportunities are limited for some individuals. The overall cost of these quick getaways is greater with plane travel than bus or car travel, but some travelers are willing to pay more for the convenience of time.

Tours of greater distances typically last several days to several weeks and frequently use multiple modes of transportation. For instance, a plane may transport a group to Europe. Once on that continent, though, the travelers may use rail travel to move from country to country.

Rail Excursions

Another travel mode for tours is using rail passenger travel. Although not as popular today as it once was, rail travel for special, private lines such as Rancho Grande Tours in El Paso, Texas sell very well. This rail line tours through the Copper Canyon of Mexico. Travelers are treated to features such as oversized windows for viewing, reclining seats with ample leg room, full bar and dining service cars, and lounge cars. While winding through passes, gorges, and canyons, tour participants experience breathtaking views of the canyon. The tour company then provides overnight stays at hotels along the rail line and side visits to native Indian villages and other historic sites.

Some smaller rail lines operate very successfully, too. The Whitewater Valley Railroad is Indiana's most scenic railroad. On summer, fall, and December weekends, the coal-powered locomotive pulls passenger cars sixteen miles from Connersville to Metamora. At Metamora, the passengers disembark for several hours of shopping at craft and antique shops. Passengers on the train may bring their own food and beverage items, giving a casual, relaxed atmosphere to the trip.

Other types of rail tours that have been popular in recent years are wine train tours and mystery train tours. These special-interest tours attract clients due to their unique themes and the mode of transportation. Amtrak does not sell these specialized tours, but through the company passengers can obtain help with planning sightseeing excursions for attractions on the way or at their destination.

Cruise Trips

Cruise lines offer another alternative for tour travel, and cruises may last from three days to as long as several weeks. Cruise lines have rapidly grown in their volume of business. Guests appreciate the chance to have a wide variety of experiences on board, such as incredibly fine dining, multiple amenities (like massages and physical conditioning), sport activities, entertainment, and gaming. Many of the cruise lines have now purchased their own islands to offer the travelers opportunities to relax on private beaches, swim, snorkel, and scuba dive. Of course, the port calls made by the ships are a prime feature, and the cruise lines set up special land tour packages to help their guests see as much as possible when docked.

Cruising as a tour may take other forms than that of the large vessels holding thousands of passengers. Some tour travelers desire a more intimate or unique way to travel. The paddle boats that cruise the rivers of the United States offer such appeal, as do the tall ships that elegantly set sail. Smaller vessels are also available; for example, passenger boats may transport only 100 passengers and may cruise through the pristine waters off the coast of Alaska. Depending on the destination of these smaller ships, the cruise may be as short as one day.

LOOKING AT TOUR SETTINGS

Destination choices for tours range from anywhere in the United States to anywhere in the world. The settings are varied to meet the interests of a wide group of travelers. The sites visited may be historic, educational, theme-related, natural wonders or natural beauty, competition-related, exotic, cosmopolitan, rural, artistic, and/or cultural.

Historic sites have always been and will continue to be attractive settings for tour companies. Customers have a desire to see places that they have read about. The tour company may select sites that have been a key part of America's history. A tour of Philadelphia would offer stops at Independence Hall, the Liberty Bell, and other historical places.

Theme tours are also perennial favorites. An example of a theme-related setting is a trip to Branson, Missouri that permits tour customers to attend their favorite country singer's performance. Las Vegas is another theme-setting choice, with its wide variety of big-name entertainers and gaming.

Sporting events attract the interest of tour-planning companies. Many tour customers request trips organized with lodging, tickets, and even souvenirs from special athletic events. The 1996 Olympics in Atlanta, Georgia had special package one-day trips organized and sold through Leisure Clubs International. The Olympic Games' One Day Tripper Program featured a flight to Atlanta in the early morning with return in the late evening from selected major cities around the United States. Customers could select two events to attend. Transportation to and between the sports venues was provided by Leisure Clubs. Special Olympic merchandise was included as souvenirs.

Cosmopolitan settings such as New York City and Chicago offer multiple attractions for tours. One idea which has been growing in popularity is "big city" Christmas shopping. Tour companies organize one-day or weekend shopping excursions that allow the tour participants to "shop 'til they drop." For example, trips to Chicago focus on the traditional locations such as Water Tower Place and the Magnificent Mile, but also include outlet shopping stops at huge discount centers such as Gurnee Mills mall, just north of Chicago. Holiday shopping tours require planners to minimize transit time so shopping time can be maximized.

LOOKING AT A CAREER AS A TOUR GUIDE

Guiding tours is a good introductory position with a tour operations company. The primary task of the guide or escort (either term can be used) is to ensure that the trip occurs as planned. This means being responsible for guest safety, providing an interesting experience, organizing the daily itinerary, handling all problems, alleviating emergency situations, interacting with suppliers, giving narratives about sites, and completing daily report forms to summarize the activities, meals, and accommodations. Additionally, a tour guide or escort serves as the host for a trip. An escort is responsible for keeping a trip on its daily schedule; organizing the customers during transit and when stopped for touring, dining, or sleeping; assisting with customers' special needs; resolving daily problems that may occur; educating the customers about the sites being visited; and entertaining them whenever needed.

An escort is, on one hand, performing a role that might be described as "babysitter" since every minute detail is planned and every guest's need is taken care of. On the other hand, the escort is a leader, educator, negotiator, problem solver, and entertainer. These diverse activities and responsibilities can be very demanding. Typically, the escort is the first one to rise in the morning and the last one to get to bed in the evening.

If the tour has international stops, the tour escort may or may not serve as the guide speak telling about the sites. The tour operator may hire locals to serve as the guide speak. This can add a more authentic flavor to a trip, since a local person can give tremendous insight into the people, their customs, and their culture. Other benefits of using local guides are that they can relate safety do's and don'ts, help with language barriers, and assist with money equivalencies, exchange rates, and exchange procedures.

ON-THE-JOB RESPONSIBILITIES

Tour guides' lives are very busy when peak season for tours arrives. Due to weather and traditional calendars for schools, most people—whether an empty-nester family or one with school-age children—tend to use the months of May through September for excursions. Even retired senior citizens who can travel at any time are more likely to choose these months since winter travel may conflict with the holiday season or simply be months with unpredictable weather.

When tour guides have a group to escort, their main goal is for every customer to be happy with the trip. In order to fulfill this goal, they typically work twelve to fourteen hours per day. They start each day, each activity, each change in location with one thought: "Did I double check—even triple check each detail of the trip?" This is likely to be the number-one activity performed throughout a day on the job to ensure that everything goes as planned.

In the morning, the tour escort is awake early. He or she checks the breakfast service for readiness at least one hour before guests on the tour are to eat. As the travelers arrive for breakfast, the guide greets them and reviews the itinerary for the day. While the guests are eating, the escort checks at the hotel front desk to verify that check-out procedures are completed. At this time, it is important to check that travelers have paid for any incidental charges (charges not included in the cost of the trip, such as long-distance telephone calls). The guide also talks to the bus driver to determine that the customers have loaded their luggage and confirms departure time and route for the day. Calling ahead to the day's destination sites to verify arrival times is another duty at this time. In addition, planned lunch stops, if any, need to be reconfirmed at this time, as well as lodging for the evening.

When all of these checks have been made and the guests are seated on the bus, the guide re-welcomes them and reviews the day's activities. This is a time for questions and concerns to be answered. While in transit, the guide offers activities for the travelers which may include magazines to read or movies to watch. To help the travelers learn about the next destination, the tour guide will have information available about the site—possibly from a chamber of commerce, from the site itself, or from books and magazines featuring the destination. The guide also prepares the customers by giving them facts and tips acquired from previous trips to the site.

Upon arrival at a site, the guests are reminded of the activities and the time schedule. Depending upon the destination, the guide may simply "turn the guests over to the site" or may lead them around the site, serving as a guide speak. As a guide speak, the escort tells the travelers all the important facts and unique information about the site. Either way, time management of the group is the escort's top priority. If lunch and/or dinner are included with this stop, the guide's day is simplified.

After the hours or day of activities at this site are completed, the bus is reloaded. Once the day's activities, which may include other stops, are completed, the top priority for escort and guests becomes getting to the hotel for rest. Once the group arrives at the lodging property, room assignments are checked and, if needed, dinner or evening snacks take place. The guide previews the next day of activities for his group and makes sure everyone gets settled for the night. Once in his or her room, the guide completes all of the paperwork required by the company and reviews the next day's responsibilities. Since every detail for this day was double-checked and triple-checked, it has been a successful day. Now the guide must go through the same process for the next day to ensure its success, too.

PREPARATION FOR A CAREER AS A TOUR GUIDE

Training is usually on-the-job so tour guides can learn the procedures and policies of their employer through observation. This on-the-job training might consist of taking several trips with an experienced escort to assist in all of the responsibilities required to keep a group moving through the schedule. Training would include education on the destination sites or attractions so that the guide will be informative to the customers. Escorts will also be taught about common pitfalls of serving as a guide. Handling people is very demanding. Some individuals want constant attention, for example, and training would give appropriate solutions to help the guide give some extra attention to a demanding guest, but not at the expense of the other customers.

SPECIAL ATTRIBUTES OF TOUR GUIDES

Qualifications include being a "people person," being good with oral and written communications, being an entertainer, being able to resolve problems, and being able to handle a crisis. Tour guides need to be knowledgeable about reading maps and meticulous in handling details. A degree credential is very advantageous, but so, too, are decision-making skills, multicultural skills, and organizing skills, which can be learned in other work experiences. Part-time or full-time work experiences in other types of hospitality businesses (restaurants, hotels, cafeterias, concessions, exhibitions, and/or conventions) would offer useful exposure in these areas and are valuable to the individual who seeks employment with a tour operations company. Physically, tour guides must have an excellent stamina level in order to work the long days required while on tour. Guides and escorts spend long hours on their feet in environments that can be very inclement. Fitness is essential to coping well with the challenges and stresses of guiding tours.

SALARY AND FRINGE BENEFITS

Tour guides receive hourly wages of $40.00 and up per day, with a meal allowance of approximately $20.00 per day. Their wages depend upon the complexity of the trip. Factors that would command a greater daily rate are: unusually large groups, tours made up of travelers with special requirements (for example, handicapped travelers), particularly long trips, and a large number of activities. While tipping is not expected from customers, extremely pleased guests will give a gratuity to the guide as a thank-you for an enjoyable trip. Tips can give a large increase to a tour escort's annual income.

Companies do offer free trips to destinations as part of establishing itineraries and/or preparation for an inaugural trip to a new location. This is an excellent benefit. Only guides who work full-time year-round will receive benefits such as life insurance, health insurance, and retirement programs. Guides who are seasonal employees do not usually receive these benefits.

THE REWARDS OF BEING A TOUR GUIDE

Tour guides frequently cite the opportunity to see new places as the greatest advantage of this career choice. If the company is involved in international tours, visiting foreign countries is an attractive possibility. Related to the excitement of traveling extensively is the opportunity on each trip to meet new people who vary widely in their interests, backgrounds, and ages. In addition, there is the companionship that develops between the tour guide and the clients. Whether the trip is one day or several weeks in length, a special bond develops between the guide and the group members as they share in the excitement of the trip. Group members have a certain dependence on the tour escort and look to this individual for assistance in all areas. The escort, too, makes the trip come alive for the customer, and that intangible aspect brings about an unique relationship between the guide and the guests.

Tour escorts have another advantage in their careers. Since very popular trips are repeated annually or even more frequently, the contact people at the attraction sites and lodging properties can become close working associates. With each tour repeated to a destination, the guides and the employees of other businesses have opportunities to pool their efforts to make certain that the travelers have the best possible experience. Working together results in a "win-win-win" situation. The customers win since they have a great total tour experience. The tour operation company builds an outstanding reputation, so they win by gaining new customers while keeping previous customers. The win for the destinations, hotels, and restaurants is a tour company that brings more travelers to them.

THE DISADVANTAGES OF BEING A TOUR GUIDE

With the diversity of clients on a tour—even a tour focused on a rather specific interest—guides are challenged to please all of their customers all of the time. The purchasers of a tour package generally represent some degree of differences in economic, social, geographical, cultural, educational, and age backgrounds. Tour guides must be sensitive to differences and address them effectively.

Another challenge for tour guides is maintaining good spirits among all of the clients. Traveling and touring can be tiresome for the customers. When nerves become frayed, the guide must work to bring harmony and humor to the group. Another drawback to tour escorting is repetition of locations. Some tour-planning businesses do not frequently change destinations, and guides may find multiple visits to a site monotonous. Tour guides must draw upon their personalities to sincerely convince the guests on each and every trip that this trip is exciting. Guides cannot reveal their boredom to the customers.

Finally, problems do occur despite the best planning efforts to ensure a perfect tour. An escort will be responsible for using contingency planning to handle problems and provide guest satisfaction through the chosen resolutions. Contingency planning requires examining the problem and all possible solutions. Furthermore, alternatives must match company policies and procedures. Within this framework of responsibility, the guide selects an alternative that best fits the situation at hand.

LOOKING AT A CAREER AS A TOUR PLANNER

Large tour businesses, whether they sell wholesale or retail, have employees who plan the trips. The planners research the popularity and demand for specific sites, investigate all costs, negotiate prices, establish travel dates and times, and coordinate with other companies whose services might be needed for transportation, lodging, food, and/or entertainment. (Transportation may not be included in these duties since some companies own the means of travel, such as buses or planes. In these cases, the companies would also hire drivers or pilots.)

In large companies, tour planners may not have the opportunity to work closely with customers, since a guide would serve that role. The planning and sales of a tour depend upon knowing the customers' demographics: age, income, and interest. It is very important to organize trips that are appealing to customers' particular interests. Planners must also be aware of quality businesses that can be used as part of the trip. A destination trip can nearly be ruined, for example, if the planner selects a restaurant that is understaffed, overpriced for the quality, and/or unclean. The tour planner's rewards are found in the satisfaction of planning and overseeing the execution of a flawless tour.

As part of the research for destination selection, tour planners have occasion to visit the sites under consideration. This gives the tour planner a first-hand experience in a country, state, or city to see the special attractions and to evaluate the food and lodging facilities. This is very important in creating a quality trip; therefore, this visit benefits the tour company's potential success as well as giving the planners knowledge for accurate planning.

LOOKING AT OTHER CAREERS IN TOUR OPERATIONS

Reservationists have the first contact with customers, so they must be pleasant and skilled at determining the interests of the customers. Eliciting information about customers' interests is necessary so that the customers can receive marketing information that will help sell a tour. The sales staff follows up on all customer contacts, hoping to turn each lead into a booking. Both reservationists and sales staff are rewarded for the quality and quantity of selling.

Tour companies of substantial size also employ people for organizing the promotion and advertising of the tours. Advertising can be done in traditional forms through brochures, which the salespeople might design in conjunction with the planners. With software word processing packages available, salespeople do much of their own creative work for advertising. The sales staff must also stay current with new trends in marketing, such as using the World Wide Web to feature their company and its trips. If it is a wholesale company, the sales staff may visit key sites or attend marketplace meetings for wholesalers from around the country to feature their planned activities and get leads on bookings. Similarly, tour companies with retail sales staffs determine the advertising media to use and may also set up general travel seminars that are free to the public. At these seminars, the sales personnel can promote their planned activities, answer questions about travel, and get interested customers to make deposits. After bookings are made, the sales staff would oversee confirmation of deposits. They would also send out all needed information on the tour—information on climate, weather, and appropriate clothing; travel requirements such as birth certificate or passport; and pertinent materials about the destinations.

Support Services for Tour Operations Companies

Finally, the large tour companies employ people to provide the support services in the accounting and in the human resources departments. In accounting, the employees help with the financial records of the company. They oversee deposits and final payments for tours, and check disbursements for services used at hotels, restaurants, and tour sites. Human resources takes care of payroll records and benefit packages.

Working as an Owner/Operator of a Tour Company

Small tour operation companies use a "wearer-of-many-hats" approach for their companies. One or two people are employed, and their positions include planning, marketing, selling, and escorting. Their jobs encompass every aspect from initiating a plan for a trip through the evaluation of the trip's outcome. The incredible variety of tasks performed by the owner/employee of a small tour operation company makes it a necessity for this individual to be highly organized, very detail oriented, a quick thinker, excellent decision maker, and personable with customers.

PREPARATION FOR A CAREER IN TOUR OPERATIONS

To work in tour guiding, planning, and/or sales, educational requirements include a minimum of a high school education. High school courses in communications and business management are good to establish knowledge and skills in dealing with people and completing paperwork. Membership in student organizations, holding a leadership role as officer or committee chair, is valuable to help learn organizational and leadership skills. Clubs such as Distributive Education Clubs of America (DECA) and Future Homemakers Association/Home Economics-Related Occupations (FHA/HERO) are excellent choices. Both have in their organizational structure many opportunities to participate in contests that demand problem solving and use of people skills, in addition to offering the obvious leadership development positions of holding a local, state, or national office. Managing a sports team is another way a high school student can obtain some job-related preparation. Teams travel, and they need help packing equipment and supplies for their trips.

Larger tour companies or companies specializing in itineraries with international or educational settings may require a two-year or a four-year college degree. Preferred majors are tourism and hospitality management, with their emphasis on business management, service management, and food and lodging operations. To complement a hospitality degree, a minor in liberal arts, especially foreign languages, history, or sociology, is an excellent choice. Computer courses, as a minor, are an excellent complement to a hospitality major, for skills in promoting and selling the trips and for purposes of record keeping. A communications degree would be very beneficial as another choice for a major or minor since good communications can serve tour operators. Business specialties in marketing and/or accounting would help prepare the tour operator for strategies to sell the trips and to assure financial profitability. This would be a good choice as a major or a minor in a degree program.

Some professional organizations associated with tours and travel offer a variety of programs that can give further credentials to a tour operations employee. A Certified Travel Counselor (CTC) designation is granted by the American Society of Travel Agents. The National Tour Association has a program for Certified Tour Professionals (CTP). A Certified Travel Industry Specialist (CITS) is a certificate program available through the American Bus Association.

SALARY AND FRINGE BENEFITS

Fringe benefits such as life insurance, medical benefits, paid days off, and/or retirement programs vary widely in availability depending on the size of the tour operation company and the number of full-time employees. Since many tour operation companies use a small skeleton staff of full-time employees to plan, organize, and sell trips, benefit packages are not too common. Full-time employees in planning, sales, or support areas earn competitive salaries typically in the range of $20,000 to $30,000. Obviously, those people who own tour operation companies have much greater salaries than their employees. It would appear that the potential to earn a liberal income is unlimited.

MORE JOBS IN TOURS

Destination management companies have a "one-stop shopping" philosophy of business. These businesses have expanded on the tour business by not only planning and executing tours but selling other types of services to the customer too. For example, if an association is planning its annual convention, the members might want tours, entertainment, program speakers, food and lodging arrangements, airport meet-and-greet services, and/or myriad other possible services.

The destination management company is hired to provide all of the services for the customer. Jackson's Hole in Jackson, Wyoming is an example of a destination management company that specializes in providing all services for customers interested in outdoor activities and adventure experiences. The activities they can organize include bicycle tours, fishing expeditions, four-wheel drive trips, game hunting camps, dude ranch stays, hiking and backpacking, horse pack trips, river rafting, rock climbing, and wagon train treks. With this diverse array of choices, any group could find experiences that would appeal to their members.

As the intermediary, the destination management company listens to the wishes of the customers and then arranges for the activities they have selected. For their customers, the destination management company saves time and energy by completing all of the details for a group's choices of activities.

To work for a destination management company, the required skills are: to be patient with people; to be forthright with customers by informing them of what is really involved in each activity; to advise customers on the time, cost, and overall quality of possible activities; to be credible in dealings with customers by delivering the quality that is expected; and to be respectful of the other businesses whose services you contract. Destination management companies are finding a growing market for their services because customers like working with a single business to make all necessary arrangements for a group of people.

LOOKING AT THE FUTURE

Tour companies are stable, with modest growth in the past decade. However, operators are particularly susceptible to changes in the economy. Local, national, or international economic variances may affect individuals' discretionary spending. When the economy is in a slow-down period, people delay a trip. Likewise, the wholesale tour operator will find that business diminishes when the economy is slow or stagnant since large organizations may postpone incentive or award trips for their employees.

FOR MORE INFORMATION

For more information, visit local tour operations companies and interview tour escorts, planners, and sales staff. The National Tour Foundation, located in Lexington, Kentucky, has a wealth of materials available regarding courses, internships, and colleges and universities that offer tourism courses and/or degrees. A list of these institutions is included in appendix C.

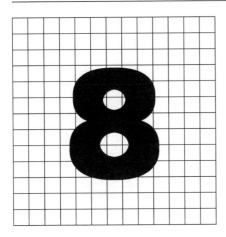

WORKING IN AMUSEMENT PARKS

Amusement parks are found all around the country in various sizes, from the colossal Disney World in Orlando, Florida to small water parks in many communities. No matter how large or small amusement parks are, the guests are in a happy mood, relaxed, and excited about being in the park. Coupled with this carefree attitude of the customer is the wide array of rides that appeal to guests of all ages. Many amusement parks have various sizes and shapes of roller coasters and other breathtaking attractions to excite visitors. The advertisements and the promotions used to attract guests highlight the speed, size, and thrills of these rides. The employees' jobs are made easier because guests have selected a park in order to experience these thrills. A major benefit, then, of working in an amusement park is serving guests who are interested in having a good time.

The same is true for parks with a greater emphasis on show entertainment. Visitors to Opryland in Nashville, Tennessee and Sea World in Aurora, Ohio both have high levels of anticipation for the shows featuring "stars." In the case of Opryland, Garth Brooks might be the star, while a killer whale could star in a Sea World show. At Walt Disney World in Orlando, Florida, the stars are Mickey Mouse and his friends.

SETTINGS OF AMUSEMENT PARKS

Very large parks such as Disney World have multiple, separate areas within the park complex. Disney World includes the Magic Kingdom, Epcot, Disney–MGM Studios, River Country, Pleasure Island, Disney's Blizzard Beach, Typhoon Lagoon, Discovery Island, the Disney Institute, and Walt Disney World Speedway. The Disney Institute is new to the Disney World complex and features a fresh concept in merging entertainment and personal enrichment. Guests can learn about animation, culinary arts, photography, storytelling, show business, landscape design, and interior design. Using choices made by the guests, Disney World has them participate in workshops and hear renowned speakers in the various areas of Disney World's expertise. To complement the educational component, guests choose fitness and life-style classes to expand their personal enrichment.

The Walt Disney World Speedway is also new to the park. Expansion into sports is being accomplished by sponsoring a site for Indy car racing. A Sports Complex is currently under construction and will open to the public in 1998. Facilities such as the Speedway and the Institute will further expand Disney World's appeal to guests.

For any guest at Disney World, leisure activities (golfing, biking, tennis, boat-ing, and fishing) are available throughout the complex, too. Disney World has forty-three square miles in the amusement park, but has expanded the park by opening the Vero Beach Resort on the Gulf side of the Atlantic for those who wish to be at the beach and experience the Disney magic all at once.

In contrast with the multi-entertainment complexes, there are smaller amuse-ment parks such as Holiday World and Splashing Safari in Santa Claus, Indi-ana. This park offers traditional rides, entertainment, and water rides. The 100-acre park uses three different themes to appeal to customers: Christmas, Halloween, and Fourth of July. Smaller parks also strongly emphasize service. For example, Holiday World and Splashing Safari was voted the World's Friend-liest Theme Park for 1995 by the readers of *Inside Track* magazine.

Other settings for amusement parks are those that have that down-home appeal. The rides, attractions, and entertainment at Dollywood Park in Pigeon Forge, Tennessee have this flavor.

Other amusement parks are associated with cartoon characters. A new amusement park planned for Plainfield, Indiana will feature Garfield, a cat who has been a long-standing hit of the comic page of newspapers.

Universal Studios selected a setting of television and major motion pic-ture-making to attract visitors. With opportunities to see and participate in major motion picture technology, guests learn and have fun at the same time. Ride attractions such as *E.T.* and *Back to the Future* frequently have long lines of riders waiting to have an experience that simulates the action of the movie.

Water parks became popular attractions in many locations around the country in the 1980s and early 1990s. These parks use slides, fountains, rivers, and pools to appeal to guests. Water activities are enjoyed by people of all ages, so these parks have an enormous appeal. They may operate independently from any other park or may be a facility within a larger amusement park complex.

Other settings of amusement parks focus on activities other than rides. One example is the Sea World parks, which specialize in having an in-depth repre-sentation of ocean life. Customers are attracted to the educational aspect of the park, and they are given the opportunity to be up close to ocean creatures. Another interest area for amusement parks is the inclusion of wild game ar-eas. People are fascinated by exotic creatures, and some parks set aside an area where these animals roam freely. The park guests are moved through the wild game area on a tram or bus to observe the animals in a natural setting.

WORKING CONDITIONS

The very large amusement parks offer year-round employment which is an advantage for employees. Mid-size amusement parks such as King's Island in Cincinnati, Ohio and Opryland in Nashville, Tennessee offer extended seasons, operating on a full-time basis from late spring through early fall. These parks reopen in December for the Christmas season on a full-time basis because they have found that guests enjoy shopping and viewing the decorative splendor there. Many parks are open on weekends in late fall and early spring, but even those parks may be closed in the winter months. Closure for several months does present an employment disadvantage for amusement park workers. Most of these workers must find another job on a temporary basis or consider the park job as a second job.

Jobs in amusement parks offer considerable flexibility in working hours. Many parks have a seven-day work week and operating hours of 9:00 a.m. through twelve midnight. This allows employees to plan a work schedule that allows them to attend to other activities. Employees can coordinate school schedules or other employment situations with the hours of the amusement park. With the tremendous range of hours, personal preferences like those of the "late sleeper" or "early riser" can be accommodated.

The amusement parks generally have very precise codes that govern the dress and appearance of all employees. Grooming requirements usually include guidelines on hair length and arrangement, hands and fingernails, and facial hair. There are guidelines governing the wearing of jewelry and the exposing of body tattoos.

There is considerable repetition in some amusement park positions, which can make a job monotonous. Ride operators are frequently required to give the same long narratives during rides, and grounds department workers can find themselves repeatedly traversing the same areas to sweep up debris and empty trash containers.

Most employees who deal in any way with the public must constantly appear upbeat and exude an attitude of friendliness. This can be challenging when dealing with frustrated parents and cranky children. No matter how they feel, the employees must be able to be an "actor" or "actress" and give a performance that lets the customers know they are special. This must be sincerely done. If the employees are insincere in their attitudes toward customers, the guests will see a fake façade of friendliness and be disappointed in the park's hospitality.

LOOKING AT JOBS IN AMUSEMENT PARKS

Amusement parks have many departments in order to provide their services and products to customers. From entry-level positions through management levels, these departments are staffed with tens to hundreds of employees. Some employees work year-round, but many work only through the peak season. Examples of these departments are: food preparation and service, attractions operations and maintenance, transportation and parking, guest services, groundskeeping, entertainment, wardrobe, laundry, and lodging services. There may also be other departments, depending on the types of attractions and the amenities offered at the park. For every position in every department, the most important responsibility is to be friendly to the amusement park guests.

Working in Ride Operations

A department that employs large numbers of entry-level employees is attractions operations. Ride operators have many responsibilities. Amusement parks frequently use rides as the prime marketing tool to attract visitors. Ride operators need to support the advertising promotion of the ride by contributing to the mood of the ride. Major thrill rides such as roller coasters, where speed, hills, and turns offer elements of excitement and adventure, require the operators to build to this mood through their interactions and communications with guests.

It is also very important that the ride operators have full knowledge of the safety requirements for guests using a ride. Some rides are not safe for individuals who have heart conditions, motion sickness, or back problems. Pregnant women may not safely ride on some rides. Young children may also be hurt on certain rides. Therefore, the ride operator must carefully screen all riders to see that no one who would be at risk gets on the ride. This requires tact and diplomacy to help direct customers to make another choice for a ride. This is especially true for young children who want to be able to enjoy the most thrilling rides in the park.

Another responsibility is the correct operation of the ride. Guests must enter and exit the ride without risking possible injury. The ride operator must oversee this activity. Equipment checks must be made on a regular basis to determine that there are no problems. Severe weather changes may affect the safety of operating a ride. Ride operators are required to report any condition that might impact the safe operation of a ride and to close the ride if the supervisor instructs them to do so.

Ride narratives may be another task performed by the employees in ride operations. For rides that simulate an underwater dive or an earthquake, for example, the narration sets the scene for the guests, builds their level of anticipation, and makes them feel the total experience of the ride. For each group that boards these rides, the operators give the same basic "acting" performances.

Working in Ride Maintenance

Sharing responsibility for the operation of rides are the employees of the maintenance and repair department. Personnel in this department conduct regular inspections of seats, harnesses, belts, tracks, doors, and latches as well as the entrance and exit areas of attractions to make sure that everything is in good working order. Any possible deficiency for safe operating is put on a work order. The priority is to continue the operation of the ride safely, so all maintenance possible is done on a prevention basis—that is, before a minor difficulty becomes a genuine hazard. However, sometimes repairs must be made in emergency situations during peak business times. The ride maintenance department's employees must be able to respond quickly to make the appropriate repairs. If repairs cannot be made within a short time, then maintenance workers report to their supervisors so that decisions can be made to close a ride for part of a day or even a full day.

Working in Water/Pool Recreation Areas

Water activities play an important role in most theme parks. On hot summer days, the water attractions of a park are filled with crowds of people. Pools, streams, slides, and sprays are all fun activities for customers, whether these guests participate or watch. Other water activities that appeal to guests are boating, skiing, jet-skiing, sailing, canoeing, and paddle-boating. Employees' responsibilities in water/pool recreation departments are to provide for the safety of the guests, oversee the number of guests using a water space or floating device, train guests on the safe operation of equipment, and check equipment for operating safety. These employees must be able to perform water rescue and administer CPR.

Working in Park Maintenance

General maintenance of an entire park offers various positions in painting, air conditioning and refrigeration, carpentry, masonry, electrical and mechanical systems, pest control, plumbing, and audiovisual technology. The employees in these areas provide preventive checks on all types of equipment, fixtures, and furnishings in the park. Their primary responsibility is to keep the park looking clean and new by having everything in good working order. Another key function of maintenance work is to provide safety for guests. Any accident that occurs due to a broken or unrepaired piece of equipment or a fixture would be a major liability to the park. Whenever possible, maintenance tasks are completed when the parks are closed for the day.

Working in Retail or Food Outlets

Surrounding the rides are an assortment of gift and souvenir shops, food and beverage stands, restaurants, and carnival stands for game playing. These support areas are always located near premier rides, since they offer diversions to guests waiting to get on a ride and activities to occupy guests who are waiting for friends and relatives to complete a ride. Employees in these departments need good customer skills to promote interest in eating, shopping, browsing, relaxing, or game playing and to make customers content while they wait. Also, employees in these areas order stock, complete inventories, prevent shoplifting, keep accurate sales records, and control cash.

Working in Entertainment

Many amusement parks have a substantial number of entertainment attractions. These programs focus on quick-movement, high-energy shows that please everyone in a crowd. The entertainers must be musically and athletically talented, personable, and able to relate to the audience to get and keep the spectators' attention. Entertainment is not typically the focus of the amusement park; rather, it is an opportunity for park attendees to relax and rest from the thrills of the rides. By having a type of "quiet time" activity within the park, the park can increase the length of time visitors stay. This is a critical factor in the park's financial success, so the shows have an important supporting role. The entertainers sing and dance, tell jokes, and solicit involvement from the audience. Audience participation brings guests in, so interactive themes for the shows are very common.

Some of the amusement parks have characters who provide entertainment by mingling with the guests. At Disney World, children and adults flock to the characters. Cartoon characters like Donald Duck, movie characters like Snow White and the Seven Dwarfs, and many other characters regularly rotate through shifts of being walking entertainers. These characters meet and greet the customers, pose for photographs, and promote the friendliness of the park.

Working in character requires a special type of entertainer. As a member of the cast of characters, contact with the guests is constant. While they are entertaining, the characters must let all guests know that they are special and give them a few seconds of their time. They do this using only nonverbal communication, which makes these positions extremely demanding and requires very creative and patient employees. Another challenge which occurs for the costumed characters that are very well-known, like Mickey Mouse, is that of crowd control. The popularity of some characters is so great that excessive crowds quickly form. These characters must keep moving without appearing to slight any fan. Frequently, one or two security personnel accompany the most popular characters to ensure safety of the character and of the park guests.

A primary feature of Sea World's entertainment is to have the mammals perform for the guests. Killer whale shows and dolphin shows are very popular. The entertainment depends then on individuals who are talented and personable, but who are also trained in sea life. These employees are responsible for the training of the animals and for their care. Since the mammals are captive, they receive routine exams to ensure their health.

Water shows with skiing tricks and boat maneuvers also entertain the guests at amusement parks. Employees in these shows must be talented in the use of different types of skis and be able to perform acrobatic stunts such as jumps and twists and the formation of human pyramids or chains. The Dells at Wisconsin Dells, Wisconsin features a variety of water shows.

Working in the Wardrobe Department

All members of the entertainment department and all employees in ride operations and retail outlets have special costume wardrobes that must be maintained. Keeping the costumes cleaned, repaired, and inventoried requires a large department of employees. Laundry, pressing, and alterations are typical tasks performed in this department. These employees may also have the responsibility of designing and constructing new uniforms to meet the needs of new rides or retail stores opening within a park.

Working in the Transportation and Parking Services Department

Employees of this department have the important role of getting thousands of vehicles and all of the occupants of these vehicles into and out of the park. At the opening and close of the day, the many employees in the transportation department are very busy. They may be assigned to direct parking in the guest parking lots or may operate shuttles from the lots to the park. Their most important responsibility is traffic flow. Whether people are on wheels or on foot, t_____ This is especially true for all c_____ pation and eagerness may c_____ eir safety.

_____ attention from transporta-
_____ elchairs or motorized carts
_____ enjoy the park. Transpor-
_____ e guests in an appropriate
_____ ctions to the entrance, and
_____ ations are other tasks com-
_____ rtation department.

Working in the Security Department

_____ want to know that they are in
_____ rtment to provide for every
_____ the responsibilities of locat-
_____ g out for shoplifters or pick-
_____ idual who might have illegal
_____ around the food vendors, the
_____ ese are areas within the parks

Working in Support Services Departments

_____ support service personnel of
_____ nd accounting departments.
_____ ve a variety of tasks to com-
_____ spaces and communicating to
_____ servationists perform. Knowl-
_____ be attending the park that day,
_____ ns employees prepare to per-

_____ tionists offer opportunities to
_____ ns require speed and accuracy,
_____ tuation, and spelling. Other re-
_____ mmunications skills, excellent
_____ tention to detail. Furthermore,
_____ fidentiality of records and pre-
_____ tain to the proprietary nature of

the park or to personnel files.

Accounting department employees compile the costs for each area of the park's operations and compare them to the sales generated by the park. Their results are used by management to determine which rides and venues are operating efficiently and to determine ways to improve efficiency in less profitable attractions.

The staff in human resources has the important tasks of determining staff needs in operations and support services, recruiting potential employees, collecting and reviewing applications, conducting interviews, providing orientation to new hires, and documenting performance by keeping thorough and accurate records on all personnel. Recruiting potential employees is a challenge for most parks, but especially so for the parks with seasonal positions. Human resources employees use creative means to discover possible employees, such as conducting college recruiting around the country. Disney World has an extensive college recruiting program to help fill positions within the park. Recruiting high school students, stay-at-home moms, and retired people helps expand the pool of employees.

Other support departments within an amusement park are marketing, group sales, development, and construction. Each of these departments is critical to the overall success of the park. The key role for employees in marketing is to determine the groups that should be targeted for advertising campaigns so the number of visitors can be increased. Group sales personnel work with associations and businesses who may want to bring in a large group of people. Sales employees help plan the budgets and activities for the big groups, ensuring that these visiting groups enjoy as much of the park as possible.

Employees in the development department create ideas for new attractions. New concepts must be continually researched. This helps give the park a competitive edge as an attraction. As population demographics change, the development department staff works with the marketing department staff. They recognize that the appeal of certain types of attractions may increase or decrease as the age, ethnic background, and socio-economic status of the guests change. These employees work to keep a balance of activity choices within the park to appeal to all guests.

Amusement parks use construction departments to build or remodel the park as designed by the development department. Cost efficiency and construction schedules are important responsibilities for this area. Since many parks are in continuous operation or operate nearly year-round, construction areas must be carefully secured from visitors to prevent accidents. Also, planning must be done to move guests around the construction with as little inconvenience as possible. Guests must be able to get to all areas of the park so that no part of the park loses its traffic flow and customers.

PREPARATION FOR BECOMING AN AMUSEMENT PARK EMPLOYEE

It is never too early to prepare for a career at an amusement park because many of the entry-level positions are filled by students attending high school. Six Flags Over Mid-America, an amusement park in Eureka, Missouri, recruits many high school-age employees. To work in their department of food service, employees need be only fifteen years old. Sixteen is the minimum age for jobs in the admissions, retail, ride operations, entertainment, and wardrobe departments. To work in the areas of cash control and guest relations, employees must be eighteen years old, while security positions require employees to be twenty-one.

These young employees must demonstrate through their high school activities, grades, and attendance that they are outgoing, motivated, and responsible. The amusement parks value participation in school or community groups or on athletic teams since this can indicate an ability to work with others as a team member. Teamwork is very important in the operation of amusement parks.

High school courses in communications, foreign languages, and business management are good selections for young people wishing to prepare for amusement park employment since these courses will help them learn about people and about business operations. It is also important to have a solid attendance record since amusement park employers look at these records as measures of maturity and responsibility.

To work in supervisory positions in the various departments or in semi-skilled positions, employees need to have a high school diploma and some type of postsecondary training. The range of positions within amusement parks is so extensive that generalizing about the most desirable type of postsecondary education is impossible. Examples of appropriate postsecondary education for positions in some different departments are as follows. For positions in the maintenance department, a technical school certificate or a degree from an associate or baccalaureate institution is needed to work in electrical, mechanical, or air conditioning and refrigeration jobs. For positions in departments such as development and design, computer software and hardware expertise and a college degree are required to use computer-aided design (CAD). For customer service positions in retail or in hospitality departments, a certificate, an associate's degree, or a bachelor's degree in food service and lodging management, culinary arts, or business management may be needed.

Whatever discipline is chosen for a major, individuals considering employment in amusement parks should plan to take multicultural management and communication courses. Previous work experiences in any type of hospitality industry (food service, lodging, clubs, or concessions) is valuable because these positions require development of customer contact skills. These skills enable new employees to work more effectively with park guests and to be ready for supervisory positions.

TRAINING NEEDED

All entry level employees at amusement parks receive on-the-job training. Typically, videos and workshops are used to teach new employees the responsibilities of their jobs and to train them in customer interaction. Since customer service is the most important aspect of every employee's job, the parks plan training to emphasize and reemphasize the importance of working with guests in a warm, friendly way. Again, the focal point of training is that every employee learn to interact positively with each guest.

SPECIAL EMPLOYEE ATTRIBUTES

Amusement park employees will be happy in their work if they genuinely like people. Since park employees must interact with guests of different backgrounds, they need to be good communicators, patient, and positive. With the international appeal that all parks—large and small—have, all employees need to be people-oriented. Satisfaction of the guests' needs is critical to the success of the park.

ADVANCING UP THE CAREER LADDER

One advantage of working for a large amusement park is the opportunity to move laterally or vertically in job positions. With thousands of employees, many moves can be made to other departments or to other parts of the park. This provides variety in the employment opportunities with the park, helps to cross-train employees, and serves as a means of preparing outstanding employees to move into supervisory or management positions.

SALARY AND FRINGE BENEFITS

Entry-level positions in amusement parks may begin at minimum wage. However, hourly wages for entry-level jobs in areas of the country where the employment rate is high may be substantially above minimum wage. Higher entry pay is necessary in these locations for employers to attract and retain employees. In 1995, Disney World used a rate of $5.95 per hour for entry-level positions in the departments of food and beverage, laundry, wardrobe, merchandise/retail, ticketing, and transportation.

Some positions within parks require some training, education, skills, previous work experience, and/or credentials. For 1995, hourly pay at Disney World was $6.30 for a lifeguard. A culinary assistant started at $6.20 per hour. The starting pay for reservationists was $6.95 per hour. Entry positions in security paid a minimum of $6.87 per hour. These wages would be typical of most amusement parks.

Skilled positions are available in every department at amusement parks. Wages in these positions may vary from $7.00 to $9.00 per hour in clerical/secretarial areas. To receive this pay, previous secretarial work experience, typing at fifty words per minute, and familiarity with word processing software, Lotus 1-2-3™, and Excel™ would be required. Sous chefs work under the executive chef in directing food preparation. Their pay would range from $7.00 to $9.00 per hour depending on kitchen experience and training. Audiovisual technicians and computer staff employees would have pay scales similar to clerical employees.

Benefits typically include medical, dental, and life insurance for full-time employees. Depending on the size of the park, part-time employees may have some of these benefits, too. Overtime hours may be offered at time-and-a-half rates, which can be advantageous. Other benefits given to amusement park employees include free admission to the park. Many of the parks provide guest passes when a minimum number of hours have been worked with a corresponding level of competency. In addition, special get-togethers are planned for park employees. These might include picnics and other social outings. Employees get free parking, and uniforms and their maintenance are provided. Amusement parks also offer their employees discounts at the retail stores.

REWARDS OF WORKING IN AN AMUSEMENT PARK

Amusement park employment is in a fun-filled, high-energy environment. One reward of working in a park is the chance to be around customers who are enjoying themselves and appreciate the part that each employee plays in providing an opportunity for them to have fun. Amusement park employees get to see customers of all ages laugh, scream, and squeal with delight. Interaction with guests is very satisfying.

Working for an amusement park means working as a member of a team or family. All of the employees are treated with respect by their managers because the managers know that it is the employees who have the responsibility of meeting the customers' expectations. Working together to provide a quality experience for the guests is satisfying for amusement park employees. Also, cross-training is rewarding, as employees see the development of skills and their career.

A DAY IN THE LIFE OF AN AMUSEMENT PARK EMPLOYEE

Ken Gleason works as a part-time cast member at Disney World. There, employees are called cast members because they are "on stage" presenting a show for the guests. Ken is a high school teacher in the Orlando area who finds teaching very stimulating but likes to be involved with people in other ways. Working at Disney World keeps him motivated to stay in good physical condition. Disney World employs Ken as a lifeguard at the Yacht and Beach Club Hotel. Since Ken is certified in lifesaving, he easily met the requirements for this position. However, Disney World requires its lifeguards to be certified specially through Disney, so Ken has first aid certification, CPR certification, and rescue skills certification.

Ken's day at Disney World begins at 7:00 a.m. To report to duty, Ken parks at the employee parking area and then walks to the hotel. Ken does not need to report to wardrobe since costumes for lifeguards are considered personal belongings, and the cast members must be responsible for their swimsuits and t-shirts. After clocking in, Ken reports to the lead guard stand for cleaning assignment. He and the other lifeguards spend two hours a day preparing the pool and the deck area for the guests. Pre-opening requirements are to clean and vacuum the pool, sweep and hose the deck, "pick and pull" (pick up trash and pull the chaise lounge chairs into rows), and wipe all tables and chairs.

At opening time, the guards meet at the lead guard stand for their daily assignments. On a typical day, each guard works three shifts of thirty minutes each at different stands and is then off stand for thirty minutes. This rotation keeps the guards fresh and alert. Ken's training at Disney World and in life-guarding keeps his eyes keenly focused on the activity in the water. The guards use whistles for communication, so guards must be very attentive to sounds while on duty. While in their off period, the guards complete in-service training consisting of physical conditioning, CPR practice, and water rescue procedures. At the end of their workday, Ken and the other guards are "bumped" by the guards who work the closing shift. Ken clocks out and exits to the cast members' parking lot.

A TYPICAL DAY FOR PARK ADMISSIONS EMPLOYEES

To work in the Magic Kingdom admissions area, cast members usually report for a morning shift at 8:00. All cast members use the cast parking area and take the VIP Cast Member Shuttle through an underground tunnel to the wardrobe department. Cast members are assigned a specific wardrobe window in order to get their apparel. Personal belongings are stored in lockers, and the cast members change in the dressing rooms.

Using the tunnel, the cast members go to their appropriate area and clock in. Each employee has a plastic identification card to be scanned. After reporting for duty to the admissions office, the cast members receive their assignments, which vary from taking tickets to working at the monorail gates. Cast members never work at any one station for an excessive length of time; they are regularly bumped to new areas. The philosophy is to move people to keep them "fresh. The shift responsibilities revolve around traffic flow and answering questions. Guests need to know operating hours, directions, restroom locations, times for special shows, whether dinner reservations are mandatory, and myriad other things. At the end of the day's shift, the cast members return to the wardrobe department via the tunnel, change clothes, and clock out.

LOOKING AT THE FUTURE

Amusement parks have a tremendous opportunity to grow and expand their sales for a variety of reasons—a growth that will increase the need for employees. With the wide variety of their attractions, amusement parks appeal to people of all ages and backgrounds. Featuring quality venues that are exciting and entertaining and providing quality service that is warm and friendly are important goals of parks. If park management can continue to offer these attractions to their guests, then patronage will continue to grow at amusement parks.

Regardless of the size or the number of rides or the type of entertainment, amusement parks represent a value to customers. Families can enter with one charge paid at the gate for almost any type of activity they may want to participate in, and they may stay for as long as they like in the day. This promises value to the guest, and it has been successful at helping parks develop and grow.

Parks are perceived as a value in other ways. Many people no longer feel safe when at a public beach or in a public shopping area. Visitors do not have this concern when visiting an amusement park. This significantly contributes to the volume of business for amusement parks. While amusement parks cannot guarantee that there will never be a guest safety incident, every effort is made to provide for the safety and security of the guest. Guest safety is accomplished through control of traffic flow, operation of rides, and crowd control through queuing or directing people to attractions through roped lanes. Safety in the park is part of every employee's responsibilities. Security personnel keep a close watch over all guests by searching for individuals whose actions and movements might be suspect. This keeps purse snatching and pickpocketing activities to a bare minimum. Security checks all employees for identification badges, so the park is certain that only its screened employees are in sensitive areas.

OTHER JOBS RELATED TO AMUSEMENT PARKS

There is a need for employees all around the country to work in the amusement ride industry at county and state fairs. Working in this industry may mean being a part of a traveling caravan of rides and attractions. These companies contract with fair boards to arrive on a given date. The rides and attractions are set up and operated for the length of the contract for a site. When the fair closes, the traveling amusement park packs everything and departs for the next community.

This type of business presents many unique situations for employees. First, of course, is the near-constant travel. A ride company covers hundreds of miles each week as it fulfills its obligations in one town and moves on to the next. Another unique aspect is the skill, speed, and safety requirements involved in erecting and dismantling the rides at each site. Employees work long days and nights to be ready to open a fair or to move onto the next community quickly. A third characteristic of these traveling ride operations is that the rides are located at county fairs where the main attractions are animal exhibits and homemaking projects. The rides are an added attraction to support this primary purpose, so the fair board will negotiate for the best price and the greatest number of operating hours.

FOR MORE INFORMATION

All amusement parks have printed information that explains their various departments and requirements for employment. The parks are happy to send materials to prospective employees. The International Association of Amusement Parks and Attractions, located in Alexandria, Virginia, can be a source of information about parks. College-age students may find out more about working in parks through their university career offices since many of the large amusement parks recruit all over the country to meet their needs for employees.

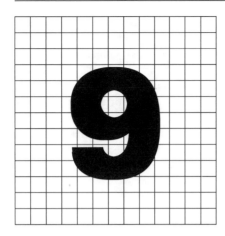

WORKING IN NATIONAL, STATE, AND LOCAL PARKS AND ORGANIZED CAMPS

Parks have attractions of rivers, lakes, mountains, deserts, and geological formations to entertain and enhance the traveler. Parks also feature historical attractions, bringing American history to life. Millions of tourists visit parks each year hoping to see animals, scenery, or historic sites that they may have only read about previously. Many also return to parks year after year to enjoy the recreational aspects of these sites. Employees at the parks expand visitors' knowledge by explaining the ecology of the parks as well as any historical events that occurred there. They also maintain the quality of the park environment and ensure the safety of the visitors. Outdoor recreational opportunities are not limited to parks. Many people, especially children, enjoy organized camps.

SETTINGS FOR PARKS

The first parks were set aside as hunting areas for royalty and the nobility in ancient Egypt and Rome. Today's parks are for everyone. Millions of people visit these parks every year. Altogether there are more than 100,000 national, state, and local parks. And each of these parks is a workplace for from a few employees more than 1,000.

National Park Settings Yosemite was America's first national park. It was established in the majestic Sierra Nevada Mountains of California in 1864. The establishment of America's national parks is based on the need to set aside natural, cultural, and historic areas for the enrichment of the citizens. The parks conserve natural scenery, protect wildlife and historic sites and objects, and provide for the public enjoyment of these areas in such a manner as to leave them unimpaired. The settings for national parks can be divided into these three categories: natural, recreational, and historical and cultural.

Natural areas include national parks that cover a large land area and preserve one or more distinctive natural land forms, wildlife habitats, or plant forms. Geysers, volcanos, caves, glaciers, waterfalls, and mountain peaks are some types of nature's creations that are protected in parks. For example, Carlsbad Caverns in New Mexico includes massive underground chambers in a park of 48,755 acres. National monuments are not as diverse or as large as parks; they each preserve one nationally significant natural or historic resource.

Other settings for national parks are locations where recreational activities flourish due to water and terrain. Recreational areas include recreation reservoirs, national seashores and lakeshores, national rivers, national parkways, and national trails. Within this category is Lake Mead in Arizona and Nevada, which covers 62,000 acres and provides a variety of outdoor and water activities for visitors; the natural lakeshore at the Indiana Dunes on Lake Michigan is also in this category. And so are the Blue Ridge Parkway and the 2,000-mile-long Appalachian Trail that goes from Maine to Georgia. A unique water trail in the Everglades National Park in Florida is also classified as a recreational area. Using a kayak or canoe, visitors can enjoy the setting of the Everglades while traveling ninety-nine miles through mangrove trees and bays and observing alligators, wild birds, porpoises, and manatees.

In the historical and cultural category, parts of the history of the United States are preserved in the parks. Such tangible things as the buildings, houses, and artifacts of a group of people as well as intangible things reflecting customs, religion, and family structure are on display. The settings include historical parks like Appomattox Courthouse in Virginia, historical sites like Lincoln's birthplace in Kentucky, and historical memorials like Mount Rushmore in South Dakota.

National Forest Settings

About twenty-five percent of the land areas of the United States are classified as forest lands and are under the protection of the U.S. Forest Service. This includes 155 national forests, 19 national grasslands, and 18 "land utilization projects." The areas are in forty-four of the fifty states and include a total of 190.8 million acres of land. The major uses of these forests are as a water supply for people and crops; forage for grazing sheep and cattle; a home for hundreds of species of animals, fowl, fish, and insects; water recreation for the public; and timber harvesting for management of the country's resources. One national forest is Mount Hood in Oregon, with 1,058,400 acres of land featuring glaciers, lakes, springs, and alpine meadows. Here, visitors can fish, camp, take saddle-and-pack trips, and enjoy the scenery.

State Park Settings

States have adopted an approach similar to the federal government in developing parks to provide outdoor activities for their citizens. States recognize that they must protect, enhance, preserve, and wisely use natural, cultural, and recreational resources for the benefit of their citizens. Each state determines what is historically and culturally significant. Environmental interests determine land and water locations to be held by the state. So settings for state parks and forests could be acreage in forests held as nature preserves as well as settings designed to educate visitors about the geography, geology, and wildlife native to the state. Other outdoor settings are streams, rivers, and lakes that are state-owned and state-managed to provide public access. Water sites are very important to state park programs because water activities such as boating, skiing, fishing, and swimming are leisure activities valued by the public.

Local Park Settings

County parks and city parks are most often found in large metropolitan areas. "Green space" is a term used for small tracts of land held in the public domain and used by citizens to rest, relax, and play. Municipalities may use both larger parks and green spaces to meet people's needs for a place to enjoy outdoors recreation. Rarely is any special historical, geological, or environmental concern the basis of the selection for the site or the primary purpose of the site. Swimming pools, shelters, picnic areas, walking paths, bicycle trails, and sports facilities are typically included in city parks. And during the summer, programs are set up to provide activities for school-age children.

Parks in smaller communities have picnic areas and playground areas as their typical amenities, and some may have swimming pools and community centers. Although these communities generally do not have extensive daily programs, they may organize tennis tournaments and musical programs in their parks. These parks are places for community residents to gather for socializing and relaxation.

WORKING CONDITIONS

The natural settings that encompass most parks are beautiful and peaceful, which is an advantage of working in a park. The serenity of the outdoors contributes to a relaxed job environment. Furthermore, the diverse range of activities, facilities, and natural attractions contributes variety to the job and stimulates creativity and problem solving. Also, a park's management team is allowed latitude in management, decision making, and implementation of plans for the parks as long as budgetary guidelines are met and the plans fit within the mission of the park's operation. Since public funds exclusively support operations at many of the parks, the various legislators who determine the budgets for parks may reduce funding, compelling park employees to do more with less. When this situation occurs, working in the park system at any level can be frustrating.

Maintaining a balance between visitor needs and wildlife needs is a challenge to employees at many parks. There is an increased interest in finding places to relax and vacation. While people may wish to develop wetlands, river beds, and forests for recreational purposes, the development may endanger the environment. If parks expand to accommodate more visitors and add facilities like lodging, restaurants, and retail businesses, the employees are criticized by environmental groups. If they don't, those wanting more public access and facilities will complain. Furthermore, many parks are now over-crowded at times, which forces employees to turn people away from these popular sites. This is not well received by the public.

Closely related is the problem park employees have in managing the balance between wildlife and plant life. When the food chain is not in a state of natural balance, the predators of some species may be limited in number, contributing to an unhealthy number of another species. Deer, for example, over-run many parks and destroy the vegetation. Without the vegetation, other species may be endangered. In the Grand Canyon National Park, the wild burros have damaged the natural vegetation, in turn creating the problem of what to do with the burros. The decisions made by park management in these cases are always controversial.

LOOKING AT DIFFERENT JOBS IN PARKS

Many park jobs are available that allow employees to help visitors enjoy the park and nature. Positions vary from working as the superintendent who over-sees the operation of a national park to entry level positions as part-time rangers. There are also many jobs in park services, from working in concessions to lifesaving. Every park employee seeks to provide through his or her position a memorable experience for the visitor. The size or type of the park does not affect this goal.

Working as a Park Superintendent

State parks and national parks, depending on the size and the purpose of the park, may have only one manager or superintendent. More commonly, however, at national parks there is a superintendent with several assistant superintendents reporting to him or her. The superintendent's responsibilities are to preserve natural and historical features and make these available to the public for their enjoyment. The assistant superintendents are responsible for the departments of natural and historical features, interpretation, law enforcement and protection, park facility maintenance, and administration.

At a state park, a manager is the top authority. Several department heads report to this person. The number of departments depends on the size of the park. Some examples of departments that the manager would oversee are the nature center with interpretation and education, buildings and grounds maintenance, and office operations.

At a city park, the superintendent would monitor the recreation programs and recreation facilities. This could involve multiple sites. For example, the superintendent of the South Bend, Indiana Parks and Recreation Department has six locations to oversee, with different programming at each site. To reduce operating costs, some municipalities try to extend their operating capabilities by using volunteers to help the staff answer telephones and monitor leisure and education activities. While using volunteers does lower operating costs, these people must all be trained and observed, which adds to the park superintendent's responsibilities.

Working as a
Park Ranger

The exact tasks that rangers have depend on the type of job held and the park where the ranger is employed. Many rangers work in the area of law enforcement, which involves seeing that park visitors follow all laws and regulations. Duties in this area could include patrolling the waters of a lake or a ski slope. Rangers also serve as naturalists or interpreters; in this capacity they explain the history or physical features of a park to visitors, create programs, and answer questions in information centers. Administrative work is another duty. This can involve issuing visitor permits, keeping records, handling public relations, following budgets, and supervising employees. Two other areas are maintenance work (such as building trails, roads, and facilities) and conservation work designed to protect a park's ecosystem.

In many states, rangers have rankings or levels. The position of ranger level I requires rangers to carry out a wide variety of safety and security assignments. This means knowing all park rules and the state conservation laws. At this level, rangers interact with the visitors to maintain safe and acceptable conditions in the park. These criteria are met when the rangers verify that the land, buildings, and water are used for the purposes intended. Rangers check regularly to make certain that the visitors travel where permitted on paths, trails, and roads instead of entering areas preserved for animals.

Rangers must monitor use of the park's resources so that the visitors do not endanger the park's ecological balance. Counts of visitors may need to be made to avoid overcrowding. In parks with camping or lodging spaces, the number of guests must not exceed space available. And rangers must check picnic areas, shelters, hiking trails, climbing areas, and water activity areas to ensure that they are not so busy that safety problems occur. Other activities include monitoring fishing and hunting limits, boating safety, and forest fire safety.

As the rangers' level increases so does the depth of responsibilities. For example, a level III ranger functions as either the supervisor of a department in a large park or as the park manager on duty in the absence of the regular park manager at a smaller park. These responsibilities would be typical of a ranger at a national park, too.

Working as a
Recreation Forester

Recreation foresters promote and practice good forest stewardship. Their primary responsibility is to preserve the forests for the benefit of current visitors and future visitors while at the same time keeping the integrity of the forest as a home for wildlife. To achieve this goal, a recreation forester must communicate with the public, plan and monitor recreational facilities for the public to use, collaborate with biologists to protect wildlife, and work with businesses and the public in managing the forest's timber.

Working as a
Park Naturalist

Naturalists conduct educational sessions for visitors on such topics as how to spot indigenous animals and plant life. They may guide tours through the park to highlight the park's natural resources. These tours are often conducted in the early morning or in the evening so animals can be seen in their natural habitats. Naturalists teach in truly unique classrooms—from former coal mines to sand dunes to wetlands. A major part of their job is helping the public understand the fragile balance between humans and nature and between different species.

Working as a Recreation Leader

In city parks the focus is on the use of the land and space for recreation. Recreation leaders are the enthusiastic and creative individuals who plan, direct, organize, and evaluate recreational programs for all of the people in a city. They must know the interests of the population and the limitations of the park in terms of space, equipment, and budget. Working with this information, recreation leaders plan individual, group, and team activities, which can include sports, games, hobbies, art, crafts, and special events.

PREPARATION FOR BECOMING A PARK EMPLOYEE

In local, state, and national parks, entry-level jobs are unskilled positions in such departments as concessions, housekeeping (when the park includes lodging facilities), grounds maintenance, and level I ranger. These positions are likely to be seasonal, depending on the weather and park usage. Previous job experience is not necessary but is helpful. A high school diploma is not required, since many of these entry-level positions are filled by high school-age people. Because parks must have reliable employees in these positions, an excellent attendance record in high school is important. The entry-level worker will find courses in communications and business helpful in understanding how to work with people and how organizations operate. As an extracurricular activity, scouting can help high school students because the scouting program teaches many of the same skills that park employees need.

Most positions in parks require some skills or training. In local parks, semi-skilled positions would include lifeguard, recreation leader, athletic supervisor for sports programs and/or referee, clerical support, technician, and level II ranger. Since these positions are so different, it is not possible to generalize on the type of training needed for each one. Here are the educational requirements for certain unskilled positions. Level II ranger: the completion of two years of college with twelve or more credit hours in outdoor recreation or park management combined with six months or more of park or related work experiences. Erosion control technician: college training not required, but knowledge of farming practices and soils and computer data skills are essential. Biology aide: laboratory science classes that teach skills in obtaining samples, completing testing, and writing reports. In place of formal educational experience, preparation for all of the semi-skilled positions can be demonstrated by a work history clearly showing reliability and an ability to learn.

Highly skilled positions are held by those who work in park management. The basic educational requirement for managerial positions is a college degree. A bachelor of science degree in natural resources or resource management provides needed information on resources (land, water, animals, and plants) and how to manage these resources to benefit the park visitors and environment. Another choice would be a degree in parks and recreation, a course of study that teaches about recreation activities and managing the equipment and facilities used in those activities. People who want to work in cultural and historical parks will gain expertise from degrees in anthropology or history. Besides meeting educational requirements, candidates for highly skilled positions may need to take civil service tests to secure employment.

For individuals wanting to work with the United States Forest Service, degrees in forestry, wildlife sciences, or biology are good choices. A forestry major is a combination of mathematics, botanical and physical sciences, human relations, sociology, engineering, salesmanship, and business management. These are all areas where expertise is needed in working in forestry. Biology and wildlife sciences focus more on the environment, so these degrees would be good preparation for individuals who want to monitor animal habitats in forests or preserves. Business, engineering, communications, and human relations would be excellent choices for a minor in a degree program.

A typical urban-area park manager would benefit from a degree in parks management, recreation and leisure studies, or physical education. Counseling, business management, public relations, and communications are preferred as minors in a degree program. Secondary or elementary education degrees are also excellent backgrounds for this position.

SPECIAL ATTRIBUTES OF PARK EMPLOYEES

Park employees spend a large part of their days working with people. Many of these contacts are with visitors who do not know the park and its resources, so the same questions may be asked and answered repeatedly. Communication skills are important. Park employees must be quick thinkers. The park and its resources must be protected at all times and the visitors must be safe, so employees must be able to respond without hesitation when making a decision. Patience is necessary, too. Visitors have come from many different parts of the country or world to see the resources of the park. They are curious and eager to see all of the park. Park employees need to be sensitive to their interests to give them an enjoyable visit.

SALARY AND FRINGE BENEFITS

Unskilled personnel employed in parks may earn minimum wage. Higher wages will be paid if the supply of these workers is limited. Due to the seasonal nature of many entry-level positions, fringe benefit packages of health, dental, and life insurance may not be offered.

Salaries for rangers can start at $10,000 for level I. Level III rangers average $40,000. The size of the park and whether the jurisdiction is state or national make a difference in ranger salaries. Their fringe benefits include health, dental, and medical insurance; paid vacation days; and paid sick days. Retirement plans are provided. As employees of a federal or state government or local municipality, the salary and benefits package is controlled by the governing body. As political leaders leave office and new officials assume responsibilities, budgets for wages and salaries may be reduced, stay the same, or be increased.

City parks superintendents earn a salary based on the size of the park or park system. A city park director could earn $25,000 or more, depending on the extent of the activities and the number of park sites to be supervised. Entry-level employees at city parks receive the minimum wage or slightly higher hourly wages depending on local employment trends. Qualification for fringe benefits depends on full-time employment. The benefits package for entry-level employees is determined by the city or county government, but typically health insurance, life insurance, paid vacation days, and retirement plans are included.

THE REWARDS OF BEING A PARK EMPLOYEE

Working to preserve a part of the state or country is an intrinsic part of a ranger's job. It is also the most fulfilling part of the job. For centuries the earth has provided resources for the people to use and enjoy, and rangers protect these resources and help people enjoy them. Rangers also oversee the cultural and historical preservation of our country's development, keeping the link from the past to the present strong. Knowing that they are the key to keeping living records of history is very rewarding for rangers. Educating the visitors about the environment in parks is rewarding, too. Many other park employees receive satisfaction from their contribution to maintaining and improving the environment in parks.

THE PERSONAL STORY OF A PARK MANAGER

Larry Brown is the park manager for Fort Benjamin State Park—Indiana's most recently opened state park. Formerly a U.S. army base, the facilities will now be used for different purposes. The former officers' quarters will be a bed-and-breakfast, while the officers' dining hall has become the park inn. New roads and trails are planned to give visitors hiking and biking recreation activities. A nature center will be built to educate visitors on wildlife and plant life species.

Larry supervises employees in three departments: the nature center, buildings and grounds maintenance, and office operations. Fourteen full-time employees and eighteen seasonal employees are on the park staff.

As the administrator, Larry must be certain that the park provides a friendly, educational experience for guests. Activities in the park must be planned and facilities maintained so that visitors will be able to enjoy themselves. Since this is a new park converted from another use, a great deal of staff time is spent overseeing the remodeling and construction. As parts of the park are completed and visitor traffic is increased, Larry and his staff of rangers will spend more time interacting with the visitors.

THE PERSONAL STORY OF A PARK RANGER

Before applying for a position as a ranger, Shelton Johnson worked for two summers for a concessionaire at Yellowstone National Park. Through this position, he learned about the day-to-day operations of the park. Because the West Entrance supervisor was impressed with Shelton's work experience and educational background (he was working toward his master's degree), Shelton was accepted as a seasonal ranger. It can be very difficult to get full-time status as a ranger. Some employees have taken as long as ten seasons to pass this hurdle; however, Shelton succeeded in his fourth season.

In his first job as a seasonal park ranger at Yellowstone, Shelton was a gate ranger at the busy West Entrance Ranger Station. This job involved taking money, selling passes, issuing permits, and answering all kinds of questions (even though seventy cars and their occupants might be waiting behind the questioner). In his second year at the gate, Shelton also worked as a firefighter on the North Fork and Fan Fires that burned thousands of acres in Yellowstone. The next season he worked in the superintendent's office in public affairs, where one of his jobs was to take the media on naturalist tours as a follow-up to the fire. When Shelton obtained permanent status, his job shifted to the chief ranger's office, where his duties were primarily clerical. However, in the winter he had the challenge and excitement of delivering the mail on a snowmobile on a 150-mile route on which he experienced nature at its best and worst.

After several other assignments, Shelton became a ranger naturalist at Yosemite National Park. His day begins at 11:30 a.m. when he goes to work at the visitor center in the park. At first, his time is spent doing program development work and handling mail and correspondence. Then he works at the visitor center for several hours, answering questions from the location of the closest restroom to the name of a flower or bird a visitor saw on a walk. He also may have to fix audiovisual equipment, help people find a place to stay, and in general orient people to their new surroundings. Next, Shelton prepares for his nature walk and then leads a ninety-minute walk. Then he returns to the visitor center for another work session. His day ends after he leads another ninety-minute nature walk.

LOOKING AT JOB OPPORTUNITIES

The country's population is growing, creating a greater need than ever before for outdoor spaces for fun, relaxation, and environmental education. At the same time, various species of mammals, reptiles, insects, and birds have experienced changes in their natural habitat that threaten either nature's balance or extinction of a species. Based on these two factors, the need to expand parks is great. This should result in a need for more park employees.

Funding for parks, however, has been somewhat limited in recent years due to economics. Budget cutbacks have been experienced by parks at all levels—federal, state, and local. Parks have not been closed, but the number of employees who serve the guests has been reduced. The future appears to be a situation of continuing the current status. Public officials recognize the needs of the people for recreation, the country's environmental needs, and the need to preserve the history and culture of the country.

Severe cuts in funding are not likely to be made. Moderate cuts in funding could occur, depending on the philosophy of elected officials and the budgeting of monies for the operation of federal, state, and local parks. Moderate cuts would mean fewer operating days, shorter hours, a reduced number of programs, and fewer employees, especially those in full-time positions.

It is important to understand that seasonal peaks and valleys of employment occur for park employees no matter how much funding is available for parks. Parks will employ a small staff of full-time, year-round employees. Rangers and a small support staff of clerical and maintenance employees make up this group. When the peak season approaches for a park, many part-time and some full-time seasonal employees must be hired to help handle the increased volume of business. Furthermore, competition is extremely intense at all times for certain positions. For every applicant who succeeds in getting a job with the National Park Service as a ranger, 100 qualified applicants fail to get a job. Competition is also very rigorous for part-time seasonal jobs, as these jobs can lead to obtaining full-time positions.

FOR MORE INFORMATION

The following organizations have career information about becoming a ranger:

> National Recreation and Park Association
> 2775 South Quincy Street, Suite 300
> Arlington, VA 22206

> U.S. Department of the Interior
> National Park Service
> 1849 C Street, NW
> Washington, DC 20240

The Society of American Foresters has a career packet with basic information on careers as foresters and forest technicians. The packet also has a job seekers' guide and a list of schools with Society-recognized programs for these careers. The schools will provide more career information. The Society's career packet is available from:

> Society of American Foresters
> 5400 Grosvenor Lane
> Bethesda, MD 20814-2198

LOOKING AT ORGANIZED CAMPING

Traditionally, the term "camping" has been associated with children attending a camp for a week or more. Today, camps serve other purposes to meet the needs of a wide variety of populations. These special camps may use the facilities of traditional youth camps, including lodges, dining halls, recreation halls, and outdoor activity areas. However, the campers are there with purposes such as church/fellowship, leadership, education, personal enrichment, crafts, and sport activities. One type of residential camp that has become very popular in recent years is the sports camp for both adults and children. Frequently, this type of camp is organized by a well-known sports star to develop athletic skills in aspiring athletes. One example is the Reggie Miller Basketball Camp. Miller, a player for the Indianapolis Pacers, is a leading scorer in the National Basketball Association. At his basketball camp, participants drill and scrimmage for one week to learn basketball skills. Being able to meet a superstar and learn skills has made sports camps successful. During the summer, major universities sponsor sports camps, staffing their camps with school athletes and coaches. This serves to promote the image of the university, and the young athletes receive excellent coaching. Participants stay in school dormitories. Adults frequently attend golf and tennis camps that last from a weekend to one or more weeks. Some of these camps are held at well-known resorts. And both adults and children may attend wilderness camps that teach survival skills.

Trip camps involve using tents for shelter or carefully spaced campsites while a group of campers journey to a destination. The journey may be made by walking, biking, canoeing, sailing, horseback riding, skiing, or snowmobiling. The purposes of trip camping can be for team building, personal development, outdoor education, and/or viewing and exploring the outdoors.

Careers in Organized Camping

At many camps, the only full-time employee is the camp director. This individual oversees the entire operation of a camp and is often responsible for organizing and publicizing the next year's program. The director hires the staff, which includes the two key positions of director of programs and the head of the housing and food—individuals essential to the success of the camp.

All of the employees at a camp must know health and safety procedures; site, facility and equipment maintenance procedures; and customer relations skills. Salaries range from $10,000 to $45,000, depending on the level of the position and the size of the camp. Room and board are typically included. Due to the small size of most camp staffs, medical insurance is usually not offered.

Individuals who are interested in camp management should take college degree programs in recreation management and camp leadership. Minors in counseling, business, physical education, human relations, and hospitality management are excellent complements to this degree. Many entry-level positions are available in camps as counselors. High school students may qualify for these positions based on their skills and leadership experiences.

Leads on job opportunities can be obtained from churches, boys' and girls' clubs, 4-H extension offices, universities, Girl Scouts, Boy Scouts, and the YMCA. *The Guide to Accredited Camps* has information on careers in camp leadership. It can be obtained by contacting:

American Camping Association Bookstore
5000 State Road 67 North
Martinsville, IN 46151-7902
Phone: 1-800-428-CAMP

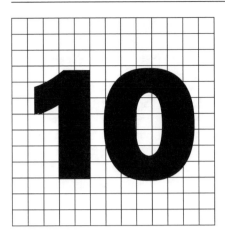

WORKING AT
TOURIST ATTRACTIONS

When people are on vacation, in addition to visiting amusement parks and national parks, they also visit tourist attractions. Some of these attractions (such as the Hearst Castle in California) may command a day or more of the tourists' time. Others, like mansions, zoos, caves, and aquariums, may be easily seen in just a few hours or even less time. Within the United States, there are thousands of tourist attractions—from well-known ones like the Empire State Building to roadside attractions featuring alligators and other reptiles. All of these places, large and small, require employees to guide tours, sell food and souvenirs, maintain the attraction, market it, and manage the operation.

SETTINGS OF TOURIST ATTRACTIONS

Almost anything can become a tourist attraction if people show enough interest in learning more about it. The diversity of tourist attractions is immense. There is the Corn Palace in Mitchell, South Dakota; Mark Twain's home in Hannibal, Missouri; the Winchester Mystery House in San Jose, California; quaint communities like Zionsville, Indiana; old mining towns like Virginia City, Nevada; Boys Town in Omaha, Nebraska; pioneer villages, and museums displaying cars, trains, planes, James Dean memorabilia, doll collections, jewels, radiator caps, and just about everything imaginable. What follows is a closer look at several popular settings for tourist attractions.

Homes and Villages

Historic homes showcase the background and lifestyle of some of the most famous citizens of our country. These citizens include politicians, inventors, writers, political leaders, scientists, architects, actors, singers, sports heroes, wealthy industrialists, and other celebrities. The purpose for having these homes open as tourist attractions is to share these famous people, their families, their lifestyles, and their contributions to the American culture with the public. Graceland Mansion in Memphis, Tennessee is an example of a celebrity's home that attracts millions of visitors each year. Elvis Presley's fame as a musician and his eccentric lifestyle have fueled a large element of curiosity that draws people to see his home. People are also drawn to seeing the homes of former presidents. Two very popular tourist attractions are Thomas Jefferson's Monticello and George Washington's Mount Vernon.

Some historic homes have become tourist attractions because they are good representatives of homes of a certain period in history. Natchez, Mississippi is the oldest city along the Mississippi River. Here thirteen homes are open throughout the year to acquaint the public with plantation-era homes and the lifestyle of wealthy southern landowners.

Another setting for historical tourist attractions is an entire community. The Amana Colonies in Amana, Iowa let tourists see a community that a group of religious immigrants settled after arriving in the United States in 1842. This community was one of the first communal colonies in this country. The people lived and worked together to preserve a lifestyle of religious freedom. Their lifestyle fascinates the large number of people who visit each year to learn about the early settlers as well as how this colony functions in today's world. The Village of Kohler in Kohler, Wisconsin, built in 1917 by Walter Kohler and the Olmsted Brothers, was carefully laid out and designed for the workers of the Kohler Company, a plumbing and fixture business. Today, this perfectly preserved village is listed on the National Register of Historic Places. It is a multi-purpose attraction, as it is also one of the Midwest's premier resorts.

Some cities represent a unique cultural aspect of present-day life and have multiple tourist attractions. One of these cities is Nashville, Tennessee, which has country and western music as its theme. Included in the attractions is the restored Ryman Theatre, where many of country music's most famous singers have performed. Nashville's Opryland Theme Park has theaters and live telecasts featuring country and western music. Within the park, the Grand Ole Opry broadcasts five hours of musical programming each day from its 4,000-seat auditorium.

Museums and Halls of Fame

Many types of museums are located throughout the country. The purpose of a museum is to preserve a unique part of the country's culture. For example, early automobiles are kept in museums to educate visitors about the development of the car as a means of transportation. The Studebaker Museum in South Bend, Indiana illustrates how the Studebaker Brothers switched from making wagons to manufacturing automobiles. Special types of cars also have museums to showcase them. The Corvette Museum in Bowling Green, Kentucky shows the evolution of the design of this sports car. Race cars and racing also have museums. The Indianapolis Motor Speedway Museum in Indianapolis, Indiana exhibits race cars and racing memorabilia.

Some museums are "living museums," which recreate the life of a period through interpreters. A replica of an 1840s Indiana village is the basis for Conner Prairie Museum in Noblesville, Indiana. As visitors walk through the homes and businesses of the village, the interpreters dress, speak, and act as if they were part of the past.

The Rock and Roll Hall of Fame in Cleveland, Ohio gives visitors an idea about how this style of music developed and celebrates the musicians who wrote and played it. Many sports also have halls of fame, such as the well-known Baseball Hall of Fame in Cooperstown, New York.

WORKING CONDITIONS

Many major tourist attractions are open year-round, so employees have the advantage of full-time employment on a yearly basis. This contributes more readily to career development than seasonal employment would. Smaller attractions, however, may have limited hours and shorter seasons, which means many of their employees will be able to work only part-time.

Nearly all tourist attractions are educational in nature. Visitors learn something new about people, places, the past, animals, the American culture, sports, and a great variety of objects. Many employees at tourist attractions take on the role of educators. Because tourist attractions appeal to a wide audience, employees work with people of all ages, from young children to senior citizens. One advantage to being employed at these attractions is that most visitors have a high interest level in the attraction, since they have chosen to see it. Furthermore, many visitors are on vacation, so they are relaxed and easy to please.

There are downsides to working at tourist attractions, especially for employees dealing directly with the visitors. Typically the attraction's features do not change. Since the employees have nothing new to learn, they must relate the same information each day. The visitors, of course, are new to the attraction, but they tend to ask the same types of questions, so responding to questions is repetitive. Employees must be wary of letting an element of boredom creep into the workplace. Additionally, it can be difficult to explain attractions to visitors of such disparate ages and backgrounds. The presentation may go over the heads of the youngest visitors or lose the attention of the more mature visitors.

LOOKING AT DIFFERENT JOBS AT TOURIST ATTRACTIONS

Even though there is a great variety of tourist attractions, many of the same jobs are available at each attraction. There will be very well-defined jobs at major attractions while employees at smaller attractions will find themselves playing many roles—including ticket seller, guide, maintenance worker, food server, and souvenir salesperson.

Working as a Guide

One job found at almost every attraction is that of guide. This individual has the task of leading tourists through the attraction, whether it is a historic home, the Astrodome, or a wolf farm. To educate and tell the story about the attraction's focus and exhibits is the job of the guide. Guides need to be very knowledgeable about every aspect of the attraction. They must commit to memory dates, facts about significant developments, and names. A good guide couples facts with unique or unusual pieces of information. Blending these two types of information keeps the audience's attention, which is very important in guiding. It is crucial, however, that the guide never embellish the narrative to fascinate the visitors. Information must be accurate as proven by records or other forms of data. Good guides must do some research to be interesting presenters.

Guides must keep their groups moving on schedule so that each group has an equal opportunity to see and hear about the attraction. Guides must end each tour on time so they are ready to take the next group through the attraction. Guides must also be observant of the actions of the visitors, making sure that everyone stays with the group. This is for the safety of the visitors and for the protection of the exhibits.

Working in Security

Nearly all tourist attractions have employees involved in security even though employees at small attractions may have other job responsibilities. One of the unique problems faced by the staff of the security department is that of keeping all parts of the exhibit in place. For different reasons, visitors to tourist attractions like to take home the "real" thing from an attraction rather than purchasing a replica or a souvenir from the attraction.

Working in Retail Sales

Sales of products and food will be large departments at major tourist attractions. Retail sales play a very important role in generating income for these attractions. Souvenirs and other commemorative items are sold at nearly every attraction. Managers of retail departments must have a selection of souvenirs to appeal to different age groups and different budgets. They also will need a staff of full-time and part-time salespeople. On the food side, employees will be needed to manage restaurants and other food outlets, prepare food, serve food, and clean the facilities.

Working on the Administrative Staff

The larger a tourist attraction is, the more employees it will have working in an administrative capacity. Some attractions will have large sales and marketing, accounting, computer, and human resources departments. Clerical employees will also be needed. So will individuals to respond to consumer inquires and provide for the operating needs of the tourist attraction. Positions will be available in several areas including reservations, ticket sales, and tour programming. Large tourist attractions will need professional management teams to direct all aspects of the attraction.

Working in Maintenance and Groundskeeping

The appearance of tourist attractions is vital for capturing new visitors and repeat visitors. Likewise, it is essential to provide for visitor safety. Due to the age of some of the structures, upkeep can be a very challenging responsibility. Some attractions have buildings listed on the U.S. Register of Historic Places, and maintenance must be done to be in compliance with this registration. Both skilled and unskilled employees are needed in the maintenance and groundskeeping department, as well as supervisory personnel.

PREPARATION FOR BECOMING A TOURIST ATTRACTION EMPLOYEE

Education requirements vary with an employee's position. Some of the entry-level positions may be held by high school-age employees. A young employee could work in guiding or in retail. Employers will want a mature and responsible high school student with good communication skills. Membership in student organizations as officers or committee chairpersons would be an excellent way to develop maturity, responsibility, and people skills. Participation in athletics would contribute the same qualities. Previous work experience in hospitality or other service industries is a good preparation for a career in tourist attractions. Service industry positions give excellent customer service experiences.

Other positions will require a high school diploma or a college degree. The amount and type of education depends on the focus of the attraction. For example, a living museum will need department heads to oversee the exhibits or possibly even to conduct the tours. The depth of knowledge needed to create and develop exhibits requires a college degree. Depending on the type of museum, beneficial majors include anthropology, history, and museum studies.

Restaurants and food service at the attraction would require operations management expertise. Majors that would be beneficial are culinary arts, hospitality management and/or business administration. For marketing and public relations positions, majors in business, communications, and media would be good choices.

SALARY AND FRINGE BENEFITS

Entry-level hourly positions are likely to pay minimum wage since these are non-skilled positions. In areas where the rate of unemployment is low, the tourist attractions may offer higher wages to attract and keep employees in these positions. Positions that require some skills—such as security and maintenance—will pay more per hour. Department heads or managers earn salaries starting in the range of $20,000 to $25,000 and may earn more depending on the level of education and experience a job requires.

Fringe benefit packages depend on the number of employees for the attraction. Attractions that employ larger staffs are able to economically offer health and life insurance, retirement plans, paid vacation days, and paid sick days. Not all of these benefits would be available at attractions that employ smaller numbers of people.

LOOKING AT THE FUTURE

Successful tourist attractions have focal points that interest their customers. The changing demographics of the population of the United States may impact the demand for certain types of attractions. For example, the baby boomers (individuals born between 1946 and 1964) are reaching middle age. They are likely to have more leisure time and more discretionary dollars. Owners of tourist attractions will want to have a focus that would appeal to this large group of potential customers. This change in demographics is what makes the

Corvette Museum popular and is also a major factor behind the opening of the Rock and Roll Hall of Fame. This does not mean, however, that any other type of attraction will have no customers. It simply means that the management of attractions should be aware of the interests of this large group of people. When possible, attractions should target their marketing strategies to explain why their particular site would appeal to the baby boomers.

Classical and historical attractions will always have business, because people want to see the lifestyles, homes, and communities of our country's pioneers. These tourist attractions are particularly interesting to school groups and senior citizens' groups. The goal of these types of attractions is to keep the authenticity of their attraction.

OTHER JOBS RELATED TO TOURIST ATTRACTIONS

Many communities around the country have tourist attractions that are open only for short periods of time. These commonly take the form of a festival that may be celebrating some specific theme, such as pioneer days, covered bridges, flowers, or a racing event. The focus of a festival may be to highlight an ethnic group of people—as in the St. Patrick's Day celebration in Chicago. The March 17th parade and supporting activities are planned to attract thousands to the city. Festivals like the Blueberry Festival in Plymouth, Indiana spotlight foods that are plentiful and important to a region. On Labor Day weekend, this community organizes a variety of activities, from antique car shows to entertainment to food treats (featuring blueberries, of course). The Azalea Festival in Tyler, Texas attracts many visitors who drive through the town to see the colors of the azaleas in bloom, along with other spring flowers and the flowering dogwood. Restaurants and hotels are jammed with out-of-town visitors for two weeks while these flowers are in full bloom.

Unlike tourist attractions, which are typically managed as for-profit, year-round businesses, festivals are not organized as money-making events for a particular business and are not managed by one business owner. All of the businesses of a community benefit financially from the success of a festival, and all of the community's business leaders will help organize the festival. The Chamber of Commerce is often the community organization that spearheads a festival. The overall success of a festival comes from a total commitment of the community and relies heavily on volunteers to carry out the activities associated with a festival.

WORKING IN ADVENTURE RECREATION

Adventure recreation features an outdoor activity with elements of risk, physical stress, mental stress, and fear. It matches participants against elements in the environment. The goal for the participants is to overcome the challenges of the natural setting through personal skills and will. Some individuals are very interested in using their leisure time to pursue adventure recreation. This is the type of vacation or get-away activity that appeals to them. The individual who guarantees the success of a recreation adventure is the guide.

SETTINGS FOR ADVENTURE RECREATION CAREERS

The settings for adventure careers are as diverse as the activities. These activities are associated with land, water, air, snow, or ice and include hiking, climbing, tracking, spelunking, biking, horseback riding, motorcycle riding, skiing, sky diving, canoeing, rafting, and scuba diving.

Survival Schools

A survival school like Tom Brown's in Asbury, New York is one setting for adventure recreation. This school offers seventeen courses that are typically a week long. They are offered throughout the year in New York, Pennsylvania, New Jersey, and California. The school's philosophy of being one with the earth has led to three major categories of classes in survival: tracking, nature awareness, and the ancient philosophy of the earth. The classes are personally taught by the owner, Tom Brown. He does use volunteers to assist with courses, but any volunteer must have completed Brown's basic survival course.

Whitewater Schools

Whitewater schools prepare people to be commercial whitewater guides; however, anyone who wants to become an expert in whitewater rafting may attend. Participants learn oar- and paddle-powered raft navigation, expeditioning, knot tying, river rescue and safety, equipment repair, trip logistics, guiding, menu planning, and meal preparation.

Camps for Adventure Recreation

Adventure recreation camps are found in a variety of settings and are designed for children, teenagers, and families. At Teton Valley Ranch in Kelly, Wyoming, school-age boys and girls learn photography, horse packing, hiking and backpacking, swimming, ham radio operation, horseback riding, and archery while they become accustomed to being outdoors and gain readiness for handling unusual situations. The development of decision-making skills is stressed. Employees in children's adventure recreation camps must be able to work with young learners.

In recent years, camps for pre-teen and teenage groups have become popular. The adventure activities of the camps appeal to these young people, and educators recognize that the camp activities can help students learn teamwork, learn about themselves, and learn to take responsibility.

Teens can experience backpacking, horseback riding, technical climbing, kayaking, river rafting, fishing, glacier climbing, and wilderness survival at Wind River Wilderness Camp in Wyoming. Having recreation coupled with teamwork and decision-making skills is the program's goal. Camp employees must present challenges appropriate for a less-mature audience than when working with adults.

Families at the Yellowstone Institute camp in Wyoming participate in nature studies of bears, birds of prey, plant life, wildflowers, and natural phenomena like geysers. Handling family units requires the camp employees to meet the needs of a wide variety of ages through the activities.

Scott Valley Ranch in Mountain Home, Arkansas is a family guest ranch featuring horseback riding, water sports (jet skiing, sailing, and scuba diving), and fishing. Families at this guest ranch can be as active as they choose because these milder adventure activities can be done without direct supervision. The responsibilities of the employees are to have the equipment and facilities in good working order and instruct the participants in their use.

Horse packing schools in Dubois, Wyoming have the guides or outfitters teach beginning and intermediate riders in a week-long course. The first two days are spent in camp; the participants learn how to use equipment, tie knots, and gain expertise in horsemanship. On the trail for five days, the participants learn natural history, geology, and land ethics. The guide helps direct the use of the skills learned in camp as situations occur on the trail.

Single-Activity Adventure Recreation Settings

Unlike schools or camps where adventure recreation is concentrated on multiple activities, some adventure recreation programs concentrate on a single activity, such as mountain climbing or mountain biking. Usually, participants pick an activity because they have had some experience with it. Sometimes, however, a novice chooses one of these activities for the adventure experience. Skill level and ability are critical for these activities. It is up to the employee—the outfitter or the guide—to determine the readiness of participants. They must be certain that all participants are capable, since others may be at risk if one individual is less capable than the group.

Some settings can be just mildly adventurous, such as a self-guided houseboat excursion on a lake. However, even then there must be basic instruction on how to participate in the activity and use the equipment. So even though there may be less risk, there is no risk-free situation or activity. All employees must educate the participants on safety and other procedures relevant to the adventure recreation.

Narrow-Audience Adventure Recreation Settings

Adventure recreation activities can focus on a particular audience. One example is the Women's Mountain Tune-Up Mini Spa, a four-day workout in Summit County, Colorado at the Keystone Resort. This adventure program is for women of any age with a real desire to change their lives and a commitment to building and balancing a healthy body and mind. A typical day includes hiking, biking, aerobic workouts, gourmet meals, lectures, and hot tubbing, plus the encouragement and motivation the employees give to the participants. The leaders or guides direct all of these activities as they encourage participants to challenge their bodies, minds, and spirits.

Specific-Interest Adventure Recreation Settings

Sea kayaking in Mexico's Bay of Whales is an example of an adventure attraction appealing to participants with a specific interest—water and sealife. Participants spend one week seeing whales, sea lions, porpoises, bird life, and natural beaches. Motorboats carry food and water to the kayakers while en route and supply them at night while they are camped on the beaches. During the day, the participants paddle along the coast observing nature's beauty. Guides on this adventure must have the ability to supervise people moving at different paces. They must also educate the participants on what they are seeing as well as closely monitor weather conditions to keep all participants safe.

Another example of a specific-interest recreation activity is a mountain-climbing trek in the Grand Tetons in Jackson Hole, Wyoming. All of the participants must be in good physical shape, because as the climbers move from an altitude of 6,500 feet to 11,600 feet, they encounter all types of weather conditions and rock formations. Several days of instructions are given in camp before the two-day climb. Training focuses on learning rope handling, climbing signals, climbing harnesses, methods of anchoring, and placing protection. Leaders train the participants and judge their readiness and capabilities. Throughout the climb, the leaders make certain that everyone is using correct techniques.

WORKING CONDITIONS

Depending upon the activity or activities an adventure recreation company offers, the season may last for several months or may be year-round. Seasonal employment is very common for adventure recreation employees because so many activities like river rafting are dependent upon the weather. Adventure recreation employees must then find other employment for the remainder of the year.

Guides are expected to work long days, typically from twelve to fourteen hours. Guides, as well as outfitters for adventure recreation companies, primarily work outdoors. Their work environment includes swirling waters, lofty mountain peaks, and native forests. And they work closely with the participants taking adventure recreation vacations. Supporting the work that guides do in conducting adventure recreation activities is the ownership/management of the adventure recreation company. In small companies, the owner and head guide are the same person. Seasonal guides are hired to help with the excursions. Larger adventure companies will have a year-round staff of ten to thirty employees. These people carry out the marketing, adventure trip planning, purchasing of supplies, accounting, and human resources functions. In small companies, the owner will handle most of these responsibilities.

Adventure recreation activities can be risky. Guides must always be focused on the safety of the participants. They may have to change routes or postpone an activity if the weather or other event causes unsafe conditions. Making decisions affecting the participants' safety can be stressful for guides.

LOOKING AT A CAREER AS A GUIDE

The major responsibility of guides is to oversee the safe undertaking of an adventure. Included in this are the tasks of educating and training the participants, checking equipment, keeping track of weather conditions, leading the group, organizing meals and overnight stays, and keeping the group informed of pertinent information regarding the weather and terrain. The safety aspect of the adventure is of primary importance. During the trip, the guide must be aware of the actions of the participants at all times. In a group activity, one individual's careless action can endanger everyone. Safety is preached by the guide and must be practiced by everyone.

PREPARATION FOR BECOMING AN ADVENTURE RECREATION GUIDE

Part-time or seasonal jobs in support areas help prospective guides learn about an activity. Developing a personal interest in a particular recreation activity and following it as an avocation is another helpful step in becoming a guide. Survival schools can give a future guide solid knowledge of the precautions and common sense applications necessary for potentially dangerous adventure activities. Learning from other guides is probably the most common method of preparation for adventure recreation careers. Some of the principles can be learned in classrooms or books, but the best education for recreation that is risky is by doing.

While in high school, students can begin to prepare for careers in adventure recreation. They can get CPR certification and the first aid training all guides must have. Also, courses in life sciences, physical sciences, history, and communication should be useful in any kind of adventure activity. Extra-curricular activities in high school such as joining a ski club, climbing club, or walking club would provide experience in outdoor activities and equipment use and maintenance. Leadership activities in these clubs or in any group would be helpful in learning to work with and direct the activities of other people. An understanding of group dynamics is essential to knowing how to get group cooperation. Scouting activities present many opportunities to prepare for this career because the principles learned in scouting are valuable in any type of outdoor job. College degrees that may be helpful are geography, geology, forestry, wildlife, and anthropology.

Attending a Whitewater School

Specific skills must be learned by adventure recreation guides. Learning whitewater rafting skills can be accomplished by going to a whitewater school. Most whitewater outfitters require their guides to have school training. Whitewater schools prepare people for the different degrees of difficulty of rapids and teach them how to use equipment and employ safety measures. Swift water rescue training is also taught, along with CPR and first aid.

On-the-Job Experience

New whitewater rafting guides are hired as assistant guides. The main responsibility for the assistant guide is to row boats with baggage and help on shore whenever possible. By first accompanying an experienced guide, future guides have genuine on-the-job training as they are broken in on the rivers. They quickly become acquainted with the mix of skill levels typical rafting groups possess. After a few trips or a season of working as an assistant guide, an individual is ready to be hired as a guide.

SPECIAL ATTRIBUTES OF A GUIDE

Guides must be excellent decision makers. Good judgement and common sense are important characteristics to support a guide's ability to make sound decisions. Maturity and a calm manner are key personality traits, as the participants may react with concern in situations where the danger risk becomes uncomfortable. Guides assess the degree of danger, and if conditions are such that injury could occur, they make alternatives plans and activities. If the degree of risk is appropriate for the skill level of the group, the guide will direct them to proceed. The calmness of the guide will convince the participants of the correctness of this decision.

Guides must be in good physical condition. Their work hours are very long, and during the workday they must perform many very strenuous activities. Physical conditioning to maintain their stamina and strength is essential.

SALARY AND BENEFITS

Guides earn from $80 to $100 per day and work four to five days a week. Their jobs may last for several months or be full-time jobs. Those who work for very small companies or work part-time do not usually receive benefits. Larger adventure companies with many full-time employees will offer life and health insurance. Salaries for these individuals would be in the range of $20,000 to $30,000. Company owners/operators have the greatest opportunity to make larger salaries.

A TYPICAL DAY AS AN ADVENTURE RECREATION GUIDE

Guides complete many diverse activities every day. In the early morning hours, they check the travel conditions for the day. Then they may take part in the setting-up, service, and cleanup of breakfast. After the morning meal, guides check to make certain that all of the participants are ready, and equipment checks are completed. If camp is being broken, they oversee all of the packing for transportation.

Before embarking on the day's adventure activity, guides review safety procedures. As the group readies for the activity, guides encourage them with reminders. Leading the group through the activity requires the guides to use the technical skills required by the activity. Additionally, they promote teamwork, watch out for emotions or fright on the part of the participants, watch for signs of fatigue, and look out for carelessness or clowning around, which might contribute to an accident. During the day, guides point out and discuss interesting facts about the area and its plants and animals. They answer questions from the participants. The guides pace the activity of the group, allowing for rest breaks, snacks, and meals.

At the end of the day, guides oversee the setting-up of the camp and the preparation of the evening meal. Equipment checks are made and any necessary repairs are initiated. The next day's activities are previewed and the weather is checked for any changes in the forecast. Finally, after a long day, the guides are ready to rest.

LOOKING AT THE FUTURE

Adventure recreation companies have a good potential for growth. More people are learning about these vacation activities, and at the same time, several groups are beginning to use the activities of adventure companies for a wide variety of purposes. Businesses see adventure recreation as a team-building exercise and may use it for their employees. This type of activity can be enlightening; group dynamics come into play and business associates learn to appreciate the value of being a team member. Some judicial courts use adventure recreation as a way to help direct troubled juveniles in the right direction. Learning responsibility for their actions, building self-confidence, and accepting directions from the guide are outcomes youths can achieve from adventure recreation. Some authorities believe that using adventure recreation, especially survival schools, is one possible solution to the problem of troubled youth.

FOR MORE INFORMATION

Individuals who are interested in adventure recreation can obtain helpful information from the National Outdoor Leadership School, P.O. Box AA, Lander, Wyoming, 82520. The Outward Bound National Office (Field Point Road, Greenwich, Connecticut, 06830) has pertinent materials and leadership experiences activities. The Wilderness Association (Route 1, Box 3400, Driggs, Idaho, 83422) offers outdoor leadership training materials.

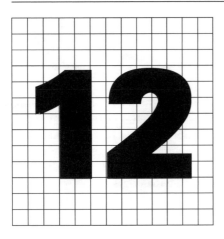

WORKING IN MEETING PLANNING

Meeting planning is a relatively new career in terms of its formal title. People have been planning get-togethers for the purpose of conducting business, socializing, and training for decades. With the changes occurring in business and industry, more meetings than ever are being held to keep employees informed and updated. Professional and social organizations use meetings as a major form of communication within their groups. So while meeting planning is not a new concept, it has become a formal career.

A meeting planner may plan menus, set up exhibits, secure famous people as speakers, and write marketing pieces to promote a meeting. Meeting planners may have their own businesses where they contract with associations and companies to plan meetings as needed. Or they may work within large corporations to plan any type of event that the corporation needs for its employees.

SETTINGS FOR MEETINGS

Settings for meetings can be hotels, conference centers, convention centers, exhibit halls, restaurants, parks, reception halls, community buildings, or simply the outdoors. The setting depends on the type of meeting being held. Meetings can be general sessions, concurrent sessions, breakout sessions, seminars, independent conference groups, workshops, roundtable discussion groups, panel presentations, retreats, forums, field trips, recreation/sporting events, exhibits/displays, combined meal/speaker presentations, awards programs, and socials. Each type of meeting serves a specific purpose for the attendees.

WORKING CONDITIONS

Meeting planners have an opportunity to work in different locations since meetings may be held at different sites within a city or in different cities around the country. The activities that a meeting planner plans, organizes, coordinates, markets, and controls are unlimited. Big band entertainment may be part of a social gathering. Selecting a panel of experts to give their opinions on an issue can be the job of a meeting planner. This great variety of activities means that the meeting planner has new experiences every workday.

In many instances, meeting planners have control and flexibility over their work hours. Independent meeting planners can choose to plan as many meetings as they can competently handle. Contracting to do a large number of meetings can make a heavy work schedule. On the other hand, if meeting planners wish to work less intensively for a period of time, they can decide not to contract any business or to contract a lesser volume of business.

Meeting planners who are independent operators must continuously submit proposals to obtain business. Hard work goes into preparation for a proposal, and the planner may or may not be selected. This gives an element of uncertainty to the life of the planner.

During the actual days of a meeting that has been planned, meeting planners are on site or on call twenty-four hours a day. They must be available to resolve any problems that arise. These long days at meetings can make it difficult to handle other clients, as well as to spend time with families and friends.

ON-THE-JOB RESPONSIBILITIES

The meeting planner has the overall responsibility for the quality of a meeting. Attendees' time at a meeting is wasted unless they can concentrate, function properly, and leave with new insights or information. Furthermore, poorly planned business meetings waste valuable company time, and employees are disgruntled because they could have been doing something more meaningful. Failing to plan a meeting properly can result in lost business in the future for independent meeting planners.

Here is a list of the many steps that a meeting planner must follow to ensure a quality meeting. The planner initiates all plans for a meeting, including setting objectives, creating themes appropriate to the meeting's purpose, designing the agenda, and estimating time for all activities (including breaks, refreshments, and movement between areas). Planning the budget and selecting the meeting site are also a planner's responsibility. Organizational tasks include coordinating with needed support groups such as the staff of a hotel, restaurant, or caterer; arranging transportation; planning the menu; selecting speakers; marketing literature on the meeting to obtain the maximum number of attendees, if necessary; and arranging the exhibits. The planner must also determine how much a meeting will cost or stay within a previously agreed-upon budget. The final step is for the meeting planner to evaluate the meeting using as criteria every aspect of the meeting—time, location, cost, food, lodging, quality of speakers, and entertainment.

The independent meeting planner must include in the plans and budget figures a consideration for the compensation of organizing the meeting. Independent meeting planners may opt to set a flat fee for any or all services needed to plan and execute a meeting. Other alternatives for compensation could be to charge by the hour or the day. Whatever method is used, planners will want to be certain that the compensation is fair to the organization using their services and fair to themselves.

PREPARATION FOR BECOMING A MEETING PLANNER

A meeting planner is not required to have a degree; however, professional organizations for the industry, like Meeting Professionals International, highly recommend post-secondary training. Solid choices of a college major for this career are hospitality management programs either focusing on operations management or, if offered in the curriculum, using courses in meeting and convention management. These courses help future planners learn the principles and procedures of meeting planning. Other majors that would be appropriate are business administration, marketing, communications, and public relations. Any of these areas can serve as a major, and the use of another of the areas as a minor would be excellent academic preparation. If coursework is offered in media, this would support the activities of a meeting. Other important courses to include in the college curriculum are computer applications.

Whether an individual completes a degree or not, professional certification is recommended. Meeting Professionals International has training and an examination to become a certified meeting professional.

Related work experiences in the hospitality industry in hotels or with catering companies can be beneficial. These experiences provide an excellent opportunity to work with groups and get a general feel for some of their activities. This information can then be used as a basis for future meeting planning.

Volunteer experiences can also enhance a career in meeting planning. In high school, organizing a prom or a fund-raising function teaches organizational and event-coordination skills. Similarly, college students can gain experience through organizing a fraternity or sorority pledge process, a blood drive, or a marathon race.

SPECIAL ATTRIBUTES OF A MEETING PLANNER

Attention to detail is one characteristic that all meeting planners must have. Every aspect of a meeting needs to be considered and planned for. To help plan and administer such a large number of details, meeting planners often use checklists. A meeting planner must also be cool, calm, and collected. Even carefully constructed plans are not always followed by other individuals. Mistakes will happen. Accidents do occur. The job of the meeting planner is to create feasible alternatives. The most important thing is to not panic.

SALARY AND FRINGE BENEFITS

Meeting planners' incomes vary with the complexity of each meeting. On a hourly basis, meeting planners may make as little as $10 per hour or a rate that is ten times higher or more. As previously mentioned, compensation must be carefully negotiated between the planner and the person requesting his or her services. Independent planners will generally need to provide their own insurance and retirement plans, and so will their staffs. If a planner is a part of a large organization, the company's fringe benefits package will typically include health and life insurance, paid vacation days, paid sick days, and retirement benefits.

LOOKING AT THE FUTURE

The future looks very promising for meeting planners. Businesses have found meetings to be an effective and efficient way to educate employees on new developments or to update skills. Associations meet on regular schedules for monthly, quarterly, or annual meetings to conduct the business of the association. There is a solid demand for meeting planners. Furthermore, hotels, resorts, conference centers, convention centers, and exhibition halls have space available to accommodate the smallest and largest groups of people. With the demand that exists for meetings and the locations available to hold those meetings, meeting planners should be busy bringing these two elements together.

FOR MORE INFORMATION

Meeting Professionals International has career materials available. This organization can be contacted at 1950 Stemmons Freeway, Suite 5018, Dallas, Texas 75207-3109. Other associations to contact are:

> Convention Liaison Council
> 1575 I Street, NW
> Suite 1200
> Washington, DC 20005

> Exposition Service Contractors Association
> 1516 South Pontius Avenue
> Los Angeles, CA 90025

> Foundation for International Meetings
> 1400 K Street, NW
> Number 750
> Washington, DC 20005

> Hotel Sales and Marketing Association International
> 1400 K Street, NW
> Suite 810
> Washington, DC 20005

> International Association of Conference Centers
> 362 Parsippany Road
> Parsippany, NJ 07054

International Association of Conference and Visitor's Bureaus
1809 Woodfield Drive
Savoy, IL 61874

International Conference Industry Associations
1400 K Street, NW
Suite 750
Washington, DC 20005

Society of Company Meeting Planners
2600 Garden Road
Suite 208
Monterey, CA 93940

OTHER JOBS RELATED TO MEETING PLANNING

Special event planning is closely tied to meeting planning. Events, shows, expositions, celebrations, dances, and competitions are examples of special events. Events are scheduled for the enjoyment of the audience and/or the participants. Commonly, the event is a one-time affair. Reasons for holding special events include religious celebrations, cultural events, technical show-cases, economic conferences, entertainment, political conventions, sporting events, fund-raisers, and recreational exhibits. These events rarely focus on business matters. And the event may be open to an entire community of people rather than participants who are aligned with a particular organization or business. Individuals who organize special events plan in the same detail-oriented fashion as meeting planners.

One example of a special event is the Gus Macker basketball tournaments. This basketball competition moves its tournaments from location to location around the country, using both outdoor and indoor locations. The tournament directors hire a special event company at each site to take care of all local arrangements. The special event planners must secure a location that is large enough and conveniently located. Other details that the event planners handle are securing advertising, finding food vendors, meeting city licensing requirements, removing trash, monitoring safety and parking, and coordinating temporary staffing needs for the weekend event. On the weekend of the competition, the special event planner and team of employees are there on site to oversee the execution of all of the planning. Everyone works long hours in the days directly before the event and during the event to make it possible for this tournament to be successful.

WORKING IN HOTELS AND MOTELS

While hotels and motels often have restaurants and shops, the core business of hotels and motels is lodging. Providing places for people to stay is not a new business. The first inns, established around 3000 B.C., were rooms in private homes. There was not enough space in these inns for individual rooms; in some inns there wasn't even enough space for individual beds. The Bible story of Joseph and Mary being turned away from an inn in Bethlehem is a familiar one. At that time, people traveled only out of necessity. By the Middle Ages, more people were traveling because of the increased numbers of roads and coach routes. In fact, in England, travelers could encounter an inn every fifteen miles along certain routes.

With the arrival of the colonists in 1607 came the first known hotel in North America—the Jamestown Inn, located in Virginia. As the pioneers journeyed west, more hotels were built. In new settlements, hotels were often the first buildings constructed. American innkeepers were the world leaders in hotel development during the 1800s. These hotels were still very simple, with many beds, no lobbies, and no security locks to protect the guests. The first hotel to provide private rooms and locks on doors was the Tremont House in Boston, in 1829. The Tremont was also the first hotel to provide indoor plumbing and a lobby. Not until 1881 would a hotel have electric lights.

After the railroads began to make travel more comfortable in the early 1900s, people traveled more for pleasure and the quality of inns began to improve. In the eastern part of the United States, resort hotels emerged and began opening health spas for the comfort of their guests. Hotel building, however, almost stopped during the Great Depression.

THE ADVENT OF THE MOTEL

During the 1940s, increased automobile travel led to the construction along the major highways of "tourist cabins," which were later developed into motels. These first motels were usually managed by resident owners, with very few paid employees. These motels were small and simple, generally having fewer than twenty guest rooms. They were usually located at the edge of town because land costs were lower there than in the city. The first motels had one-story construction because this design was significantly less expensive than the downtown highrises. The largest single cost in many lodging facilities is capital cost. If the land and building expenses were lower, the savings generally lowered the rates of the rooms. A great number of people appreciated the lower rates and patronized the motels that offered them. Many travelers also preferred the motels' informal atmosphere compared to the hotels' formality. Another appeal was that the motels did not require reservations, and travelers could easily tell by the vacancy sign whether rooms were available.

After World War II, a new kind of lodging emerged that would combine the convenience of motels and the services of hotels. It was Kemmons Wilson, a Memphis businessman, who revolutionized the lodging industry. He took his family on a vacation and was disturbed by the inconsistent standards of the motels and the high prices of the hotels. Wilson developed the Holiday Inn, which offered standardized units at affordable prices.

Within a few years, motels became larger and started offering more services. There was an increased focus on the needs of the business traveler, and motels began having dining rooms, meeting rooms, and cocktail lounges. Motor hotels began to appear; these hybrids offered the convenience of a motel and the comfort of a hotel. Telephones and televisions became staples in every room, and swimming pools were installed to accommodate traveling families.

As the motel industry grew, chains began to emerge. These motel chains consisted of two or more motels that were owned by one person or company. Over the years, many hotel and motel chains have grown by means of franchising. In the franchise system, an individual or company purchases the right to own and operate the lodging facility. The franchisee receives the advantage of using a well-known name and standardized product.

The distinctions between hotels, motels, and resorts began fading during the 1960s and 1970s, as all of these establishments began offering the same options to compete for business. Motels were becoming an accepted part of the hotel business. The American Hotel Association even changed its name to include the motels. It is now called the American Hotel and Motel Association (AH&MA). Except for the small-motel operators, who continued to maintain their own state and national trade associations, the larger motels gladly joined forces with the hotel fraternity. The term *motel* (meaning motor hotel) is not used as much now.

During the 1980s, the hotel and motel chains moved back toward segmentation. New chains were created that catered solely to business travelers, the vacation market, or longer-staying customers. It was also during this time that the all-suites hotel emerged, featuring living room areas and kitchens along with its bedrooms. Widespread hotel building in the 1980s resulted in an oversupply of facilities in the late 1980s and early 1990s.

Figure 1   Organization chart for a small lodging facility.

Figure 2   Organization chart for a large lodging facility.

Source: Educational Institute of the American Hotel and Motel Association

HOTELS AND MOTELS IN THE 1990S

By the mid-1990s, the demand for hotel rooms had increased once again. Furthermore, this industry has emerged throughout the world as one of the largest generators of jobs. Today, there are more than 45,000 hotel and motel properties in the United States. These establishments provide a wide choice of accommodations. There are facilities that meet the needs of every group, from senior citizens to corporate travelers to families. Hotels today fall into the following categories:

  all-suites hotels
  budget hotels
  economy hotels
  full-service mid-priced hotels
  full-service upscale hotels
  luxury hotels
  resort hotels

THE ORGANIZATION OF HOTELS AND MOTELS

From the very first hotel to today's hotels and motels, the key ingredient for the success of the lodging is the personnel. The larger the lodging, the greater the number of employees. Some large facilities may have as many as 1,000 employees. Each hotel or motel will have its own organization, and job responsibilities will vary from lodging to lodging. There is, however, a similarity in the way lodging facilities are organized. And the larger the facility, the more specialized the jobs will be. The two simple organizational charts in Figures 1 and 2 show how a small and a large lodging could be organized. Figure 1 shows the organization of a small lodging facility of 100 to 150 rooms that does not have food or beverage service. Figure 2 depicts the organization of a large facility with a great number of departments.

The following section examines in detail some of the departments and divisions that would be found at a large hotel or motel. It discusses some of the positions available in each area, as described by the Educational Institute of the American Hotel and Motel Association.

Front Office

The front office is often regarded as the "nerve center" of the hotel. The front office is where the guests check in and out, make payments on their accounts, and exchange messages. The front desk staff should be people-oriented, good at solving problems, and attentive to details. The actions and attitudes displayed toward the guests are a big part of what the hotel is selling—service. The positions at the front office include rooms division manager, front desk clerk, reservationist, front office manager, mail and information clerk, and switchboard operator.

Housekeeping

A lodging property's main product is the guest room. The housekeeping personnel are responsible for keeping the rooms ready for guests. They take pride in maintaining property cleanliness and are constantly monitoring guests' comfort and safety. The positions in housekeeping include executive housekeeper, inspector, floor supervisor, houseperson, room attendant, laundry personnel, and linen-room worker.

Marketing and Sales

Without guests, no hotel can survive. It is the job of the marketing and sales personnel to discover what the guests want, know how to build guests' needs into the services sold, and know how best to reach potential guests. The creative efforts of this team can bring in the business that makes a property a success. Positions in marketing and sales include the marketing director, sales manager, public relations, account executive, advertising representative, banquet sales manager, and convention services representative.

Food and Beverage

Food and beverage sales can mean big business. They may provide many good opportunities for advancement for employees in this department. The quality of the food being served and the quality of service are the keys to a successful department. Positions in the food and beverage department include the food and beverage director, host/captain/maitre d'hotel, chef/cook, wine steward, dietitian, food server, banquet services worker, steward/dishwasher, baker, cashier/checker, restaurant manager, dining room manager, kitchen manager, and shift leader.

Security

The members of this department must master the fine art of balancing guest relations with safety and security. The security staff is charged with protecting the safety and security of the guests, fellow employees, and the property. They are also in charge of developing and directing all emergency procedures. Positions on the security staff include the director of security and house officer.

Human Resources

More and more emphasis is being placed on the human resources area as the hospitality industry is affected by today's labor shortage. This is the department responsible for recruiting, selecting, and training qualified applicants. It also administers benefits programs and handles other personnel matters. Positions in human resources include the benefits administrator, employment manager, human resources director, and training manager.

Facility Maintenance and Engineering

The engineering and maintenance staff members are responsible for property equipment and systems. Fixing and maintaining electrical systems, plumbing, heating, ventilation, air conditioning, and refrigeration are highly skilled and highly respected jobs in the hospitality industry. This is a job for "nuts and bolts" types of people. Positions in the facility maintenance and engineering field include engineer, grounds maintenance worker, plumber, painter, electrician, and carpenter.

Uniformed Service

The members of the uniformed service staff greet guests, assist with travel plans, and much more. These employees are always on the go and play a vital role in making guests feel welcome. The positions in this department include the bell captain, concierge, parking attendant, door attendant, and courtesy van operator.

Accounting and Financial Management

Accounting and finance personnel use their professional foresight to help guide management decisions, make important financial recommendations, and even forecast industry trends to help the hotel succeed. This department records sales, controls expenditures, calculates costs, and keeps close track of overall profits. Positions in accounting and financial management include controller, accountant, bookkeeper, purchasing agent, cashier, auditor/night auditor, clerk, credit manager, and computer systems worker.

LOOKING AT "FRONT-OF-THE-HOUSE" AND "BACK-OF-THE-HOUSE" JOBS

In the lodging industry, employees are usually described as having jobs in "the front of the house" or "the back of the house." Employees who work directly with the guests have jobs in "front-of-the-house" departments, which include front office, marketing and sales, food and beverage, security, human resources, uniformed service, and accounting and financial management. The "back-of-the-house" departments are housekeeping and facility maintenance. Although employees in "back-of-the-house" departments may not have much direct contact with guests, their work is vital to guest approval of a lodging facility.

LOOKING AT A FRONT DESK CLERK'S JOB

There are more than 100,000 hotel and motel desk clerks working in front office departments. They perform a variety of services for guests in lodging establishments. The term "desk clerk" is actually an inadequate and even misleading one to use. The term suggests only the clerical aspect of the job, which in fact is one of the least important and least demanding parts of the job. Since front desk clerks are often the first people to greet guests and deal directly with them, the clerks play a major role in establishing a hotel's reputation for service and courtesy. It is their job to consider the guests' preferences in assigning rooms while at the same time trying to maximize the lodging's revenues. Besides assigning rooms and registering guests, they answer questions about services, checkout times, and the local community. They keep records of room assignments so they can tell housekeepers, telephone operators, and maintenance workers which rooms are occupied. They also collect payment for rooms and issue receipts. In addition, they may also take registrations for future stays at the facility. In smaller hotels and motels that have minimal staffs, the desk clerk may also act as bookkeeper, advance reservations agent, cashier, and/or telephone switchboard operator.

WORKING CONDITIONS

A front desk clerk's job offers very flexible work schedules. A full-time front desk clerk can work any of three different eight-hour shifts. More than one in five clerks, however, will work part-time. And some clerks in resort areas may be only seasonal employees. Lodging facilities are located throughout the world, making these jobs available in most locations. One factor that favors the employment of hotel and motel desk clerks is the very high turnover rate associated with this job. Each year thousands of clerks move to different occupations that offer more advancement opportunities and higher pay, and many more leave work altogether to assume family responsibilities, return to school, or for other reasons. Opportunities for part-time work should continue to be plentiful since the front desk must be staffed twenty-four hours a day.

TRAINING AND ADVANCEMENT

When hiring a front desk clerk, most lodging facilities prefer applicants with at least a high school education and experience in the field. Most high schools offer courses in bookkeeping and computer skills that give clerks the clerical skills they will need on the job. Throughout their high school years, future desk clerks can gain important work experience by having a part-time job or summer employment in an office or a retail store, or an entry-level position in a lodging facility. It is even better for applicants to have specialized training in a technical school or a community college. These schools have hospitality-specific vocational or college-level courses. Furthermore, the Educational Institute of the American Hotel and Motel Association offers solid training through correspondence courses.

Many desk clerks are trained on the job by an experienced front desk clerk or manager. The clerks who have more job experience and a better education in the field are more often considered for advancement to managerial positions. Most large lodging facilities offering managerial training programs will begin their trainees in front desk clerk positions to have them gain experience in hotel services. After gaining the requisite knowledge and experience, trainees will then begin to advance up the career ladder to positions such as reservations manager or front office manager.

SPECIAL ATTRIBUTES OF FRONT DESK CLERKS

Since such an important part of front desk clerks' jobs is dealing with people, this position requires individuals to have a friendly, outgoing personality and a desire to serve people. Because clerks are in the public eye, they need to be well-groomed, polite, dependable, and sincere. A good memory for faces and names as well as an understanding of human nature are also good qualities for clerks to have. Most clerks will need computer skills, and clerical, mathematical, and bookkeeping skills are also quite helpful.

SALARY AND FRINGE BENEFITS

The income that front desk clerks earn depends on factors such as geographical location and size of the lodging facility, the type of employing organization, and the experience and training of the individual worker. The average weekly income for starting clerks ranges from $225 to $280 per week; more experienced workers earn between $260 and $335. In some lodging facilities, the front desk clerks may also receive such benefits as paid vacations, reduced lodging rates, free meals, and medical insurance.

THE PERSONAL STORY OF A FRONT DESK CLERK

Seth Fulk began his career in hospitality as an assistant manager at a pizza restaurant while he was in high school. He chose to work in hospitality because he was intrigued by people. People are his "passion." Seth is now a freshman at a vocational/technological college studying hospitality management. His school requires him to work 500 hours in the hotel/restaurant field to receive his degree. The school helped Seth get his present job as front desk clerk at an all-suites hotel in a major metropolitan area. He is working an eight-hour day five days a week while still attending school. His shift varies from day to day. One day he may work from 2:00 p.m. until 10:00 p.m., while another day his work schedule is from 7:00 a.m. to 3:00 p.m.

Besides being a front desk clerk, Seth handles a variety of other services for the hotel, depending on the hours he works and the occupancy of the hotel. Seth usually works with another clerk at the front desk. His responsibilities include checking guests in and out, fulfilling guest requests, taking reservations, and assisting all management personnel. On the night shift, especially, he may find himself helping other departments—for instance, making beds for housekeeping at 10:00 p.m.

Seth received his training on the job—primarily from co-workers but also from the manager. According to Seth, the necessary skills for this job are people skills, problem-solving skills, and basic computer skills. His future plans include graduating from college with a bachelor's degree in hospitality management, then completing his master's degree in project management.

ANOTHER PERSONAL STORY OF A FRONT DESK CLERK

Bill Funkhouser has been in the hospitality field for about six years. Before he became interested in this field, he worked in construction after graduating from high school. The construction job did not fulfill his expectations of having a steady job, so he decided to go back to school. He took courses in general business and hospitality management and began to work as a front desk clerk.

At present, Bill works at an economy lodging facility with 108 rooms that does not have a restaurant. Bill's job consists of doing "a little bit of everything." He is going through cross-training in all departments of the facility, including maintenance, laundry, housekeeping, and administration. He enjoys the cross-training because he likes to move around, doesn't have to do the same job every day, and has many responsibilities. While at the front desk, Bill's duties include handling phone reservations, checking guests in and out, collecting payment, answering the phone, transferring calls to guests, making wake-up calls, and handling requests of the guests. He also has to know the area around the lodging facility so he can supply the guests with information about restaurants, banks, bank machines, and entertainment. Bill believes front desk clerks need to be personable, help the guests with whatever they need, and have common sense.

LOOKING AT CAREERS AS MANAGERS AND ASSISTANT MANAGERS

For vacationing families and out-of-town businesspeople, a comfortable room, good food, and a helpful hotel staff can make being away from home an enjoyable experience. It is the job of the hotel and motel managers and assistant managers to ensure that each guest's stay is a pleasant one. These managers are responsible for the efficient and profitable operation of the establishment where they are employed. The duties of a manager depend on the size, type, and location of the lodging facility. In smaller lodging facilities, a single manager may be in charge of all aspects of the operations. However, in large facilities, managers may be aided by a number of assistant managers who head different departments.

General Manager   The general manager has the overall responsibility for the operation of the hotel. The owners and executives of the hotel chain establish the guidelines, and within those guidelines the general manager sets room rates, allocates funds to the different departments, approves expenditures, and sets the standards for guest service, decor, housekeeping, food quality and service, and banquet operations.

Assistant Managers   Assistant managers must make sure that the day-to-day operations of their departments meet the managers' standards. They assign department workers to shifts, give out work assignments, schedule staff vacations, and promote workers within the departments. This position is generally filled by employees already working at a facility.

Resident Managers   Resident managers live in hotels and are on call twenty-four hours a day to resolve any problems or emergencies, although they normally work an eight-hour day. As the most senior assistant manager, a resident manager oversees the day-to-day operations of the hotel. In many hotels the general manager also serves as the resident manager.

WORKING CONDITIONS

Since lodging facilities are open 24 hours a day 365 days a year, working nights and weekends is not uncommon for hotel and motel managers. Most lodging facilities' managers work more than 40 hours per week. Managers sometimes experience the pressures of having to coordinate a wide range of functions. Conventions and large groups of tourists may present unusual problems. Dealing with irate patrons and difficult employees can be stressful.

TRAINING AND ADVANCEMENT

Reaching the managerial level is based upon training, experience, and individual initiative. In the past, most managers were promoted from the ranks of front desk clerks, housekeepers, waiter and chefs, and hotel sales workers. Today, post-secondary training in hotel or restaurant management is preferred for most hotel management positions, although a college liberal arts degree may be sufficient when coupled with related hotel experience. Experience working in a hotel—even part-time while in school—is an asset to all persons seeking hotel management careers.

A bachelor's degree in hotel and restaurant administration provides a strong starting point for a career in lodging management. More than 150 colleges and universities offer bachelor's and graduate programs in this field. These programs usually include instruction in hotel administration, accounting, economics, marketing, housekeeping, food service management and catering, hotel maintenance engineering, and data processing—reflecting the widespread use of computers in hotel operations. See Appendix D for a list of colleges and universities offering hospitality degree programs. Part-time or summer jobs in a lodging facility or restaurant often are encouraged by colleges since the experience gained and the contacts made with employers may benefit students when they look for full-time employment after graduation. Some colleges even have campus lodging facilities where students can work. Individuals who cannot afford to attend college can prepare to advance themselves up the hospitality career ladder by taking correspondence courses from the Educational Institute of the American Hotel and Motel Association. This gives them access to hospitality training developed by the industry for the industry. Participants can earn world-recognized certificates backed by the American Hotel and Motel Association.

Sometimes large hotels sponsor specialized on-the-job training programs that let trainees rotate among various departments to gain a thorough knowledge of the hotel's operation. After demonstrating their knowledge and administrative ability in lodging operations, the trainees may advance to department heads and on to assistant managers and managers. And some hotels may help finance the necessary training in hotel management for outstanding employees.

Most hotels promote employees who have proven their ability. Large hotel and motel chains may offer better opportunities for advancement than small, independently owned establishments, but relocation every several years often is necessary for advancement in these chains. Career advancement can be accelerated by completion of certification programs offered by industry associations.

SPECIAL ATTRIBUTES OF LODGING MANAGERS

Lodging managers need to have people skills that equip them to get along with all kinds of people, even in stressful situations. They also need to have initiative, self-discipline, and the ability to organize and direct the work of others.

SALARY AND FRINGE BENEFITS

What managers and assistant managers earn varies greatly according to their job responsibilities and the size of the hotel in which they work. According to a 1993 survey conducted for the American Hotel and Motel Association, the annual salary of assistant hotel managers averaged $32,300. The assistants who were employed in large hotels with more than 350 rooms averaged nearly $38,400, while the assistants in hotels with no more than 150 rooms averaged more than $26,000. Salaries of assistant managers also varied because of differences in duties and responsibilities. For example, food and beverage managers averaged $41,200, according to the same survey, whereas the front office managers averaged $26,500. The level of experience that the manager has also plays an important factor in his or her salary.

The salaries of general managers in 1993 averaged more than $59,100. The average salary for a general manager in a facility with no more than 150 rooms was $44,900, while general managers in large hotels with more than 350 rooms earned an average of $86,700. In some hotels, managers may earn bonuses of up to fifteen percent of their basic salary in some hotels. In addition, they and their families may be furnished with lodging, meals, parking, laundry, and other services. Most managers and assistants receive three to eleven paid holidays a year, paid vacation, sick leave, life insurance, medical benefits, and pension plans. Some hotels offer profit-sharing plans, educational assistance, and other benefits to their employees.

THE PERSONAL STORY OF A GENERAL MANAGER

Michael Conner decided on a career in the lodging industry after a family trip that included stays in hotels. The day after he graduated from high school, he went to a Marriott Hotel in Indianapolis and secured a position as a busperson. Even though he was working full time, he enrolled in a vocational college and took fourteen hours of classes in the hotel and restaurant management program. The management staff at the hotel knew of Michael's interest in a career in hotel management and tried to give him experience by cross-training him. Michael worked in catering and reservations and also had jobs as a desk clerk, telephone operator, bellperson, and reservationist.

After Michael received his associate's degree, he stayed on at the school and started working as a culinary assistant. In this job, Michael assisted the chef, did purchasing for the school's culinary classes, and arranged catering functions with the chef. During this time, he also worked, when needed, at the hotel in the catering department. After working for a year at the school, he heard about a new Marriott that was opening. It was a 146-room Courtyard Hotel that was designed specifically for business travelers. Michael secured a job there as a desk clerk. At the same time, he vowed to get into the Marriott Hotel's management training program. Within six months he was in the program, which was a great hands-on learning experience. Soon he was involved in the opening of a new hotel. Then he was promoted to front desk manager. Basically, he was an assistant manager taking care of front desk administrative tasks, including overseeing reservations, administering staff payroll, and the hiring and disciplining of employees. After a company restructuring that phased out other department heads, he became assistant general manager of the hotel and was running the housekeeping, maintenance, restaurant, and sales and marketing departments. During this time, he always volunteered for Marriott programs. He spent time on the road doing computer updates, training safety and security people in CPR, and doing seminars.

When Michael was in college, he set the long-term goal of being a general manager by the time he was thirty. He achieved this goal when he was only twenty-five years old and was assigned the task of opening a new Courtyard property for Marriott. This hotel was a new style—only 78 rooms, as the company was trying to introduce a smaller hotel in a smaller market in a mid-size town in Illinois. He saw the hotel being built from the ground up and had the responsibility of selecting the entire staff of twenty-three people. Michael was charged with the responsibility of having the hotel ready to open four weeks after it was built; he exceeded all expectations and had it ready in two weeks. At this facility, the management team consisted of Michael, an assistant general manager, and two department supervisors—front desk and housekeeping. The hotel received the Marriott "Best of the Best" award, signifying that it was number one in hospitality and service all four quarters of its first year.

After two years as a general manager, Michael was recruited by Red Roof Inns to return to his home state as general manager of a 108-room economy property that did not have a restaurant. At the present time, this is the fastest-growing segment of the hotel industry. Michael is the only manager at this lodging facility and has the responsibility of running the housekeeping, front office, and maintenance departments.

Michael is not yet thirty years old. However, he has already had experience working at a full-service hotel, a business-class hotel, and an economy lodging. He definitely sees himself continuing in the hospitality industry. His next career move may be to a resort facility. While Michael is busy rapidly climbing the hotel management career ladder, he is also busy doing substitute teaching at his vocational college to "give back" to the school all he gained from it. In addition, he is serving as vice president of the school's hospitality alumni association and is working on recruiting more young people to the hospitality industry.

A DAY IN THE LIFE OF A GENERAL MANAGER

John Stewart works at an all-suites hotel in a large southern city. This lodging facility was designed to accommodate corporate and extended-stay travelers and is part of a chain. It has 116 suites. At the hotel, there are six managers: housekeeping, sales, front office, accounting, maintenance, and complimentary services. One of these managers will check into the hotel each weekend and be the weekend manager. All the managers are on call twenty-four-hours a day, and John says that he is "married to his pager."

John did not have any formal education in hotel and restaurant management. While in college, he secured a summer job as a front desk clerk at a hotel. He enjoyed the environment so much that he kept the job for two years. John's managers were very encouraging and were willing to teach him what he wanted to know. Then he went to the corporate office, where he secured a job installing computers at hotel front desks and training the people to operate them. John then transferred to a regional office as a sales coordinator overseeing sales and marketing for eighteen hotels. This job taught him how to sell hotel rooms. After working in sales for five years, John decided he wanted to manage a hotel. He moved to another company and became the manager of an all-suites hotel, where he stayed for two years before changing companies again. At that time he moved to Virginia to manage another all-suites hotel.

At the facility where John now works, little is routine. He starts work between 8:00 a.m. and 9:00 a.m. and ends between 6:00 p.m. and 7:00 p.m. five to six days a week. When he arrives at work, he reviews the accounting reports of the previous day, the revenue reports, and the night audit reports so he will know how the inn did in the past twenty-four-hour period. He also talks to everyone about how things are going at the hotel. Here is a list of the tasks that John accomplished in one day after doing his routine start-of-the-day work.

- looked at the forecast for the next two months to help anticipate staffing needs and expected revenue
- worked with a group planning to stay at the facility in July to make sure they were definitely coming and were sending in a deposit
- met with a painter to get an estimate for painting the exterior of the lodging
- met with outside vendors about cleaning the curtains
- discussed with the front office manager changes that he wants to make in the reservations system
- held a meeting with the front office and sales managers to talk about how reservations changes will affect sales and revenues
- met with the employee in charge of preventative care about installing new locks
- inspected new locks
- met with the executive housekeeper and the room inspector to discuss the quality of cleanliness in the rooms, especially the issue of what the mirrors look like
- talked at considerable length with the local fire chief about fire department services
- spent considerable time at desk in lobby talking to guests
- faxed a business contract to a company
- checked how the changes in the reservations system are working

John has his own managerial style, which features sitting at a desk in the lobby so he can observe what is taking place around him and so that the guests know where to find him. He believes this makes his inn "management friendly." He believes that responding to what the guests need is critical to his facility's success According to John, the inn must make sure that the guests receive what was promised to them. Another critical facet to John's job is generating revenue. This means setting the room prices within the parameters that earn the most revenue. If a room is not sold on a given night, that revenue is lost forever.

THE PERSONAL STORY OF A DIRECTOR OF HUMAN RESOURCES

As the director of human resources, Rose Lloyd is responsible for managing the human resources department of a 525-room full-service upscale hotel in a major metropolitan area. She is responsible for hiring all new employees, handling employee relations, and training hotel personnel. In selecting individuals to fill top-level management positions, she coordinates her efforts with the general manager. At all times, she must make sure that there are enough people to do all the jobs in the hotel. Rose handles her many tasks with the help of a training manager, a human resources coordinator, and a department secretary. Because the job market in the area is tight, Rose must have excellent contacts within the community to recruit workers. In her job as director of human resources, she must play the roles of judge, jury, mom, teacher, and truant officer in dealing with hotel employees.

Rose is very enthusiastic about career opportunities in the hotel and motel industry. Two great advantages of working in this industry are the many opportunities for advancement and the abundance of jobs in many different areas. Rose also points out that individuals can advance up the career ladder in this field with and without schooling. The ascent will be faster, however, with schooling.

THE PERSONAL STORY OF A FOOD AND BEVERAGE DIRECTOR

Suresh Rao brings an international background to his present job as executive assistant manager of food and beverages in a large full-service upscale hotel. His climb to this position began in India. After studying economics in college, he decided on a career in the hospitality industry because he wanted to work with different hotels and see the world. His first position was as a busboy in a large intercontinental hotel chain in India. Suresh then moved to Europe where he received extensive on-the-job training that allowed him to advance within another international hotel chain. At the same time, he learned to speak several languages, including Dutch, Flemish, and German. He came to the United States almost twenty years ago to work as an assistant manager at a hotel that was part of a large international chain. He was soon promoted to food and beverage director at another hotel in the chain. Then he worked for several other chains.

Today, Suresh is in charge of the overall operation of the hotel's food and beverage department, which includes all food and beverage outlets in the hotel, catering, and room service. His responsibilities include supervising 150 people and the entire food and beverage operations. This includes overseeing the purchasing of food; ensuring the quality of the food; handling the hiring and scheduling of employees; and working for revenue growth and profitability in his department. Reporting directly to Suresh are the executive chef, the restaurant manager, the director of catering, the banquet manager, and the executive steward. These individuals supervise the staff members within their departments.

Suresh generally works six days a week and enjoys his job because it is challenging and no two days are alike. He likes seeing satisfied guests and employees enjoying their jobs. His special joy is helping people advance within the industry and achieve their career goals.

THE PERSONAL STORY OF AN EXECUTIVE HOUSEKEEPER

Archie Henderson was a police officer when he began his lodging facility career working part-time in the security department of a full-service upscale hotel. The head housekeeper noticed that Archie was always cleaning up after people and offered him a job in housekeeping. Archie started out as a management trainee called a team leader. The team leaders were each responsible for the cleaning of a section of the hotel. Archie's section was the third through seventh floors. This was a challenging job because Archie had to deal with employees who had limited education and little career enthusiasm. Archie soon discovered that he had a knack for dealing with people, and within eight months, his section was the cleanest in the hotel. Additionally, many of his workers had been recognized as employees of the month. In this job Archie did no cleaning; he just supervised and trained the workers and participated in the hiring of new employees. Typically, he would come to work at 6:00 a.m. and leave at 5:30 p.m. The cleaners would work from 8:00 a.m. until 4:30 p.m. Archie needed the extra time to handle the paperwork and to inspect each room for cleanliness and other details. This job was non-stop work—often six days a week. And the weekends were the busiest times because there were frequently more people in each room at that time.

Archie's superior work was soon recognized by the housekeeping department and was promoted to assistant executive housekeeper. Now he was working on the second shift—from 3:00 p.m. to midnight—and frequently staying later to make sure everything was done for the night. His responsibilities included checking on other team leaders, the public space workers, and the overall cleanliness of the hotel. Archie also had to manage the payroll and order all supplies while staying within the budget.

The harder Archie worked, the more promotions he received. Soon he was the executive housekeeper at the hotel where he had started just two years earlier as a management trainee. Archie points out that quite a few cleaners have worked their way up the ladder in housekeeping. They do need, however, to get some education and be able to handle numbers in order to manage the payroll and forecast future needs. As executive housekeeper, Archie delegated many of his responsibilities, yet at the same time he had to remain involved in all managerial areas. Much of his time was now involved with training and teaching team leaders. In addition, he had the responsibility of meeting corporate cleanliness standards.

Within three months, Archie went to a bigger hotel in the chain to serve as one of two assistant executive housekeepers. One was responsible for room cleanliness and training, while the other was in charge of payroll, purchasing, and public areas. They reversed jobs after six months. Within one year, Archie was the executive housekeeper at this facility, with two assistants and eleven team leaders. In this chain he needed to have a bachelor's degree in order to advance further.

Archie next left the hotel field to go into business for himself for awhile. But soon he found himself back in housekeeping at a luxury hotel as an assistant executive housekeeper working with a former co-worker who was the executive housekeeper. He was part of the team that won the Malcolm Baldridge Award, a national quality award, for this hotel for the first time. After another career interruption to help family members with health problems, he worked briefly for another hotel as an executive housekeeper before moving to his present job.

For the past three years, Archie has been an executive housekeeper at a full-service upscale hotel, handling a staff of 116 employees. When he was hired, this hotel was close to failing the chain's quality standards for cleanliness. Within four months, he had won the general manager's traveling trophy award for the most improved department. Turning the housekeeping department around involved spending a lot of time training the employees. It was a challenging task, because 22 of the workers were immigrants who spoke limited English. However, Archie's work was well-recognized: he won the training award of the local hotel plus the "manager of the quarter" award. In addition, his work at the hotel was further recognized when he was nominated for a Leadership Development Award in his city.

While working hard on the job, Archie has also been taking classes to increase his expertise in management. He has earned a Human Resources Management Certificate and is working on getting housekeeper certification from the American Hotel and Motel Association. Because Archie finds caring for people very rewarding, he anticipates that his next career move will be into the human resources department.

LOOKING AT THE FUTURE

The employment of lodging managers is expected to grow as fast as the average for all occupations through the year 2005. This is because more lodging facilities will be built and business travel and domestic and foreign tourism will continue to grow. Because of the growing share of the industry that will be composed of economy properties, the number of manager jobs is expected to grow more slowly than the industry. This is because economy properties generally have fewer managers than full-service hotels. Economy hotels offer clean, comfortable rooms and front desk services without costly extras like restaurants and room service. Because there are fewer departments in these hotels, fewer managers are needed at the hotel sites. Typically, economy hotels have a general manager, and regional offices of the hotel management company employ department managers, such as executive housekeepers, to oversee several hotels.

Even though industry growth will be concentrated in the economy sector, full-service hotels will continue to offer many training and managerial opportunities. Most openings are expected to occur as experienced managers transfer to other occupations, retire, or stop working for some reason.

FOR MORE INFORMATION

Individuals can learn more about the lodging industry by obtaining a copy of *Hotel, Motel Careers... A World of Opportunities.* Requests for single copies should include a self-addressed stamped envelope and be directed to:

AH&MA
1201 New York Avenue, NW
Washington, DC 20005-3921
(202) 289-3193

Requests for catalogs of junior and senior college programs in hotel, restaurant, and institutional management in the United States should be sent to:

Educational Foundation of the National Restaurant
  Association
250 South Wacker Drive, Suite 1400
Chicago, IL 60606

More than 1,000 vocational schools, community colleges, and universities in the United States and abroad offer courses in hospitality management. The Council on Hotel Restaurant and Institutional Education (CHRIE) offers a list of schools with hospitality programs. Contact:

CHRIE
1200 17th Street, NW
7th Floor
Washington, DC 20036-3097
(202) 331-5990

To find out how to prepare yourself for a career in the hospitality industry, contact:

Educational Institute of AH&MA
P.O. Box 1240
East Lansing, MI 48826-9924
(800) 344-3320, ext. 3160

WORKING IN RESTAURANTS

The third-largest industry in the United States is the restaurant business. This is not surprising since one in every three meals is eaten away from home. The average growth rate for the restaurant business is faster than that for any other business in the United States. Furthermore, the number of people employed in the restaurant business is more than three times the number employed in automobile and steel manufacturing companies combined.

Eating out is not a new concept. As early as 1700 B.C. people were eating in taverns. Of course, the menus were not the same as today's menus—those early "menus" consisted of a single dish—such as a combination of wild fowl, cereal, and onion. However, the restaurant business that began developing in England, France, Germany, and Sweden in the Middle Ages did have a large influence on the habits and customs found in the restaurant business in the United States today. The word "restaurant" comes from the Latin *restaurare,* meaning "to restore." It was first used to describe an eating establishment that had this message inscribed on its door: *Venite ad me omnes qui stomacho lavoratoratis et ego restaurabo vos* which meant "Come to me all whose stomachs cry out in anguish and I shall restore you."

The restaurant business truly began to grow in the United States after the start of World War II. Before this time, many Americans had never eaten in a restaurant. Away from home for the first time, many people began to eat out and to enjoy the experience. In recent years, the number of people eating in restaurants has rapidly increased due to changing lifestyles. Many women have entered the workforce, and the numbers of unmarried adults and of single parents have increased. For many people, it is just easier to eat meals in restaurants, and rising family incomes are making it easier to do so.

There are two main kinds of restaurants: sit-down restaurants, which seat customers at tables and give them menus, and fast-food restaurants. In 1994, sales in fast-food restaurants surpassed those in sit-down establishments for the first time. The history of fast-food restaurants is quite short; McDonald's was established in 1948, for example, and Wendy's in 1969.

The National Restaurant Association provides these food service industry facts that clearly show the impact the industry has on the economy of the United States:

- More than one out of every four retail outlets is an eating or drinking establishment.
- Eating and drinking places have the greatest number of establishments and number of employees among all retailers.
- Approximately five percent of the nation's work force is employed at eating and drinking places.
- Eating and drinking places are extremely labor intensive—sales per full-time equivalent non-supervisory employee are notably lower than other industries.

LOOKING AT RESTAURANT JOBS

Just like the lodging industry, restaurants have front-of-the-house and back-of-the-house employees. Typically, those working in the front of the house have contact with customers. In sit-down restaurants where customers are given menus, you will find:

bar managers	hosts/hostesses
bussers	server assistants
cashiers	sommeliers
dining room managers	waiters/waitresses
dining room supervisors	wine stewards
head waiters/waitresses	

The individuals who are involved with the preparation of food are the back-of-the-house employees. Within this group at sit-down restaurants are:

chefs	kitchen supervisors
cooks	kitchen workers
dishwashers	pastry chefs
executive chefs	prep cooks
kitchen managers	sous chefs

At fast-food restaurants, front-of-the-store jobs are the ones that customers see fast-food workers doing. These employees take orders, take money, and assemble or pack orders. Back-of-the-store employees cook and prepare food and clean the equipment.

LOOKING AT JOBS IN SIT-DOWN RESTAURANTS

Whether waiters, waitresses, server assistants, and hosts work in small, informal diners or large, elegant restaurants, all food service workers deal with customers. The quality of service they provide determines in part whether the patron is likely to return. The efficient and profitable operation of restaurants depends on the skill of their managers and assistant managers.

ON-THE-JOB RESPONSIBILITIES OF FOOD SERVICE WORKERS

Waiters and Waitresses

Waiters and waitresses take customers' orders, serve food and beverages, prepare itemized checks, and may accept payments. The manner in which they handle these tasks depends on where they work. In fine restaurants where gourmet meals are served, they work at a more leisurely pace and offer more personal service to customers. They may describe how various items on the menu are prepared and even prepare some salads and other special dishes at tableside. In less formal restaurants, waiters and waitresses are expected to provide fast and efficient, yet courteous service. They may also be expected to perform other duties that waiters and waitresses may not have at more formal restaurants—such as seating guests, setting up and clearing tables, and cashiering.

Server Assistants

Server assistants—also called dining room attendants—aid waiters and waitresses by cleaning tables, removing dirty dishes to the kitchen, and keeping the serving area stocked with supplies. They replenish the supply of clean linens, dishes, silverware, and glasses in the dining room. Server assistants set tables with clean tablecloths, napkins, silverware, glasses, and dishes and serve ice water, rolls, and butter to customers. At the end of the meal, they remove dirty dishes and soiled linens from the tables. If they work in cafeterias, they stock serving tables with food, trays, dishes, and silverware and may carry trays to dining tables for customers.

Counter Assistants

Counter assistants take orders and serve food at counters. In cafeterias, they serve food displayed on counters and steam tables as requested by customers, carve meat, dish out vegetables, ladle sauces and soups, and fill cups and glasses. In lunchrooms and coffee shops, counter attendants take orders from customers seated at the counter, transmit the orders to the kitchen, and pick up and serve food when it is ready. They also fill cups and glasses with coffee, soda, and other beverages and prepare fountain specialties such as milkshakes and ice cream sundaes. They often prepare some simple items, such as sandwiches and salads, and wrap or place orders to be taken out and consumed elsewhere. Their duties include cleaning counters, writing up itemized checks, and accepting payment.

Hosts and Hostesses   Hosts and hostesses are restaurants' personal representatives to customers. They warmly welcome guests, courteously direct customers to where they may leave coats, and indicate where they may wait until their table is ready. Their duties include assigning guests to tables, escorting them to their seats, and providing menus. They try to ensure that service is prompt and courteous and the meal enjoyable; they may also adjust complaints of dissatisfied customers. Hosts and hostesses are also expected to schedule dining reservations, arrange parties, and organize any special services that are required. In some restaurants, they act as cashiers.

WORKING CONDITIONS

Working in food service is one job where employees are on their feet most of the time. And they often have to carry heavy trays of food, dishes, and glassware. During busy dining periods, these workers are under pressure to serve customers quickly and efficiently. While the work is relatively safe, care must be taken to avoid slips, falls, and burns.

Although some food service workers work forty hours or more a week, the majority are employed part time—a larger proportion than in almost any other occupation. In addition, they are expected to work evenings, weekends, and holidays. Some work split shifts, in which they work for several hours during the middle of the day, take a few hours off in the late afternoon, and then return to their jobs for the evening hours.

QUALIFICATIONS FOR BECOMING A FOOD SERVICE WORKER

Special Attributes   Most employers place an emphasis on personal qualities. Food service workers should be well-spoken and have a neat and clean appearance because they are in close and constant contact with the public. They should enjoy dealing with all kinds of people, and a pleasant disposition and sense of humor are important. Waiters and waitresses need a good memory to avoid confusing customers' orders and to recall the faces, names, and preferences of frequent customers. They should also be good at arithmetic if they have to total bills without the aid of a calculator or cash register. In restaurants specializing in foreign foods, a knowledge of how to pronounce the house specialties is helpful.

Education   There are no specific educational requirements for food service jobs as waiters, waitresses, server assistants, counter attendants, hosts, or hostesses. However, many employers prefer to hire high school graduates for waiter, waitress, host, and hostess positions. Hotels and restaurants that have rigid table-service standards like to hire experienced employees.

ADVANCING UP THE CAREER LADDER

Due to the relatively small size of most sit-down restaurants, opportunities for promotion are limited. After gaining experience, some dining room and cafeteria server assistants are able to advance to waiter or waitress jobs. For waiters and waitresses, advancement usually is limited to becoming hosts or hostesses or finding a job in a larger restaurant where prospects for earning tips are better. Some hosts, hostesses, waiters, and waitresses advance to supervisory jobs, such as maitre d'hotel, dining room supervisor, or restaurant manager. In large restaurant chains, food service workers who excel at their work are often invited to enter the company's formal management training program. Restaurant jobs should never be thought of as dead-end jobs. According to a survey conducted for the National Restaurant Association, two-thirds of those who own or operate a restaurant today worked their way up from lower-level positions. Thirty-four percent actually started out as a busser, dishwasher, or server.

SALARY AND FRINGE BENEFITS

Excluding hosts and hostesses, food service workers at sit-down restaurants generally derive their earnings from a combination of hourly wages and customer tips. Their wages and the amount of tips they receive vary greatly, depending on the type of job and establishment. In some restaurants, waiters and waitresses contribute a portion of their tips to a tip pool, which is distributed among many of the establishment's other food service workers and kitchen staff. Food service workers who are employed full time often receive paid vacation and sick leave and health insurance, but part-time workers generally do not receive such benefits. However, many employers provide free meals and furnish uniforms.

LOOKING AT THE FUTURE OF JOBS FOR FOOD SERVICE EMPLOYEES

The future is bright for jobs as waiters, waitresses, server assistants, counter assistants, hosts, and hostesses. Most openings occur because of the need to replace the high number of workers who leave food service jobs each year. However, demand for workers will also increase as more people eat meals in restaurants. As the population grows older, it is expected that the demand will increase for employees to work in sit-down restaurants. Because earnings are highest in popular restaurants and fine dining establishments, keen competition should be anticipated for the limited number of jobs in these restaurants.

ON-THE-JOB RESPONSIBILITIES OF RESTAURANT MANAGERS

Although the cuisine offered, its price, and the setting vary greatly, the managers of restaurants have many responsibilities in common. In order to run an operation both efficiently and profitably, the managers and assistant managers of restaurants must select and appropriately price interesting menu items, order and effectively use food and other supplies, achieve consistent quality in food preparation and service, recruit and train an adequate number of workers and supervise their work, and attend to the various administrative aspects of the business.

In most restaurants, the manager is assisted by one or more assistant managers, depending on the size and business hours of the establishment. In large establishments, as well as in many others that offer fine dining, the management team consists of a general manager, one or more assistant managers, and an executive chef. The executive chef is responsible for the operation of the kitchen, while the assistant managers oversee service in the dining room and other areas of the restaurant. In these restaurants, much of the administrative work—such as payroll, paying suppliers, and keeping records of costs—is handled by bookkeepers. In restaurants that operate long hours, seven days a week, the manager is aided by several assistant managers, each of whom supervises a shift.

WORKING CONDITIONS

Managers are quite often the first to arrive and the last to leave. Frequently, they work fifty or more hours a week. They can also expect to work evenings and weekends, as these are popular dining periods. Being a manager can be a pressure-filled job, especially during peak dining hours, when the manager must simultaneously coordinate a wide range of activities, handle problems with irate customers, and deal with uncooperative employees.

PREPARATION FOR BECOMING A RESTAURANT MANAGER

Experience Requirements

Many restaurant manager positions are filled by promoting experienced food service workers. Waiters, waitresses, and chefs who have demonstrated their potential for handling increased responsibility sometimes advance to assistant manager or management trainee when openings occur. General managers need experience working as assistant managers.

Personal Requirements

Restaurant management can be demanding, so good health and stamina are important. Self-discipline, initiative, and leadership ability are absolutely essential. Managers must be able to solve problems and concentrate on details. They need good communication skills to deal with customers, employees, and suppliers. They must also have a neat and clean appearance since they are often in close personal contact with the public.

Educational Requirements

Most restaurant chains prefer to hire managers with degrees in food service management, although they often hire graduates with degrees in other areas who have demonstrated interest and aptitude. A list of colleges and universities offering degrees in restaurant management is given in Appendix D. Prospective managers not wanting to pursue a four-year degree should investigate the food service programs at community colleges and technical institutes. Some programs combine classroom and laboratory study with internships that provide on-the-job experience.

Training

Restaurant chains have rigorous formal training programs for individuals hired for management jobs. Through a combination of classroom and on-the-job training, trainees receive instruction and gain work experience in all aspects of the operation of a restaurant, including food preparation, nutrition, sanitation, security, company policies and procedures, personnel management, recordkeeping, and the preparation of reports.

Certification

Recognition of professional competence is shown by restaurant managers who have earned the designation of Foodservice Management Professional (FMP). The Educational Foundation of the National Restaurant Association awards the FMP to managers who achieve a qualifying score on a written examination, complete a series of courses, and meet work experience standards.

Finding a Job

The management application for employment at the MCL Cafeterias chain (see pages 142–145) shows the types of information prospective managers need to provide future employers. Completing an application satisfactorily is generally a prerequisite to obtaining a job interview for a position.

ADVANCING UP THE CAREER LADDER

Assistant managers can become managers. Managers typically advance by relocating to larger restaurants or regional management positions within chains. Some managers open their own restaurants, and others advance to hotel management positions in food service.

SALARY AND FRINGE BENEFITS

Earnings of restaurant managers vary greatly, depending on their responsibilities and the type and size of the establishment. Manager trainees can anticipate a median base salary of $20,000 to more than $27,900 in the largest restaurants. They can also expect annual bonuses or incentive payments of $1,000 to $3,000. Managers receive a median base salary of approximately $27,900 and can earn more than $45,000. Most will receive bonuses based on their performance, ranging from $2,000 to $8,000. Most salaried managers receive free meals, sick leave, health and life insurance, and one to three weeks of paid vacation.

THE PERSONAL STORY OF A GENERAL MANAGER OF A CAFETERIA

Jay Chandler began his restaurant career working at a pizza restaurant when he was in high school. When he graduated from college with a degree in business management, he was uncertain about what direction to take. He received two job offers, one from a bank and one from a Mexican restaurant. He chose the restaurant since the job offered more money; thus, he started his restaurant career as the general manager of a small full-service Mexican restaurant. He then transferred to a steak house in a site that had been converted from an old railroad station. Jay stayed at this job for $1^1/2$ years, often working six or seven days a week and as many as ninety-five hours a week. His next job was as assistant manager of a smorgasbord restaurant. Then this company gave him the task of opening a new restaurant and serving as general manager. The company suffered financial ups and downs, and Jay elected to leave the restaurant business and try his hand at sales work. After a short stint in sales, he returned to the restaurant world, taking a job with the company where he has worked for the past eleven years.

Today, Jay is general manager of one of the twenty-eight cafeterias of this family-owned corporation. He has worked at eleven different locations of the restaurant and advanced up the career ladder from service manager, In his present position, he oversees the entire operation of a restaurant with the help of three assistant managers. The first assistant manager is the chef, who makes up the menus and orders all the inventory for the kitchen. The second assistant is the service manager, who has a primarily front-of-the-house job making sure that the servers are doing their jobs correctly and that the housekeeping staff is doing a good job. The third assistant is the line supervisor, who has the responsibility of making sure that the food line looks neat and tidy. Altogether, the restaurant has ninety employees. To become a manager at this company, Jay had to complete a twenty-three-week training program that covered everything from cleaning to knowing the 400 different recipes that the cafeteria offers.

Jay's restaurant has a sales volume of more than $2.3 million annually— the second-highest in the chain. It also serves as the new-manager training unit, as well as a new-product test unit. During Jay's tenure at this location, the cafeteria has had four record sales years as well as four record profit years. He appreciates the fact that this company says employees will work only five days a week and means it. He also likes the fact that he is working for a stable company that cares about family values.

LOOKING AT THE FUTURE FOR RESTAURANT MANAGERS

To meet the ever-increasing demand for consuming meals outside the home, more restaurants will be built and more managers will be needed to supervise them. Future managers can expect to find more jobs working for national chains as fewer new restaurants are independently owned and operated. Job opportunities

Rev. 1/96

DATE _____

MCL CAFETERIAS
2730 EAST 62ND STREET • INDIANAPOLIS, IN 46220 • (317) 257-5425

Management Application

POSITION APPLIED FOR	**PERSONAL INFORMATION**	HOME PHONE & AREA CODE

Name _____ Social Security No. _____

☐ Yes   ☐ No

Driver's License Number	Year Obtained	Driver's License Now Valid?	Issuing State or Province

PRESENT ADDRESS _____
(STREET)   (CITY)

_____ How Long? _____
(STATE)   (ZIP)

PREVIOUS ADDRESS
(if less than five years) _____ How Long? _____

DO YOU HAVE AUTHORIZATION TO WORK IN THE UNITED STATES? _____

HAVE YOU BEEN CONVICTED OF A FELONY IN THE PAST SEVEN YEARS? _____

RECRUITMENT SOURCE?   Newspaper _____ Agency Name _____ Other _____

Have you previously applied to, or been employed by this Company?   ☐ Yes   ☐ No   When? _____

Can you perform the functions of the job for which you are applying with or without reasonable accommodations?

_____

How would you perform the tasks and with what accommodations?

_____

_____

RELOCATION: ☐ NOT NOW   ☐ AFTER 5 MONTHS   ☐ NO   ☐ YES   DO YOU PREFER: ☐ IND.   ☐ ILL.   ☐ OHIO

EDUCATION

SCHOOLS	NAMES AND ADDRESSES OF INSTITUTIONS	DATES		GRADUATED		DIPLOMA or DEGREE RECEIVED	SUBJECTS or SPECIALI-ZATION
		From Mo.-Yr.	To Mo.-Yr.	Yes	No		
COLLEGE OR UNIVERSITY							
HIGH SCHOOL							

MILITARY SERVICE

DATES IN SERVICE: From _____ To _____ Branch of Service _____

Rank and Specialization _____ Discharge Date _____

    All applicants are considered for employment without regard to race, color, creed, national origin, religion, sex, age or disability, in accordance with applicable equal employment opportunity laws.

    All information given is true and accurate to the best of my knowledge. I hereby authorize MCL, Inc. to make inquiry regarding my schools and past service with other employers and grant permission for them to release information to MCL concerning me. I understand misrepresentation or omission of facts called for on this Application is cause for dismissal.

    I understand that nothing contained in this employment application or in the granting of an interview is intended to create an employment contract between MCL, Inc. and myself for either employment or for the providing of any benefit. No promises regarding employment or duration of employment has been made to me and I understand that no such promise or guarantee is binding upon MCL, Inc. If an employment relationship is established, I understand that I have the right to terminate my employment at any time and that MCL, Inc. retains a similar right, with or without cause.

Date _____ Signature _____

An Equal Opportunity Employer

MCL
CAFETERIA

EMPLOYMENT HISTORY

PRESENT OR LAST JOB

Name of Company	Mailing Address of Company	Name and Phone Number of Area Manager
		Name and Phone Number of Your Immediate Supervisor

Date of Hire	Starting Title	Starting Pay	Ending Title	Ending Pay & Bonus
Date of Term				

Ending Job Responsibilities:

Reason for Leaving or Reason for Wanting to Leave. Explain:

Were You Discharged?   ☐ Yes   ☐ No   ☐ Let's Discuss

May we Contact this Employer?   ☐ Yes   ☐ No   If no, why not?

Interviewer Comments:

NEXT TO LAST JOB

Name of Company	Mailing Address of Company	Name and Phone Number of Area Manager
		Name and Phone Number of Your Immediate Supervisor

Date of Hire	Starting Title	Starting Pay	Ending Title	Ending Pay & Bonus
Date of Term				

Ending Job Responsibilities:

Reason for Leaving or Reason for Wanting to Leave. Explain:

Were You Discharged?   ☐ Yes   ☐ No   ☐ Let's Discuss

May we Contact this Employer?   ☐ Yes   ☐ No   If no, why not?

Interviewer Comments:

EMPLOYMENT HISTORY (Continued)

THIRD LAST JOB

Name of Company	Mailing Address of Company	Name and Phone Number of Area Manager
		Name and Phone Number of Your Immediate Supervisor

Date of Hire	Starting Title	Starting Pay	Ending Title	Ending Pay & Bonus
Date of Term				

Ending Job Responsibilities:

Reason for Leaving or Reason for Wanting to Leave. Explain:

Were You Discharged?　　　□ Yes　　　□ No　　　□ Let's Discuss

May we Contact this Employer?　　　□ Yes　　　□ No　　　If no, why not?

Interviewer Comments:

FOURTH LAST JOB

Name of Company	Mailing Address of Company	Name and Phone Number of Area Manager
		Name and Phone Number of Your Immediate Supervisor

Date of Hire	Starting Title	Starting Pay	Ending Title	Ending Pay & Bonus
Date of Term				

Ending Job Responsibilities:

Reason for Leaving or Reason for Wanting to Leave. Explain:

Were You Discharged?　　　□ Yes　　　□ No　　　□ Let's Discuss

May we Contact this Employer?　　　□ Yes　　　□ No　　　If no, why not?

Interviewer Comments:

CONTINUED ON BACK

Please explain why you feel you should be given this position. What does MCL offer you that your present or past employers have not? What are your career goals?

INTERVIEWER COMMENTS

will be best for those who have bachelor's or associate's degree in restaurant or food service management. Managers will also be needed to replace those who transfer or leave the occupation. This occupation is growing faster than the average for all occupations.

OWNING A RESTAURANT

Many restaurant owners have come up through the ranks from entry-level positions, while others have been restaurant managers. Anyone thinking about opening a restaurant needs to realize that there is no guarantee of success. The competition among restaurants is always intense, and many restaurants do not survive. Here are some of the steps that are involved in opening a restaurant:

- Gain restaurant experience before opening a restaurant.
- Develop a business plan that includes price range of the food, staffing and inventory requirements, hours of operation, and projected sales and earnings.
- Do a market study that includes the expected clientele, type of restaurant, and atmosphere of restaurant.
- Hire a lawyer.
- Select a site.
- Research codes, ordinances, and permits.
- Secure adequate financing.
- Consider franchise opportunities.
- Organize the restaurant: this includes selecting the menu, planning the layout, and choosing the staff.

THE PERSONAL STORY OF TWO RESTAURANT OWNERS

Mary and Kammel Emeish decided to open a restaurant featuring Middle Eastern food because they believed that there was a demand for this type of food, and they were familiar with this cuisine. They chose a location in an area that had high restaurant traffic. After making sure they had adequate financing, they leased a building for their restaurant. Then they designed the layout of the restaurant, with the help of an architect to maximize the use of the available space. They bought all new equipment. (They say they would buy used if they were to start another restaurant, because the cost would be cut in half.) In decorating their restaurant the Emeishes chose to create a timeless atmosphere rather than one that was merely trendy. Before opening, they had to secure a number of permits and licenses, especially liquor licenses, and to make sure that the restaurant met health board inspection requirements. They also had to establish bank procedures so that they could accept credit cards. Once they had accomplished these tasks, they started to advertise the grand opening of their restaurant and advertise for help. They wanted a small staff of dependable people who could be counted on to help with everything. The Emeishes themselves planned to work at the restaurant, with Mary doing most of the cooking.

Mary and Kammel enjoyed the restaurant that they established. They liked the feeling of success and challenges it brought them and the compliments of their customers. They did not like the fact that running a restaurant was a twenty-four-hour business for them and that they had to put their personal lives on hold. They also discovered that they could not count completely on their staff. They advise future restaurant owners to make sure that they have the money, desire, and time to commit to a business that will play such a big role in the owners' lives.

LOOKING AT THE JOBS OF CHEFS, COOKS, AND OTHER KITCHEN WORKERS

It is important to every restaurant to have a reputation for serving good food whether the establishment prides itself on hamburgers and French fries or exotic foreign cuisine. The reputation of a restaurant depends greatly on its back-of-the-house employees—chefs, cooks, and other kitchen workers. They determine the quality of the food that is served.

The type of food a restaurant serves establishes the personnel who are needed to prepare it. A restaurant with a wide variety of items on the menu that are time-consuming and difficult to prepare may need a staff with several chefs and cooks, sometimes called assistant or apprentice chefs, and many less-skilled workers. In these kitchens each chef or cook usually has a special assignment and often a special job title—vegetable, fry, or sauce cook, for example. Smaller, full-service restaurants that offer casual dining often feature a limited number of easy-to-prepare items, supplemented by short-order specialties and ready-made desserts. Typically, one cook prepares all of the food with the help of a short-order cook and one or two other kitchen workers. On the other hand, a restaurant with a menu of items like sandwiches and hamburgers that can be prepared easily and rapidly needs only a fast-food or short-order cook with limited cooking skills.

ON-THE-JOB RESPONSIBILITIES OF KITCHEN STAFF

Executive Chefs

Executive chefs coordinate the work of the kitchen staff and often direct certain kinds of food preparation. They decide the size of servings, sometimes plan menus, and buy food supplies.

Chefs and Cooks

Chefs and cooks are responsible for preparing meals that are tasty and attractively presented. Chefs are the most highly skilled, trained, and experienced kitchen workers. Although the terms chef and cook are sometimes used interchangeably, a cook generally has more limited skills. Many chefs have earned fame for both themselves and the restaurants, hotels, and institutions where they work because of their skill in artfully preparing traditional favorites and creating new dishes and improving familiar ones.

Restaurant Chefs and Cooks

Restaurant chefs and cooks generally prepare a wide selection of dishes for each meal, cooking most individual servings to order. Chefs and cooks measure, mix, and cook ingredients according to recipes. In the course of their work, they use a variety of pots, pans, cutlery, and equipment, including ovens, broilers, grills, slicers, grinders, and blenders. They are often responsible for directing the work of other kitchen workers, estimating food requirements, and ordering food supplies. Some chefs and cooks also help plan meals and develop menus.

Bread and Pastry Bakers

Bread and pastry bakers—called pastry chefs in some kitchens—produce baked goods for restaurants. They bake small quantities of breads, rolls, pastries, pies, and cakes, doing most of the work by hand. They measure and mix ingredients, shape and bake the dough, and apply fillings and decorations.

Short-Order Cooks

Short-order cooks prepare foods to order in restaurants and coffee shops that emphasize fast service. They grill and garnish hamburgers, prepare sandwiches, fry eggs, and cook French fried potatoes, often working on several orders at the same time. Prior to busy periods, they may slice meats and cheeses or prepare coleslaw or potato salad. During slow periods, they may clean the grill, the food-preparation surfaces, the counters, and the floors.

Other Kitchen Workers

Other kitchen workers perform tasks requiring less skill; they work under the direction of chefs and cooks. They weigh and measure ingredients, fetch pots and pans, and stir and strain soups and sauces. They clean, peel, and slice potatoes, other vegetables and fruits, and make salads. They also may cut and grind meats, poultry, and seafood in preparation for cooking. Their responsibilities also include cleaning work areas, equipment and utensils, and dishes and silverware.

WORKING CONDITIONS

Working conditions depend to some degree on the age of the kitchen. Many restaurant kitchens have modern equipment, convenient work areas, and air-conditioning, but others, particularly in older and smaller eating places, are frequently not nearly as well-equipped. Whether kitchens are modern or old, workers generally must work close together. And there are job hazards, too, as they are working near hot ovens and grills and lifting heavy pots and pans. Kitchen workers may slip, fall, cut, or burn themselves; however, relatively few serious injuries occur.

Restaurant work frequently includes weekend, holiday, and evening hours because these are the times that customers wish to eat out. Half of all short-order and fast-food cooks and other kitchen workers work part-time. A third of all bakers and restaurant cooks work part-time. Vacation resorts may offer only seasonal employment.

PREPARATION FOR CAREERS IN RESTAURANTS

Individuals can start working in the less-skilled jobs in restaurant kitchens with no experience. And with on-the-job training they can learn to be assistant cooks or short-order cooks. But to become a chef or a cook in a fine restaurant, many years of training or schooling are necessary. Even though a high school diploma is not required for beginning jobs, it is recommended for those planning a career as a cook or chef as it may be a prerequisite for future training or employment.

An increasing number of chefs and cooks are getting their training through high school or post-secondary school vocational programs and two- or four-year college programs. Training in these schools is primarily hands-on, and the subjects are much the same in every school. Students learn to bake, broil, and otherwise prepare food, and to use and care for kitchen equipment. Courses are often included in menu planning, determination of portion size and food cost control, purchasing food supplies in quantity, selection and storage of food, and use of leftover food to minimize waste. Students also learn hotel and restaurant sanitation and public health rules for handling food. Training in supervisory and management skills sometimes is emphasized in courses offered by private vocational schools. Those who do not desire to attend classes may be trained in apprenticeship programs offered by professional culinary institutes, industry associations, and trade unions. One example is the three-year apprenticeship program administered by local chapters of the American Culinary Federation in cooperation with local employers and junior colleges or vocational education institutions. In addition, some large hotels and restaurants operate their own training programs for cooks and chefs. The armed forces are also a good source of training for jobs as chefs and cooks.

ADVANCEMENT IN THE RESTAURANT INDUSTRY

The restaurant industry is one place where the American dream is possible. Individuals can start in entry-level positions and end up being chefs or even restaurant owners. However, individuals who have courses in commercial food preparation may be able to start in a cook or chef job without having to spend time in a lower-skilled kitchen job. And these individuals may have an advantage when looking for jobs in better restaurants. An additional asset in climbing the career ladder is to have certification that formally recognizes the skills of a chef or cook. The American Culinary Federation certifies chefs and cooks at these levels: cook, working chef, executive chef, and master chef. Certification standards are based primarily on experience and formal training.

Advancement opportunities for chefs and cooks are numerous. Many acquire higher-paying positions and new cooking skills by moving from one job to another. Besides culinary skills, advancement also depends on ability to supervise lesser-skilled workers and limit food costs by minimizing waste and accurately anticipating the amount of perishable supplies needed. Some cooks and chefs gradually advance to executive chef positions or supervisory or management positions, particularly in hotels, clubs, or larger, more elegant restaurants. Some eventually go into business as caterers or restaurant owners, while others may become instructors in vocational programs in high schools, junior and community colleges, and other academic institutions.

SPECIAL ATTRIBUTES OF KITCHEN EMPLOYEES

To be a successful chef, cook, or kitchen worker, it is absolutely essential to have an interest in food. Chefs and cooks must also be creative in concocting new recipes and must stay current with food trends. The ability to work as part of a team, a keen sense of taste and smell, and personal cleanliness are important attributes that chefs, cooks, and other kitchen workers should possess. Furthermore, it is important to have good health. Most states require health certificates indicating that restaurant workers are free from contagious diseases.

SALARY AND FRINGE BENEFITS

The salaries that chefs, cooks, and other kitchen workers earn depend greatly on where they live and where they work. The more elegant and fine a restaurant is, the higher the salary at all levels. Executive chefs may earn more than $40,000 a year. It is not unusual for "superstar" chefs to earn more than $100,000 a year. According to the National Restaurant Association, median hourly wage for cooks, assistant cooks, and short order cooks is less than $7.00.

Some employers provide uniforms and free meals. However, federal law permits employers to deduct from wages the cost, or *fair value,* of any meals or lodging provided, and some employers exercise this right. Benefits—including the typical package of paid vacation, sick leave, and health insurance—are available for full-time restaurant employees. Part-time workers usually do not receive these benefits.

In some large hotels and restaurants, kitchen workers belong to unions. The principal unions are the Hotel Employees and Restaurant Employees International Union and the Service Employees International Union.

THE PERSONAL STORY OF A CHEF

Dieter Puska was born in Austria. His family was in the retail and food business, so he has been around food all his life. Originally, he went to college to study business, but after two years he changed his major to hotel and restaurant management. He trained to be a chef and served as an apprentice for three years. Through working at different hotels and restaurants, Dieter gained more experience and also had the opportunity to travel. He was offered jobs in different cities in the United States. He selected Cincinnati and planned to stay there for only two years, to gain additional experience. However, upon arrival in the United States, he was transferred to Indianapolis to be a sous chef and has remained there ever since.

In 1976, Dieter decided to open his own restaurant, the Glass Chimney, which has been widely acclaimed for its excellence. The restaurant offers fine dining in a sophisticated setting, and the menu includes such gourmet dishes as *cotelette de veau* (provimi veal chop brushed with olive oil and fresh herbs), *carre d'agneau roti* (roasted domestic rack of lamb seasoned with fresh herbs), and *sabayon aux grand marnier* (a rich custard dessert). Dieter created the menu and was the chef.

In 1980, Dieter opened another restaurant next door to the Glass Chimney and called it Deeters. This restaurant had a more casual atmosphere than his first restaurant. It featured such menu items as shrimp or king crab cocktail, filet of beef Black Angus center cut with bearnaise sauce, soft-shell crabs pane, and cheesecake. As in his first restaurant, only the best-quality food was creatively prepared and served. Subsequently, Dieter joined with a friend to start an even more casual restaurant called Deeter's & Gabe's—a rotisserie with an open kitchen. There such items as French onion soup, woodburning-oven-roasted roast beef sandwiches, Louisiana soft-shell crab, Greek salads, and chocolate mousse are served.

Dieter's day begins when he stops at Deeter's & Gabe's about 8:30 a.m. He writes the specials of the day and then checks to make sure everything is running smoothly. Around 10:30 he arrives at his office at the Glass Chimney and does paperwork (there is considerable paperwork involved in owning three restaurants). He also runs errands to places like the post office and the bank. Then during the afternoon he checks on the operation of the Glass Chimney and Deeters. As the executive chef of these restaurants, he no longer cooks all the time. He does step in when needed. In the evenings, he usually spends some time at both the Glass Chimney and Deeter's, supervising the operation and greeting patrons. On his way home, he stops by Deeter's & Gabe's again, finally arriving home about midnight.

Dieter offers these suggestions to people wanting to have a career like his: take classes, work in good establishments, and try to get a lot of hands-on experience. He believes that dedicated chefs will always be able to get work. Dieter enjoys his career because he can be creative and try different ideas. He especially enjoys making new dishes. Another aspect of the business that appeals to him is knowing right away whether a customer is pleased or displeased with the food. He also likes the fact that customers become friends after a while. The negatives to his career are that it is hard on family life. Even on holidays, he has to make sure that everything is running smoothly and the customers are satisfied.

Overall, Dieter is very pleased with his career. The philosophy that has guided his successful career is "I can learn something new every day." Following this philosophy has enabled Dieter to create three excellent restaurants serving outstanding food.

LOOKING AT THE FUTURE

Job openings for chefs, cooks, and other kitchen workers are expected to be excellent through the year 2005. A considerable number of these positions will be in restaurants that offer table service because the average age of the population is increasing, making this type of restaurant more attractive. Skilled chefs and cooks will be needed to prepare the vegetables, fresh fruit, and breads that are becoming increasingly popular with a more health-conscious population. The employment of cafeteria cooks will also grow. While the employment of short-order and specialty fast-food cooks will continue to increase, the growth will be slower than in the past.

The demand for chefs, cooks, and kitchen workers is increasing because more people are eating out than ever before. Still, most job openings will arise from the need to replace the relatively high number of workers who leave this occupation each year. Furthermore, the pool of young workers under the age of 25 who have traditionally filled the less-skilled jobs in the restaurant industry will continue to shrink through the 1990s. This means that these workers will receive higher wages, better benefits, and more training as their employers try to retain them in their jobs.

LOOKING AT THE JOBS OF FAST-FOOD WORKERS

A job at a fast-food restaurant is often the first formal job that a teenager holds. Most workers are young people between the ages of sixteen and twenty who begin as hourly workers. Many of these young workers are in high school; however, there are also college students trying to earn money for school expenses. And recently, more and more workers in these restaurants are homemakers who want to work part-time or retirees who enjoy working or welcome the income.

ON-THE-JOB RESPONSIBILITIES OF HOURLY WORKERS

Whether fast-food workers are employed at Burger King, KFC, McDonald's, Wendy's, or some other fast-food restaurant, their duties are quite similar. Typically, an hourly worker will do a variety of tasks during each shift. And surprisingly, they will have some managerial responsibilities, especially training and supervising other workers. Here is a list of the job tasks performed by hourly workers in fast-food restaurants:

assemble or pack orders	prepare food (non-cooking)
bus or clear tables	relieve manager
clean equipment	suggestive selling
clean parking lot	supervise workers
clean restrooms	sweep/mop floors
cook food	take money
hire workers	take orders
host or hostess in dining room	train workers
order food and supplies	unload trucks
payroll, paperwork, inventory	

THE TRAINING OF HOURLY FAST-FOOD WORKERS

Fast-food workers are trained in a variety of ways. Some workers receive formal training, in which each step in the training process is spelled out in a manual. Other workers receive casual on-the-job training. They are shown what to do, and then attempt to do it themselves. Restaurants that are owned by well-known chains or a franchise that has a large number of units usually give new workers well-organized, standardized training. Besides considerable hands-on training at all restaurants, training also may consist of reading materials, listening to tapes, and watching slide shows, videos, or films.

ADVANCING UP THE CAREER LADDER FOR AN HOURLY WORKER

Fast-food is an unusual industry in that it offers entry-level workers a realistic opportunity to become managers if they demonstrate the requisite abilities. A large number of today's fast-food company executives are former hourly employees who worked their way up. The chairman of the board of McDonald's was once a grill man. And no one in the White Castle organization—except for people holding certain specialized jobs—can be in management without having started at the bottom of the ladder as a crew worker. Even graduates of the Harvard Business School must take their turn as White Castle hourly workers.

Within most large chains, the first step up from hourly crew worker is to crew trainer. In this position, workers normally perform the same jobs as crew workers and have the added responsibility of training new hourly workers. They also begin to learn the job of shift leader, the next step on the career ladder. As shift leader, their major responsibility is to manage the people on a shift, but they also may have to assume responsibility for the restaurant when the assistant manager or manager is not in the restaurant. Promising shift leaders also spend time learning the assistant manager's duties. It could take from six months to one year for a crew member to become a trainer, and six months to two years or more to become a shift leader.

SALARY AND FRINGE BENEFITS FOR HOURLY FAST-FOOD WORKERS

At one time, hourly workers were hired at the minimum wage, and that was where they stayed. But labor shortages in many areas, plus the need for more skilled workers, have made starting wages for fast-food workers more competitive with other entry-level jobs. Hourly workers also can expect regular wage increases, perhaps as many as three in the first year for effective employees.

In the past, standard benefits programs for full-time hourly workers did not begin until they had been employed for six months to a year. Because of labor shortages, full-time workers are eligible for benefits earlier, and some companies are enrolling part-time workers, too. Packages are becoming more generous. Hourly workers now often get paid sick leave and paid vacations along with health and life insurance and retirement plans. In addition, they may get free or half-price meals while they are on duty. Uniforms are free and may even be laundered free by the company.

THE PERSONAL STORY OF A DAIRY QUEEN HOURLY WORKER

Linda worked at Dairy Queen for two summers and during her senior year in high school. She worked at a small Dairy Queen store that normally employed only three workers on a shift, plus a manager. She was usually a front-of-the-store worker, although at times she worked in the back. At either task, she did some cleaning. When the manager did not have enough workers on a shift, Linda would have to cover both the front and back of the store.

When Linda worked at the front of the store, she operated the cash register and took orders. She or a helper would make the drink orders for the customers. During peak hours, she would also assemble orders. At the end of her shift, she would clean the dining room as well as stock such things as spoons, napkins, cups, and dessert dishes for the next shift.

As a back-of-the-store worker, Linda cooked food on the grill. She would also clean the back area, which included cleaning the floors and the large walk-in refrigerator. In addition, she would clean the bathrooms, take out garbage, and put new linings in the garbage pails. No matter where she was working, Linda would be assigned at times to wash windows, sweep outside, and clean the video games.

LOOKING AT THE FUTURE

Fast-food is the giant of the restaurant industry. As long as busy Americans elect to eat so many meals in restaurants, the future of fast-food is secure. Employment opportunities for entry-level workers are excellent now and are likely to remain so in the near future. There will be growth in the number of fast-food units, which creates new jobs, and there is considerable turnover in the fast-food labor force. Also, in many areas of this country, there are shortages of workers to fill both entry-level and managerial positions.

ON-THE-JOB RESPONSIBILITIES FOR FAST-FOOD RESTAURANT MANAGERS

Typically, a fast-food restaurant will have a manager, sometimes called a general manager, and one or more assistant managers who may have different titles. A restaurant that does not have a large volume of sales may not have assistant managers. Managers and assistant managers have a tremendous number of responsibilities in seeing that a restaurant runs smoothly every day. Their responsibilities include employee supervision and training, restaurant operations, and administration. They may be assigning seventy or more workers to staff different positions in a restaurant that opens as early at 6:00 a.m. and doesn't close until 2:00 or 3:00 a.m. on weekends, or even a restaurant that never closes. Furthermore, it is possible that they will be keeping track of money that adds up to more than a million dollars a year in sales in a single restaurant. There are few jobs today in which a young person can hold such a responsible position. Many assistant managers and managers are in their mid- to late-twenties. Some are even younger.

WORKING CONDITIONS

Work is demanding at fast-food restaurants for both entry-level workers and managers. The work is fast-paced. Also, it is necessary to work shifts. Some shifts begin early in the day, while others extend into the wee hours of the morning. Hours can be long, particularly for assistant managers and managers. Ten-hour days are common, as are fifty-hour weeks. In addition, weekend and holiday work is required at times.

TRAINING FOR BECOMING A FAST-FOOD RESTAURANT MANAGER

Individuals can start in an entry-level position and climb the management ladder rung-by-rung as they gain experience. Or they can start higher up the ladder by attending a two- or four-year college and then beginning as assistant managers. Most fast-food chains have formal training programs for assistant managers and managers. The first training of assistant managers usually takes place in the restaurant. Inexperienced fast-food workers will be taught what is done at each crew station and how to manage a shift. Once the basics are mastered, assistant manager trainees work side-by-side with the manager or a training manager to learn the necessary skills. A company book or manual will specify exactly what must be learned and give trainees additional information about the job. The next step in the training program of a large chain almost always is attending five days of formal classes at a regional training center. Then the trainees return to the restaurant to polish their skills. It is also possible for them to take additional one- or two-day courses at the training center. Assistant managers in chains that do not have training centers learn by on-the-job training and by reading company manuals.

Most future managers begin with in-store training by the managers, who will gradually teach them the jobs that a manager performs. The manager will also help them select the company classes and seminars they should take to increase their knowledge of the manager's job. These will usually be one-day classes. Depending on the chain, managers will often attend a one- to two-week management course at a management training center, either before they become managers or sometime in their first year in that position. These courses are often held on corporate campuses with very elaborate training facilities, like McDonald's Hamburger University and Burger King's Whopper University. Graduates of management courses are usually eligible to take further courses on a single management skill.

ADVANCING UP THE CAREER LADDER IN THE FAST-FOOD INDUSTRY

The manager is at the top of the ladder in the restaurant, but a manager can keep climbing. A talented individual may even reach the very top, as president of a large chain or a large franchise. One step up the ladder from the restaurant manager is the district manager, who is almost always promoted from within the company. District managers will generally oversee the operation of three to seven stores. With each step up the ladder, responsibilities increase. Area managers generally supervise five to ten district managers. This is the beginning of upper management. Continuing on up the ladder are the regional vice presidents, who are planning, organizing, and controlling the operations and growth of their regions. The senior vice president of operations is in charge of the operation and growth of the restaurants. And the president at the top of the ladder is responsible for all aspects of the company.

SALARY AND FRINGE BENEFITS

Managers' salaries can be good. But they become even better for assistant managers, managers, and district managers who meet performance and sales goals and are paid bonuses. Some fast-food managers with as little as five years of experience are making more than $50,000 a year. There is also the possibility of participating in profit sharing plans, in which companies share a certain percentage of the profits with their employees. Managers also receive standard benefits packages.

LOOKING AT THE FUTURE IN FAST-FOOD MANAGEMENT

Fast-food's growth makes it a good career choice for ambitious high school students and college graduates. An appealing aspect of working in this industry is the rapid advancement of management personnel. Many of the executives in high-level positions are only in their thirties and forties. For example, James B. Adamson became the president of Burger King when he was in his early forties.

FOR MORE INFORMATION

The Educational Foundation of the National Restaurant Association offers career information about chefs, cooks, and other kitchen workers; food and beverage service jobs; and managerial positions in restaurants. It can provide directories of two- and four-year colleges that offer courses or programs that prepare persons for food service careers. They also offer information on certification as a Foodservice Management Professional.

> The Educational Foundation of the National Restaurant
>   Association
> 250 South Wacker Drive, Suite 1400
> Chicago, IL 60606

For information on the American Culinary Federation's apprenticeship and certification programs for cooks, as well as a list of accredited culinary programs, write to:

> American Culinary Federation
> P.O. Box 3466
> St. Augustine, FL 32085

For general information on hospitality careers, write to:

> Council on Hotel, Restaurant, and Institutional Education
> 1200 17th Street, NW
> Washington, DC 20036-3097

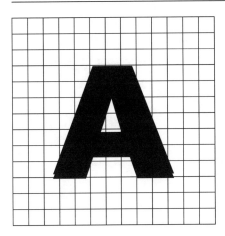

TRAVEL SCHOOLS

On-the-job experience with a travel agency was once the usual source of training for travel agents. Now most agencies require more formal training. The American Society of Travel Agents provides this list of member travel schools.

Alabama
Faulkner State Community College, Bay Minette, AL
Shelton State Community College, Tuscaloosa, AL

Arizona
American Express Travel School, Phoenix, AZ
Arizona Hospitality Research and Resource Center, Flagstaff, AZ
International Society of Meeting Planners, Scottsdale, AZ
Maricopa Skill Center, Phoenix, AZ
Pima Community College, Tucson, AZ

California
Academy Pacific Business and Travel College, Hollywood, CA
Cañada College, Redwood City, CA
Career West Academy, Chico, CA
Coastline Community College, Costa Mesa, CA
Concorde Career Colleges, Santa Ana, CA
Echols International Travel Training Course, San Francisco, CA
Empire Business College, Santa Rosa, CA
Heald Business College, San Francisco, CA
International Tour Management Institute, Inc., San Francisco, CA

Los Medanos Community College Travel Program, Pittsburg, CA
San Francisco School of Travel, San Francisco, CA
San Francisco State University Downtown Center, San Francisco, CA
Travel University International, San Diego, CA
Western College of Travel Careers, Inc., Walnut Creek, CA
West Los Angeles College, Culver City, CA

Colorado
Metropolitan State College, Denver, CO
Pickens Tech, Aurora, CO
The Travel School of Boulder, Boulder, CO
The Travel Trade School, Inc., Littleton, CO

Connecticut
Morse School of Business, Hartford, CT
Naugatuck Valley Community Tech College, Waterbury, CT
Stone Academy, Hamden, CT
University of New Haven, West Haven, CT

Florida
Art Institute of Fort Lauderdale, Fort Lauderdale, FL
Florida International University, Miami, FL
Florida National College, Hialeah, FL
Florida Travel Institute, Clearwater, FL
Mid Florida Tech, Orlando, FL
Sarasota Travel School, Sarasota, FL
Sheridan Vo-Tech Center, Hollywood, FL
Webber College, Babson Park, FL

Georgia
Omni School of Travel, Atlanta, GA

Iowa
AIC Junior College, Davenport, IA
Iowa Lakes Community College, Emmetsburg, IA
Travel Enterprises, Inc. Des Moines, IA

Illinois
Adams Institute of Travel, Schaumburg, IL
Careers in Travel, Inc., Decatur, IL
College of DuPage, Glen Ellyn, IL
Echols International Travel and Hotel School, Inc., Chicago, IL
Elgin Community College, Elgin, IL

Moraine Valley Community College, Palos Hills, IL
Northwestern Business College, Chicago, IL
Parks College of St. Louis University, Cahokia, IL
Pyramid Career Institute, Chicago, IL
Travel Education Center, Westchester, IL

Indiana
Ball State University, Muncie, IN

Kansas
Cloud County Community College, Concordia, KS
The Travel Academy, Lenexa, KS

Kentucky
International Travel Academy, Louisville, KY
Shawnee High School Travel/Tourism Department, Louisville, KY
Sullivan Junior College of Business, Louisville, KY

Massachusetts
Marian Court College, Swampscott, MA
Newbury College Dept. of Hospitality Management, Brookline, MA
Quinsigamond Community College, Worcester, MA
Salem State College, Salem, MA
Travel School of America, Boston, MA

Maine
Beal College, Bangor, ME
Casco Bay College, Portland, ME

Michigan
Conlin-Hallissey Travel School, Inc., Ann Arbor, MI
Davenport College, Kalamazoo, MI
Dorsey Business Schools, Madison Heights, MI
Lansing Community College, Lansing, MI
Suomi College, Hancock, MI
Travel Career Center, Inc., Madison Heights, MI
Travel Education Institute, Inc., Southfield, MI

Minnesota
Brainerd Staples Technical College, Brainerd, MN
Dakota County Technical College Travel Planner Program, Rosemount, MN
The McConnell School, Inc., Minneapolis, MN
Rasmussen College System, Minnetonka, MN

Saint Cloud State University, Saint Cloud, MN
South Central Technical College, Albert Lea, MN

Missouri
Central Missouri State University, Warrensburg, MO
Columbia College, Columbia, MO
Maple Woods Community College, Kansas City, MO
Trans World Travel Academy, Saint Louis, MO

North Carolina
LTS of Richmond, Inc., Greensboro, NC
Lucas Travel School, Greensboro, NC

North Dakota
Interstate Business College, Bismarck, ND

Nebraska
Lincoln School of Commerce, Lincoln, NE
Spencer School of Business, Grand Island, NE
Universal Technical Institute, Omaha, NE
University of Nebraska at Kearney, Kearney, NE

New Hampshire
Hesser College, Manchester, NH
New England School of Travel, Claremont, NH
New Hampshire Technical Institute, Concord, NH

New Jersey
Bergen Community College, Paramus, NJ
TAO Travel Services Inc., Egg Harbor Township, NJ
Travel One Travel Academy, Cherry Hill, NJ

New York
Adirondack Community College, Queensburg, NY
Brugger Inc., New York, NY
Bryant and Stratton Business Institute, Albany, NY
Bryant and Stratton Business Institute, Rochester, NY
Cornell University, School of Hotel Administration, Ithaca, NY
Genesee Community College, Batavia, NY
Herkimer County Community College, Herkimer, NY
International Institute of Travel, Inc., Syracuse, NY
LaGuardia Community College, Long Island City, NY
Monroe Community College, Rochester, NY

National Academy Foundation, New York, NY

Niagara University, Niagara Falls, NY

Rockland Community College, Suffern, NY

SUNY-College of Technology, Delhi, NY

Tompkins Cortland Community College, Dryden, NY

Travel Careers International Ltd., New York, NY

Ohio

Columbus State Community College/Hospitality Management, Columbus, OH

Hocking College, Nelsonville, OH

Northwestern College, Lima, OH

Ohio University Southern Call, Ironton, OH

Sinclair Community College, Dayton, OH

Toledo Travel School, Toledo, OH

The Travel School, Lakewood, OH

Tri-State Travel School, Cincinnati, OH

Oklahoma

Demarge College, Oklahoma City, OK

Oregon

Chemeketa Community College Hospitality Systems Management Dept., Salem, OR

Emmett Travel School, Portland, OR

Mt. Hood Community College, Gresham, OR

Pennsylvania

The Boyd School, Pittsburgh, PA

California University of Pennsylvania, California, PA

Central Pennsylvania Business School, Summerdale, PA

Harcum College, Bryn Mawr, PA

ICM School of Business, Pittsburgh, PA

Luzerne County Community College, Nanticoke, PA

Martin School of Business, Philadelphia, PA

Northampton Community College, Bethlehem, PA

Parkway West AVTS, Oakdale, PA

Reading Area Community College, Reading, PA

York Technical Institute, York, PA

Tennessee

Electronic Computer Programming College, Chattanooga, TN

Humphrey and Associates, Knoxville, TN

Texas

Access Travel Academy, Houston, TX
American Airlines Travel Academy, Fort Worth, TX
Capitol City Careers, Austin, TX
Houston Community College System, Houston, TX
International Aviation and Travel Academy, Arlington, TX
Kingwood College, Kingwood, TX
Pace Travel School, Austin, TX
Richland College, Dallas, TX

Utah

Bryman School, Salt Lake City, UT
Education Systems, Sandy, UT
June Morris School of Travel, Salt Lake City, UT

Virginia

Cal Simmons Travel School, Alexandria, VA
Fleming-Ruffner Magnet Center, Roanoke, VA
Northern Virginia Community College, Annandale, VA
Omega Travel School, Fairfax, VA
Satotravel Academy, Arlington, VA

Washington

Academy of Travel Careers, Bellevue, WA
Art Institute of Seattle Management in Travel and Tourism, Seattle, WA
Bates Technical College, Tacoma, WA
Clover Park Technical College, Tacoma, WA
The Fox Travel Institute, Seattle, WA
International Air Academy, Vancouver, WA
SST Travel Schools, Lynnwoood, WA
SST Travel Schools of the Pacific Northwest, Inc., Seattle, WA
SST Travel Schools of Western Washington, Bellevue, WA

Wisconsin

Academy of Travel, Elm Grove, WI
Gateway Technical College, Kenosha, WI
Madison Area Technical College, Madison, WI
Milwaukee Area Technical College, Oak Creek, WI

Wyoming

Sheridan College, Sheridan, WY

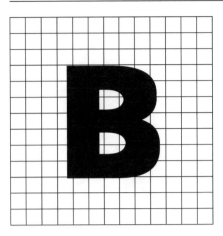

SCHEDULED AIRLINES

The airline employment picture changes constantly. Applicants should write the human resources departments of airlines for up-to-date information, job requirements, and the availability of training programs. The following list of scheduled airlines is provided by the Air Transport Association of America.

Alaska Airlines
P.O. Box 68900
Seattle-Tacoma International Airport
Seattle, WA 98168-0900

Aloha Airlines
P.O. Box 30028
Honolulu, HI 96820-0228

American Airlines
P.O. Box 619616
Dallas-Forth Worth Airport, TX 75261-9616

American Trans Air
P.O. Box 51609
Indianapolis International Airport
Indianapolis, IN 46251-0609

Continental Airlines
2929 Allen Parkway, Suite 2020
Houston, TX 77019

Delta Airlines
Hartsfield Atlanta International Airport
Atlanta, GA 30320-9998

DHL Airways
P.O. Box 75122
Cincinnati, OH 45275

Evergreen International Airlines
3850 Three Mile Lane
McMinnville, OR 97128-9496

Federal Express
P.O. Box 727
Memphis, TN 38116

Hawaiian Airlines
P.O. Box 30008
Honolulu International Airport
Honolulu, HI 96820-0008

KIWI International Airlines
Hemisphere Center
U.S. 1 & 9 South
Newark, NJ 07114

Northwest Airlines
Minneapolis-St. Paul International Airport
St. Paul, MN 55111-3075

Reeve Aleutian Airways
4700 W. International Airport Road
Anchorage, AK 99502-1091

Southwest Airlines
Box 36611 Love Field
Dallas, TX 75235-1625

Trans World Airlines
One City Centre, 19th Floor
St. Louis, MO 63101

United Airlines
P.O. Box 66100
Chicago, IL 60666-0100

United Parcel Service
400 Pertmeter Center Terraces North
Atlanta, GA 30346

USAir
2345 Crystal Drive
Crystal Park 4
Arlington, VA 22227

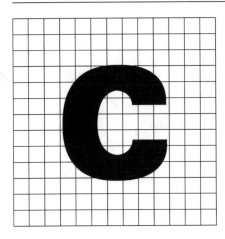

SCHOOLS OFFERING TOURISM COURSES LEADING TO CERTIFICATES AND DEGREES

The following schools offer tourism courses leading to certificates, associate degrees, and bachelor degrees. The list of schools is provided by the National Tour Foundation.

Certificate Schools

University of Calgary, Calgary AB, Canada

Nationwide Travel Training College, Richmond, BC, Canada

Tourism Training Institute, Vancouver BC, Canada

Aurora Travel School, Fayetteville, AR

Central Arizona College, Coolidge, AZ

AIT Travel School, Phoenix, AZ

Chaparral Career College, Tucson, AZ

Intensive Trainers Institute, Tucson, AZ

Pima Community College, Tucson, AZ

Mountain States Travel Training Institute, Aurora, CA

American College of Travel, Burbank, CA

Carmel Unified School District, Carmel, CA

Travel West Academy, Chico, CA

West Los Angeles College, Culver City, CA

Travel and Tourism Institute, Fair Oaks, CA

Corbett Travel Academy, Fremont, CA

Valley Travel College, Fresno, CA

Lori Kayes International Travel Academy, Hollywood, CA

Christopher Columbus Travel College, Los Angeles, CA

Trans World Travel Academy, Los Angeles, CA

California State University, Long Beach, CA

Long Beach City College, Long Beach, CA

Foothill College, Los Altos Hills, CA

Travel Expert Training School, Wista, CA

The Travel School of Boulder, Boulder, CO

Mountain States Travel Training Institute, Colorado Springs, CO

International Guide Academy, Denver, CO

Travel School of Ft. Collins, Ft. Collins, CO

Travel Trade School, Ft. Collins, CO

Colorado School of Travel, Lakewood, CO

Travel Trade School, Littleton, CO

American Educational Institute, Bridgeport, CT

Stone Institute, Hamden, CT

Gateway Community Tech, New Haven, CT

Norwalk Community Tech College, Norwalk, CT

Huntington Institute, Norwich, CT

Interamerican Institute of Tourism, Washington, DC

International Travel Training Courses, Inc., Washington, DC

Executive Travel Center of St. Petersburg, Clearwater, FL

Sheridan Vo-Tech Center, Hollywood, FL

Florida Community College, Jacksonville, FL

Advanced Career Training, Jacksonville, FL

Southeastern Academy, Inc., Kissimmee, FL

Lorraine Travel School, Miami, FL

Careers in Travel, Inc, Decatur, IL

Maki Travel Center, Inc, Downers Grove, IL

Elgin Community College, Elgin, IL

Joliet Junior College, Joliet, IL

First Class Travel Institute, Midlothian, IL

Travel Careers, Ltd., Moline, IL

Harper College, Palatine, IL

Regal School of Travel, Palos Heights, IL

Midstate College, Peoria, IL

Adams Institute of Travel, Schaumburg, IL

Travel Careers, Inc., Indianapolis, IN

Cloud County Community College, Concordia, KS

The Travel Academy, Lenexa, KS

Cranford College, Solomon, KS

CCI Travel Careers Division, Wichita, KS

Travel Career Institute, Wichita, KS

Travel Professionals Institute, Louisville, KY

The Culinary Arts Institute of Louisiana, Baton Rouge, LA

Travel Affair School of Travel, Lafayette, LA

Cameron College, New Orleans, LA

Delgado Community College, New Orleans, LA

Travel School of America, Boston, MA

Massachusetts Bay Community College, Framingham, MA

Quinsigamond Community College, Worcester, MA

Travel Careers Institute, Omaha, NE

Universal Technical Institute, Omaha, NE

Travel Education Center, Nashua, NH

Travel One Travel Academy, Cherry Hill, NJ

O Brien s Professional Travel School, Paramus, NJ

Ports of Call International Travel, Inc., Albuquerque, NM

World Travel Institute, Las Vegas, NV

Ridley-Lowell Business and Technology Institute, Binghampton, NY

Bryant and Stratton Institute, Cicero, NY

Airline Training Council, New York, NY

Sobelsohn School, New York, NY

Travel Careers International, New York, NY

Le Cordonbleu, Pleasantville, NY

Jefferson Community College, Watertown, NY

Northwest Technical College, Archbold, OH

The Travel School, Lakewood, OH

Algonquin College, Nepean, ON, Canada

Sir Sandford Fleming College, Peterborough, ON, Canada

Seneca College, Toronto, ON, Canada

Mt. Hood Community College, Gresham, OR

Emmett Travel School, Portland, OR

Northwest Schools, Portland, OR

SST Azumano Travel School, Portland, OR

Western Culinary Institute, Portland, OR

Travel Careers, Inc., Tyler, TX

TSTC-Waco, Waco, TX

Utah Valley State College, Orem, UT

June Morris School of Travel, Salt Lake City, UT

The Bryman School, Salt Lake City, UT
Western International School of Travel, Salt Lake City, UT
Cal Simmons Travel School, Alexandria, VA
Sato Travel Academy, Arlington, VA
Lucas Travel School, Richmond, VA
Lucas Travel School, Virginia Beach, VA
Academy of Travel Careers, Bellevue, WA
SST Travel Schools of Western WA, Bellevue, WA
Bellingham Technical College, Bellingham, WA
SST Travel Schools, Lynnwood, WA
Washington State University, Pullman, WA
Art Institute of Seattle, Seattle, WA
Fox Travel Institute, Seattle, WA
SST Travel Schools of the Pacific Northwest, Seattle, WA
Knapp College, Tacoma, WA
Travel Training Institute, Tacoma, WA
International Air Academy, Inc., Vancouver, WA
Trend Colleges, Vancouver, WA
Academy of Travel, LTD, Elm Grove, WI

Associate's Degree
Southern Alberta Institute of Technology, Calgary, AB, Canada
Alaska Pacific University, Anchorage, AK
Faulkner State University, Bay Minette, AL
Southern Institute, Birmingham, AL
Central Arizona College, Coolidge, AZ
Pima Community College, Tucson, AZ
American College of Travel, Long Beach, CA
Butte Community College, Oroville, CA
California State Polytechnic Institute, Pomona, CA
Cañada College, Redwood City, CA
City College of San Francisco, San Francisco, CA
Coastline Community College, Costa Mesa, CA
Condie Junior College, Campbell, CA
Empire Business College, Santa Rosa, CA
Foothill College, Los Altos Hills, CA
Golden Gate University, San Francisco, CA
Mission College, Santa Clara, CA
Palomar College, San Marcos, CA
Rancho Santiago College, Garden Grove, CA

San Bernadino Valley College, San Bernadino, CA

San Diego Mesa College, San Diego, Ca

Santa Barbara City College, Santa Barbara, CA

West Los Angeles College, Culver City, CA

Blair Junior College, Colorado Springs, CO

North Metro Technical Institute, Acworth, GA

University of Georgia, Athens, GA

Brigham Young University-Hawaii, Laie, HI

Kapiolani Community College, Honolulu, HI

AIC Junior College, Davenport, IA

American Institute of Business, Des Moines, IA

Iowa Lakes Community College, Emmetsburg, IA

Catherine College, Chicago, IL

Chicago City-Wide College, Chicago, IL

College of DuPage, Glen Ellyn, IL

Elgin Community College, Elgin, IL

John A. Logan College, Carterville, IL

Lexington Institute, Chicago, IL

Lincoln College, Normal, IL

Moraine Valley Community College, Palos Hills, IL

Northwestern Business College, Hickory Hills, IL

Northwestern Business College, Chicago, IL

Parkland College, Champaign, IL

Robert Morris College, Chicago, IL

Triton College, River Grove, IL

United American College of Travel and Tourism Careers, Lisle, IL

Indiana University Purdue University Fort Wayne, Fort Wayne, IN

Indiana University Purdue University Indianapolis, Indianapolis, IN

Indiana Vocational Technical College, Hammond, IN

Ivy Tech, Indianapolis, IN

Grand Rapids Community College, Grand Rapids, MI

Henry Ford Community College, Dearborn, MI

Jackson Community College, Jackson, MI

Lansing Community College, Lansing, MI

Madison Area Technical College, Madison, MI

Mott Community College, Flint, MI

Northwestern Michigan College, Traverse City, MI

Oakland Community College, Farmington Hills, MI

Sienna Heights College, Adrian, MI

Suomi College, Hancock, MI

Wastenaw Community College, Ann Arbor, MI

Brainerd Staples Technical College, Brainerd, MN

Dakota City Technical College, Rosemount, MN

Minneapolis Technical Institute, Minneapolis, MN

National College, St. Paul, MN

Normandale Community College, Bloomington, MN

South Central Technical College, Albert Lea, MN

Maplewoods Community College, Kansas City, MO

Penn Valley Community College, Kansas City, MO

St. Louis Community College at Forest Park, St. Louis, MO

A-B Technical Community College, Asheville, NC

Asheville-Buncombe Technical Community College, Asheville, NC

Blue Ridge Community College, Flat Rock, NC

Central Piedmont Community College, Charlotte, NC

Genesee Community College, Batavia, NY

Herkimer County Community College, Herkimer, NY

Jefferson Community College, Watertown, NY

Kingsborough-Community College, Brooklyn, NY

LaGuardia Community College, Long Island, NY

Monroe Community College, Rochester, NY

Nassau Communty College, Garden City, NY

Paul Smith College of Arts and Sciences, Paul Smiths, NY

Rochester Institute of Technology, Rochester, NY

Rockland Community College, Suffern, NY

SUNY at Cobleskill, Cobleskill, NY

SUNY New York State University, Morrisville, NY

SUNY AG Technical College, Canton, NY

Schenectady County Community College, Schenectady, NY

State University of New York, Delhi, NY

Sullivan County Community College, Loch Sheldrake, NY

Tompkins Cortland Community College, Dryden, NY

Demarge College, Oklahoma City, OK

Oklahoma Junior College, Tulsa, OK

Tulsa Junior College, Tulsa, OK

Lambton College, Sarnia, ON, Canada

Central Oregon Community College, Bend, OR

Chemeketa Community College, Salem, OR

Mt. Hood Community College, Gresham, OR

State Technical Institute, Memphis, TN
Del Mar College, Corpus Christi, TX
El Paso Community College, El Paso, TX
Kingwood College, Kingwood, TX
North Harris County College, Kingwood, TX
Richland College, Dallas, TX
St. Philips College, San Antonio, TX
TSTC-Waco, Waco, TX
Education Systems, Sandy, UT
Utah Valley State College, Orem, UT
Commonwealth College, Hampton, VA
Northern Virginia Community College, Annandale, VA
Champlain College, Burlington, VT
New England Culinary Institute, Montpelier, VT
Bates Technical College, Tacoma, WA
Clover Park Technical College, Tacoma, WA
Spokane Community College, Spokane, WA
Gateway Technical College, Kenosha, WI
Milwaukee Area Technical College, Milwaukee, WI
Moraine Park Technical College, Fond Du Lac, WI
Nicolet Area Technical College, Rhinelander, WI
Waukesha Community Technical College, Pewaukee, WI

Bachelor's Degree
University of Calgary, Calgary, AB, Canada
Alaska Pacific University, Anchorage, AK
University of Alaska, Ketchikan, AK
University of Alaska, Fairbanks, AK
Alabama State University, Montgomery, AL
Auburn, University, Auburn, AL
Shelton State College, Tuscaloosa, AL
University of South Alabama, Mobile, AL
Arkansas Technical University, Russellville, AR
Henderson State University, Arkadelphia, AR
University of Arkansas, Fayetteville, AR
Arizona State University, Tempe, AZ
Northern Arizona University, Flagstaff, AZ
University of Victoria, Victoria, BC, Canada
California Polytechnic State University, Pomona, CA
California State University at Chico, Chico, CA

California State University, Long Beach, CA
Golden Gate University, San Francisco, CA
San Francisco State University, San Francisco, CA
US International University, San Diego, CA
University of California at Irvine, Irvine, CA
University of San Francisco, San Francisco, CA
Colorado State University, Fort Collins, CO
Webber College, Babson Park, FL
Georgia Southern University, Statesboro, GA
Georgia State University, Atlanta, GA
Brigham Young University-Hawaii, Laie, HI
Hawaii Pacific University, Honolulu, HI
University of Hawaii at Manoa, Honolulu, HI
Iowa State University, Ames, IA
College of Southern Idaho, Twin Falls, ID
University of Idaho, Moscow, ID
Bradley University, Peoria, IL
Illinois State University, Normal, IL
Nothern Illinois University, DeKalb, IL
Northwestern University, Evanston, IL
Robert Morris College, Chicago, IL
Southern Illinois University at Carbondale, Carbondale, IL
St. Louis University, Cahokia, IL
University of Illinois, Urbana, IL
Western Illinois University, Macomb, IL
Ball State University, Muncie, IN
Indiana University, Bloomington, IN
Purdue University, West Lafayette, IN
Kansas State University, Manhattan, KS
Eastern Kentucky University, Richmond, KY
Morehead State University, Morehead, KY
Moorhead State University, Moorhead, MN
Rasmussen Business College, Minnetonka, MN
Southwest State University, Marshall, MN
St. Cloud State University, St. Cloud, MN
University of Minnesota, Crookston, MN
University of Minnesota-Duluth, Duluth, MN
Central Missouri State University, Warrenburg, MO
Columbia College, Columbia, MO

Southwest Missouri University, Springfield, MO
Trans World Travel Academy, Kansas City, MO
University of Missouri-Columbia, Columbia, MO
University of Southern Mississippi, Hattiesburg, MS
Montana State University, Bozeman, MT
University of Montana, Missoula, MT
Western Montana College of John Bailey, Dillion, MT
Appalachian State University, Boone, NC
Barber Scotia College, Concord, NC
East Carolina University, Greenville, NC
North Carolina State University, Raleigh, NC
North Carolina Wesleyan College, Rocky Mount, NC
Southwestern Community College, Sylva, NC
University of North Carolina, Chapel Hill, NC
Western Carolina University, Cullowehee, NC
New York University, New York, NY
Niagara University, Niagara Falls, NY
Rochester Institute of Technology, Rochester, NY
State University of New York, Morrisville, NY
State University of New York, Buffalo, NY
SUNY at Oneonta, Oneonta, NY
SUNY at Plattsburgh, Plattsburgh, NY
Syracuse University, Syracuse, NY
Bowling Green State University, Bowling Green, OH
Kent State University, Kent, OH
Ohio State University, Columbus, OH
Ohio University, Ironton, OH
Tiffin University, Tiffin, OH
Northeastern State University, Tahlequah, OK
Oklahoma State University, Stillwater, OK
Brock University, St. Catherines, ON, Canada
Fanshawe College, London, ON, Canada
Ryerson Polytechnic University, Toronto, ON, Canada
Sir Sandford Fleming College, Peterborough, ON, Canada
University of Guelph, Guelph, ON, Canada
University of Waterloo, Waterloo, ON, Canada
Oregon State University, Corvallis, OR
Southern Oregon State, Ashland, OR
Southern Methodist University, Dallas, TX

Texas A&M University, College Station, TX
Texas Tech, Lubbock, TX
University of Houston, Houston, TX
University of Texas at Austin, Austin, TX
University of Texas at San Antonio, San Antonio, TX
Wiley College, Marshall, TX
Brigham Young University, Provo, UT
Education Systems, Sandy, UT
University of Utah, Salt Lake City, UT
Utah Valley State College, Orem, UT
College of William and Mary, Williamsburg, VA
James Madison University, Harrisonburg, VA
Virginia Commonwealth University, Richmond, VA
Virginia Polytechnic Institute, Blacksburg, VA
Virginia State University, Petersburg, VA
University of Vermont, Burlington, VT
Central Washington University, Ellensburg, WA
University of Washington, Seattle, WA
Washington State University, Pullman, WA
Washington State University, Seattle, WA
University of Wisconsin, Kenosha, WI
Concord College, Athens, WV
Fairmont State College, Fairmont, WV

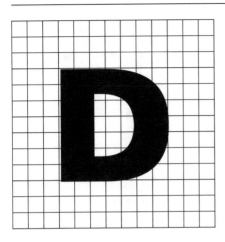

COLLEGES AND UNIVERSITIES OFFERING DEGREES IN FOOD SERVICE, HOSPITALITY, HOTEL OR RESTAURANT MANAGEMENT, OR CULINARY ARTS

There are many educational opportunities for those interested in travel, tourism, and hospitality careers. This list of colleges and universities in the United States that offer bachelor's degrees in food service, hospitality, hotel or restaurant management, or culinary arts was reprinted with permission from *Choose Food Service: It's More Than You Think, A Guide to Two-Year and Four-Year Colleges and Universities with Foodservice/Hospitality Programs, Second Edition,* by the Educational Foundation of the National Restaurant Association.

ALABAMA

The University of Alabama
Restaurant and Hospitality
  Management
College of Human Environmental
  Sciences
P.O. Box 870158
Tuscaloosa, Alabama 35487-0158

Alabama A & M University
Nutrition & Hospitality Management
4900 Meridian Street
Normal, Alabama 35762

Auburn University
Hotel and Restaurant Management
School of Human Sciences
Department of Nutrition and Food
  Science
328 Spidle Hall
Auburn, Alabama 36849

Tuskegee University
Department of Home Economics
Hospitality Management Program
204 Campbell Hall
Tuskegee, Alabama 36088

ALASKA

University of Alaska—Fairbanks
Travel Industry Management Program
School of Management
120A Bunell
P.O. Box 756080
Fairbanks. Alaska 99775-6080

Alaska Pacific University
Travel and Hospitality Management
4101 University Drive
Anchorage, Alaska 99508

ARIZONA

University of Arizona
Department of Nutrition and Food
  Service
309 Shantz
Tucson, Arizona 85721

Northern Arizona University
School of Hotel and Restaurant
  Management
P.O. Box 5638
Flagstaff, Arizona 86011-5638

ARKANSAS

University of Arkansas at Pine Bluff
Restaurant Foodservice Management
1200 North University Drive
Pine Bluff, Arkansas 71601

Arkansas Tech University
Hotel and Restaurant Management
School of Business
Corely Building
Russellville, Arkansas 72801

CALIFORNIA

**California State Polytechnic
  University-Pomona**
Hotel and Restaurant Management
School of Hotel and Restaurant
  Management
3801 West Temple Avenue
Pomona, California 91768

California State University, Chico
Foodservice Administration
School of Home Economics
117 Glenn Hall
Chico, California 95929-0002

**California State University, Long
  Beach**
Home Economics
Foodservice Systems Management
1250 Bellflower Boulevard
Long Beach, California 90840-0501

Century Business College
Food and Beverage Program
3325 Wilshire Boulevard, 2nd Floor
Los Angeles, California 90010

Golden Gate University
Hotel, Restaurant and Tourism
  Management
School of Management
536 Mission Street
San Francisco, California 94105-2968

Loyola Marymount University
Continuing Education
Hotel and Restaurant Management
7101 West 80 Street
Los Angeles, California 90045

University of San Francisco
Hospitality Management Program
McLaren School of Business
San Francisco, California 94117

San Francisco State University
Hospitality Management
School of Business 314
1600 Holloway Avenue
San Francisco, California 94132

San Jose State University
Hospitality Management
One Washington Square
San Jose, California 95192-0211

*** United States International
  University**
Hospitality Management
School of Hospitality Management
10455 Pomerado Road
San Diego, California 92131

COLORADO

University of Colorado at Boulder
Tourism Management Program
College of Business
Campus Box 419
Boulder, Colorado 80309

---

* Offers the Management Development Diploma Program from The Educational Foundation

Colorado State University
Restaurant and Resort Management
Applied Human Sciences
Department of Food Science and
    Human Nutrition
207 Gifford
Fort Collins, Colorado 80523

University of Denver
School of Hotel/Motel, Hospitality
    Management and Tourism
Business Administration
Denver, Colorado 80208

Fort Lewis College
Tourism and Resort Management
School of Business Administration
1000 Rim Drive
Durango, Colorado 81301

Metro State College
Hospitality, Meeting and Travel
    Administration
P.O. Box 173362
Campus Box 60
Denver, Colorado 80217-3362

**Metropolitan State College of
    Denver**
Hospitality, Meeting and Travel
Campus Box 60
P.O. Box 173362
Denver, Colorado 80217-3362

CONNECTICUT

University of Connecticut
Department of Nutritional Sciences
3624 Horsebarn Road
Storrs, Connecticut 06269-4017

The University of New Haven
Hotel, Restaurant and Tourism
    Administration
School of Hotel, Restaurant and
    Tourism Administration
300 Orange Avenue
West Haven, Connecticut 06516

Teikyo Post University
Hospitality Management Program
School of Business Administration
800 Country Club Road
P.O. Box 2540
Waterbury, Connecticut 06723-2540

DELAWARE

The University of Delaware
Hotel, Restaurant and Institutional
    Management
College of Human Resources
321 South College Avenue,
    Rextrew House
Newark, Delaware 19716

Delaware State College
Hotel and Restaurant Management
Department of Home Economics
1200 N. DuPont Highway
Dover, Delaware 19901

DISTRICT OF COLUMBIA

Howard University
Hospitality Management
School of Business
2600 Sixth Street, NW
Washington, DC 20059

FLORIDA

*****Bethune Cookman College**
Hospitality Management
Division of Business
640 Mary McLoyd Bethune
    Boulevard
Daytona Beach, Florida 32114-3099

University of Central Florida
Hospitality Management
College of Business Administration
Orlando, Florida 32816-1400

---

* Offers the Management Development Diploma Program from The Educational Foundation

University of Florida
Institute of Food Science and Human
　Nutrition
Food Science
359 D Food Science Building
P.O. Box 110-370
Gainesville, Florida 32611

Florida A & M University
Hospitality Management Program
Tallahassee, Florida 32307

Florida International University
Hospitality Management, Hotel and
　Food Service Management
3000 NE 145th Street
North Miami, Florida 33181

Florida State University
Hospitality Administration
225 William-Johnston Building
Tallahassee, Florida 32306

* **Lynn University**
Hotel, Restaurant and Tourism
3601 North Military Trail
Boca Raton, Florida 33431

Saint Leo College
Restaurant and Hotel Management
Division of Business Administration
P.O. Box 2067
Saint Leo, Florida 33574

Saint Thomas University
Tourism and Hospitality Management
16400 NW 32nd Avenue
Miami, Florida 33054

**Schiller International University—
　Florida**
Hotel Management
453 Edgewater Drive
Dunedin, Florida 34698

GEORGIA

* **Georgia Southern University**
Restaurant, Hotel and Institutional
　Administration
School of Health and Professional
　Studies
LB 8124
Statesboro, Georgia 30460

Georgia State University
Cecil B. Day School of Hospitality
　Administration
College of Public and Urban Affairs
P.O. Box 4018
Atlanta, Georgia 30302

Morris Brown College
Hospitality Administration
643 Martin Luther King, Jr. Drive
　NW
Atlanta, Georgia 30314-4140

HAWAII

Brigham Young University—Hawaii
Hospitality and Tourism Management
Business Division
55-220 Kulanui
Laie, Hawaii 96762

University of Hawaii at Manoa
Travel Industry Management
School of Travel Industry
　Management
2560 Campus Road
Honolulu, Hawaii 96822

Hawaii Pacific University
Travel Industry Management
College of Business Administration
1188 Fort Street
Honolulu, Hawaii 96813

---

* Offers the Management Development Diploma Program from The Educational Foundation

IDAHO

Idaho State University
Culinary Arts
School of Applied Technology
Pocatello, Idaho 83201

ILLINOIS

Chicago State University
Hotel and Restaurant Management
College of Business
9501 South King Drive
Chicago, Illinois 60628-1598

Eastern Illinois University
Hospitality Services
College of Applied Sciences
School of Home Economics
103 Khelem Hall
Charleston, Illinois 61920

University of Illinois at Urbana-Champaign
Restaurant/Hospitality Management
363 Bevier Hall
905 South Goodwin Avenue
Urbana, Illinois 61801

Kendall College
Hospitality Management, Culinary Arts
2408 Orrington Avenue
Evanston, Illinois 60201

Northern Illinois University
Food Systems Administration: Dietetics, Nutrition and Food Systems
College of Professional Studies
Department of Human and Family Resources
DeKalb, Illinois 60115

Roosevelt University
The Manfred Steinfeld Program in Hospitality Management
The Evelyn T. Stone College of Continuing Education
430 South Michigan Avenue, Room 124
Chicago, Illinois 60605

Rosary College
Foodservice Management
7900 West Division Street
River Forest, Illinois 60305

Southern Illinois University—Carbondale
Hotel, Restaurant and Travel Administration
College of Agriculture
c/o Food and Nutrition
Room 209
Quigley Hall, SIU
Carbondale, Illinois 62901

Western Illinois University
Food Service and Lodging Management Program
College of Applied Sciences
Department of Home Economics
309 Olson Hall
Macomb, Illinois 61455

INDIANA

Ball State University
Food Management
Department of Home Economics
PA 150 Practical Arts Building
Muncie, Indiana 47306

Purdue University
Restaurant, Hotel, Institutional, and Tourism Management (RHIT)
School of Consumer and Family Science
1266 Stone Hall
West Lafayette, Indiana 47907-1266

Purdue University Calumet
Restaurant and Hotel Management
School of Liberal Arts and Sciences
Hammond, Indiana 46323

IOWA

Iowa State University
Hotel, Restaurant and Institution
    Management
Family and Consumer Sciences
11 MacKay Hall
Ames, Iowa 50011

KANSAS

Kansas State University
Hotel and Restaurant Management
    and Dietetics
Justice Hall 103
Manhattan, Kansas 66506-1404

KENTUCKY

University of Kentucky
Hospitality Management
Human Environmental Sciences
103 Erikson Hall
Lexington, Kentucky 40506

Morehead State University
Hotel, Restaurant and Institutional
    Management
College of Applied Sciences and
    Technology
Department of Human Sciences
UPO 889
Morehead, Kentucky 40351

Transylvania University
Hotel, Restaurant and Tourism
    Administration
300 North Broadway
Lexington, Kentucky 40508

Western Kentucky University
Hotel, Restaurant and Tourism
    Management
College of Education and Behavioral
    Sciences
Home Economics and Consumer
    Sciences
Academic Building 302F
Bowling Green, Kentucky 42101

LOUISIANA

Grambling State University
Hotel and Restaurant Management
College of Science and Technology
P.O. Box 4248
Grambling, Louisiana 71245

University of New Orleans
School of Hotel, Restaurant and
    Tourism Administration
College of Business Administration
New Orleans, Louisiana 70148

Nicholls State University
Dietetics Management
P.O. Box 2014
Thibodaux, Louisiana 70310

**Southern University and A & M
    College**
Continuing Education
Baton Rouge, Louisiana 70819

**University of Southwestern
    Louisiana**
Hospitality, Restaurant Management
School of Human Resources
USL P.O. Box 40399
Lafayette, Louisiana 70504-0399

MAINE

University of Maine
Hotel/Restaurant/Tourism
    Management
School of Business
210 Texas Avenue
Bangor, Maine 04401

University of Maine
104 Libby Hall
Orona, Maine 04473

Southern Maine Technical College
RFO 3 Box 701
Wiscasset, Maine 04578

MARYLAND

University of Maryland
Nutrition and Dietetics
College of Agriculture
College Park, Maryland 20742

University of Maryland-Eastern Shore
Hotel and Restaurant Management
School of Professional Studies
Princess Anne, Maryland 21853

MASSACHUSETTS

Boston University
School of Hospitality Administration
808 Commonwealth Avenue
Boston, Massachusetts 02215

Endicott College
Hotel/Restaurant/Travel
    Administration Program
Liberal and Professional Arts College
376 Hale Street
Beverly, Massachusetts 01915

Framingham State College
Food Science and Nutrition
Department of Home Economics
100 State Street
Framingham, Massachusetts 01701

Lasell College
Hotel and Travel/Tourism
    Administration
1844 Commonwealth Avenue
Newton, Massachusetts 02166

University of Massachusetts— Amherst
Department of Hotel, Restaurant and
    Travel Administration
College of Food and Natural
    Resources
Flint 107
Amherst, Massachusetts 01003

MICHIGAN

Central Michigan University
Hospitality Services
Marketing and Hospitality Services
    Administration
Smith 100
Mt. Pleasant, Michigan 48859

Eastern Michigan University
Hospitality Management
Health and Human Services
Department of Human Environmental
    and Consumer Resources
108 Roosevelt Hall
Ypsilanti, Michigan 48197

*Ferris State University
Food Service/Hospitality
    Management
School of Business
901 South State Street
Big Rapids, Michigan 49307

Grand Valley State University
Hospitality and Tourism
AuSable 111
Allendale, Michigan 49401

Michigan State University
School of Hotel, Restaurant and
    Institutional Management
The Eli Broad College of Business
424 Eppley Center
East Lansing, Michigan 48824-1121

---

* Offers the Management Development Diploma Program from The Educational Foundation

Northern Michigan University
Restaurant and Foodservice
  Management
School of Technology and Applied
  Science
Jacobetti Center, Route 550
Marquette, Michigan 49855

Siena Heights College
Hotel, Restaurant and Institutional
  Management
1247 East Siena Heights Drive
Adrian, Michigan 49221

MINNESOTA

Mankato State University
Dietetics
Home Economics Department
P.O. Box 8400-MSU Box 44
Mankato, Minnesota 56002-8400

University of Minnesota
265 Food Science & Nutrition
  Building
St. Paul, Minnesota 55108

*Moorhead State University
Hotel-Motel-Restaurant Management
260 Bridges Road
Moorhead, Minnesota 56563

Southwest State University
Hotel and Restaurant Administration
Lecture Center 101
Marshall, Minnesota 56258

MISSISSIPPI

Alcorn State University
Food and Nutrition
P.O. Box 839
Lorman, Mississippi 39096

Mississippi State University
Food Science
P.O. Box 5446
Mississippi State, Mississippi 39762

University of Southern Mississippi
Hotel, Restaurant and Tourism
  Management
College of Health and Human
  Sciences
S.S. Box 5035
Hattiesburg, Mississippi 39406

MISSOURI

Central Missouri State University
Hotel and Restaurant Administration
Department of Human Environmental
  Sciences
Warrensburg, Missouri 64093

University of Missouri-Columbia
Hotel and Restaurant Management
College of Agriculture, Food and
  Natural Resources
122 Eckles Hall
Columbia, Missouri 65211

Southeast Missouri State University
Human Environmental Studies
One University Plate
Room 105, Scully Building
Cape Jirardeau, Missouri 63701

Southwest Missouri State University
Hospitality and Restaurant
  Administration
Health and Applied Sciences
901 South National
Springfield, Missouri 65804

NEBRASKA

University of Nebraska
Restaurant Management
Home Economics
Nutritional Science and Dietetics
316 Ruth Leverton
Lincoln, Nebraska 68583-0806

---

* Offers the Management Development Diploma Program from The Educational Foundation

University of Nebraska
Hospitality Management
Department of Human Resources and
     Family Science
60th and Dodge
Omaha, Nebraska 68182

NEVADA

*** University of Nevada, Las Vegas**
William F. Harrah College of Hotel
     Administration
4505 Maryland Parkway
Las Vegas, Nevada 89154-6013

Sierra Nevada College-Lake Tahoe
Ski Business and Resort Management;
     Hotel, Restaurant and Resort
     Management
Business Administration
P.O. Box 4269
800 College Drive
Incline Village, Nevada 89450-4269

NEW HAMPSHIRE

University of New Hampshire
Hotel Administration Department
Whittemore School of Business and
     Economics
McConnell Hall
Durham, New Hampshire 03824

*** New Hampshire College**
Culinary Arts
2500 North River Road
Manchester, New Hampshire 03106

NEW JERSEY

Fairleigh Dickinson University
School of Hotel, Restaurant and
     Tourism Management
FDU-H327
Hesslein Building, 1000 River Rd.
Teaneck, New Jersey 07666

Montclair State College
Tourism and Recreation Program
School of Professional Studies
Upper Montclair, New Jersey 07866

Rutgers University
P.O. Box 231
Food Science Department
New Brunswick, New Jersey 08903

NEW MEXICO

*** Gadsden Independent School
     District**
Foodservice Management
1325 West Washington Street
Anthony, New Mexico 88021

University of New Mexico
Tourism Management
Anderson School of Management
Albuquerque, New Mexico 87131

New Mexico State University
Hospitality and Tourism Services
Agriculture and Home Economics
P.O. Box 30003
Department 3HTS
Las Cruces, New Mexico 88003

NEW YORK

Cornell University
Hotel Administration
School of Hotel Administration
Statler Hall
Ithaca, New York 14853

Daemen College
Division of Business and Commerce
Transportation and Travel
     Management
4380 Main Street
Amherst, New York 14226

Keuka College
Food, Hotel and Resort Management
Keuka Park, New York 14478

---

* Offers the Management Development Diploma Program from The Educational Foundation

Marymount College
Foods and Nutrition
Department of Human Ecology
100 Marymount Avenue
Tarrytown, New York 10591

Mercy College
Hotel and Restaurant Management
555 Broadway
Dobbs Ferry, New York 10522

New York City Technical College
Hospitality Management
300 Jay Street
Brooklyn, New York 11201

New York Institute of Technology
Hotel/Restaurant Administration and
    Culinary Arts
School of Hotel Administration and
    Culinary Arts
Central Islip, New York 11741

New York University
Hotel, Restaurant and Food
    Management
School of Education; Center for Food
    and Hotel Management
35 West 4th Street
10th floor
New York, New York 10012

Niagara University
Institute of Travel, Hotel and
    Restaurant Administration
St. Vincennes Building
Niagara University, New York 14109

Rochester Institute of Technology
School of Food, Hotel and Travel
    Management
14 Lomb Memorial Drive
Rochester, New York 14623-5604

**State University of New York
    College—Buffalo (Buffalo State
    College)**
Food Systems Management
Faculty of Applied Science and
    Education
Nutrition and Food Science
    Department
1300 Elmwood Avenue
Caudell Hall 107
Buffalo, New York 14222

**State University of New York
    College—Oneonta**
Food and Business
Department of Human Ecology
Human Ecology Building
Oneonta, New York 13820-4015

**State University of New York
    College—Plattsburgh**
Hotel and Restaurant Management
Center for Human Resources
Ward Hall
Plattsburgh, New York 12901

Syracuse University
Restaurant and Foodservice
    Management Program
College for Human Development
Department of Nutrition and
    Foodservice Management
034 Slocum Hall
Syracuse, New York 13244-1250

NORTH CAROLINA

Appalachian State University
Hospitality Management Program
The College of Business
Boone, North Carolina 28608

Barber-Scotia College
Hospitality Management College
Division of Business and Economics
145 Cabarrus Avenue West
Concord, North Carolina 28025

East Carolina University
Hospitality Management Program
School of Human Environmental
  Sciences
Department of Nutrition and
  Hospitality Management
Greenville, North Carolina
  27858-4353

**North Carolina A & T State
  University**
P.O. Box 21928
Greensboro, North Carolina
  27420-1928

North Carolina Central University
Hospitality Services Management
  Program
Department of Home Economics
P.O. Box 19615
Durham, North Carolina 27707

North Carolina State University
P.O. Box 7605
Raleigh, North Carolina 27695-7605

North Carolina Wesleyan College
Food Service and Hotel
Wesleyan Station
Rocky Mount, North Carolina 27804

Western Carolina University
Hospitality Management
Human Environmental Sciences
Cullowhee, North Carolina 28723

NORTH DAKOTA

North Dakota State University
Hotel, Motel, Restaurant Management
  Program
College of Human Development and
  Education
Fargo, North Dakota 58105

OHIO

Ashland University
Hospitality Administration Program
School of Business Administration
  and Economics
401 College Avenue
Ashland, Ohio 44805

Bowling Green State University
Hospitality Management Program
Business Administration
106 Johnston Hall
Bowling Green, Ohio 43403

Kent State University
Hospitality, Food Service
  Management
School of Family and Consumer
  Studies
Nixson Hall
Kent, Ohio 44242

Ohio State University
Department of Human Nutrition and
  Food Management
Hospitality Management
265 Campbell Hall
1787 Neil Avenue
Columbus, Ohio 43210-1295

Ohio University
Food Service Management and
  Dietetics
School of Human and Consumer
  Sciences
Tupper Hall 108
Athens, Ohio 45701-2979

Tiffin University
Hospitality Management
155 Miami Street
Tiffin, Ohio 44883

Youngstown State University
Hospitality Management
410 Wick Avenue
Youngstown, Ohio 44555

OKLAHOMA

Northeastern State University
Department of Meetings and
    Destination Management
College of Business and Industry
Tahlequah, Oklahoma 74464

Oklahoma State University
School of Hotel and Restaurant
    Administration
College of Human Environmental
    Sciences
210 Human Environmental Sciences
    West
Stillwater, Oklahoma 74078

OREGON

Oregon State University
Hotel, Restaurant and Tourism
Bexell Hall 201
Corvallis, Oregon 97331-2603

Southern Oregon State College
Hotel, Restaurant and Resort
    Management Option
School of Business
Ashland, Oregon 97520

PENNSYLVANIA

Cheyney University
Hotel, Restaurant and Institutional
    Management
School of Education and Professional
    Services
P.O. Box 391
Cheyney, Pennsylvania 19319

Drexel University
Department of Hotel, Restaurant and
    Institutional Management
Philadelphia, Pennsylvania 19104

East Stroudsburg University
Hotel, Restaurant and Tourism
    Management
Professional Studies
200 Prospect Street
East Stroudsburg, Pennsylvania 18301

Indiana University of Pennsylvania
Hotel, Restaurant, and Institutional
    Management
College of Health and Human
    Development
Ackerman Hall
Room 14
Indiana, Pennsylvania 15705

Marywood College
Hotel and Restaurant Management
Department of Human Ecology
2300 Adams Avenue
Scranton, Pennsylvania 18509-1598

Mercyhurst College
Department of Hotel, Restaurant and
    Institutional Management
501 East 38th Street
Erie, Pennsylvania 16546

Pennsylvania State University
School of Hotel, Restaurant and
    Recreation Management
College of Health and Human
    Development
201 Mateer Building
University Park, Pennsylvania 16802

Widener University
School of Hotel and Restaurant
    Management
One University Plate
Chester, Pennsylvania 19013

RHODE ISLAND

Johnson & Wales University
The Hospitality College
8 Abbott Park Place
Providence, Rhode Island 02903

University of Rhode Island
Department of Food Science and
Nutrition
21 Woodward Hall
Kingston, Rhode Island 02881-0804

SOUTH CAROLINA

Clemson University
Department of Parks, Recreation and
Tourism
Box 341005
263 Lehotski Hall
Clemson, South Carolina 29634-1005

**Johnson & Wales University at
Charleston**
Hospitality Program
701 East Bay Street
PCC 1409
Charleston, South Carolina 29403

University of South Carolina
School of Hotel, Restaurant and
Tourism Administration
Applied Professional Sciences
Columbia, South Carolina 29208

Winthrop College
Nutrition
Department of Human Nutrition
701 Oakland Avenue
Rock Hill, South Carolina 29733

SOUTH DAKOTA

Black Hills State University
Travel Industry Management
College of Business and Public
Affairs
1200 University
Spearfish, South Dakota 57799

South Dakota State University
Nutrition and Food Science
Department
Box 2275 A
Brookings, South Dakota 57007-0497

TENNESSEE

Belmont College
Hospitality Business
1900 Belmont Boulevard
Nashville, Tennessee 37212

**The University of Tennessee-
Knoxville**
Hotel and Restaurant Administration
1215 West Cumberland Avenue
Room 229
Knoxville, Tennessee 37996-1900

Tennessee State University
Hotel and Restaurant Administration
3500 John Merritt Boulevard
Nashville, Tennessee 37209

TEXAS

University of Houston
Hotel and Restaurant Management
Conrad N. Hilton College of Hotel
and Restaurant Management
4800 Calhoun Road
Houston, Texas 77204-3902

Houston-Tilloston College
Hotel and Restaurant Management
900 Chicon Street
Austin, Texas 78702

University of North Texas
Division of Hotel and Restaurant
Management
School of Merchandising and
Hospitality Management
P.O. Box 5248
Denton, Texas 76201-5248

Lamar University
Restaurant and Institutional Food
Management
P.O. Box 10035
Beaumont, Texas 77710

Prairie View A & M University
Department of Human Sciences
Food and Nutrition Program
P.O. Box 4329
Prairie View, Texas 77446

Stephen F. Austin State University
Hospitality Administration
Department of Home Economics
P.O. Box 13014, SFA Station
Nacogdoches, Texas 75962-3014

Texas A & M University
Tourism Management
Department of Recreation, Parks and
    Tourism
College Station, Texas 77843-2261

**The University of Texas at San
    Antonio**
College of Business
Tourism Management
6900 North Loop 1604 West
San Antonio, Texas 78249-0631

Texas Tech University
Restaurant, Hotel and Institutional
    Management
College of Human Services
Nutrition and Restaurant/Hotel
    Management
P.O. Box 41162
Lubbock, Texas 79409

Wiley College
Hotel and Restaurant Management
711 Wiley Avenue
Marshall, Texas 75670

UTAH

Utah State University
Department of Nutrition & Food
    Sciences
UMC 8700
Logan, Utah 84322-8700

VERMONT

Johnson State College
Hotel, Hospitality Management
Johnson, Vermont 05656

University of Vermont
Food and Nutrition
HCR-31, Box 436
St. Johnsbury, Vermont 05819

VIRGINIA

James Madison University
Hotel-Restaurant Management
    Department
College of Business
515 Showcker
Harrisonburg, Virginia 22807

* **Norfolk State University**
Hospitality Management
2401 Codrew Avenue
Norfolk, Virginia 23504

Radford University
Foodservice Management
P.O. Box 6903
Radford, Virginia 24142

**Virginia Polytechnic Institute and
    State University**
Hotel, Restaurant and Institutional
    Management
College of Human Resources
362 Wallace Hall
Blacksburg, Virginia 24061-0429

* **Virginia State University**
Hotel, Restaurant and Institutional
    Management (HRIM)
Agriculture and Applied Sciences,
    Human Ecology Department
P.O. Box 9008
Petersburg, Virginia 23806

---

* Offers the Management Development Diploma Program from The Educational Foundation

WASHINGTON

Washington State University
Hotel and Restaurant Administration
College of Business and Economics
Todd Hall 245D
Pullman, Washington 99164-4742

Washington State University
Hotel and Restaurant Administration
College of Business and Economics
1701 Broadway, Room 1148
Seattle, Washington 98122-2400

WEST VIRGINIA

Concord College
Travel Industry Management
Athens, West Virginia 24712

Shepherd College
Hotel-Motel Restaurant Management
Division of Business, School of
    Professional Studies
Home Economics Department
Shepherdstown, West Virginia 25443

* **West Virginia University**
Restaurant/Food Service Management
College of Agriculture and Forestry
702 Allen Hall
P.O. Box 6124
Morgantown, West Virginia
    26506-6124

WISCONSIN

Mount Mary College
Hotel and Restaurant Management
2900 North Menomonee River
    Parkway
Milwaukee, Wisconsin 53222

University of Wisconsin
Department of Nutritional Sciences
1415 Linden Drive
Madison, Wisconsin 53706

**University of Wisconsin-Stevens
    Point**
Food Systems Administration
Human Developmental and
    Nutritional Sciences Department
College of Professional Studies
    Building
Room 101
Stevens Point, Wisconsin 54481

University of Wisconsin-Stout
Hospitality and Tourism Management
School of Home Economics
220 Home Economics
Menomonie, Wisconsin 54751

---

* Offers the Management Development Diploma Program from The Educational Foundation